COLLINS
REFERENCE

DICTIONARY OF
COMPUTING

IAN R. SINCLAIR

D1390827

COLLINS
London and Glasgow

First published as the *Gem Dictionary of Computing* in 1986
First published in this format with revisions 1988
Reprint 10 9 8 7 6 5 4 3 2

Diagrams by Gordon Barr

ISBN 0 00 434349 2

British Library Cataloguing in Publication Data
Sinclair, Ian R.
Collins dictionary of computing.
1. Electronic digital computers—
Dictionaries
I. Title
004'.03'21   QA76.5

Printed in Great Britain by Collins, Glasgow

PREFACE

No rate of change that we have ever seen in technology has quite matched the rise of the microcomputer. Computing has in a few years changed from being a mysterious occupation dominated by a few to being a hobby or a help to millions. The cause of it all has been the shrinking of computer size and price, though not necessarily of computing power, brought about by the microprocessor chip. The change has brought about computers in schools, computers in small businesses, and above all, computers in homes. This sudden ease of access means that many now need to understand terms that originated in the past of computing and which are now common expressions.

The sudden expansion in computing availability has not been matched in terms of explanations and definitions. Many users of small computers have faced an uphill struggle, starting with no background knowledge, to learn the language of a very young and rapidly changing science. A few years ago, no dictionary would have included the word 'microprocessor'. A dictionary of computing meant either a school reference book of computer science, rooted in the practices of the 50s and 60s, or a vast tome for the specialist. Many meanings have changed since these books were first written, and the emphasis has shifted from the huge machines of the past to the tiny personal computers of the present and the near future.

This book is an attempt to cater for the new computer user as well as the traditional student of computer studies. The emphasis is very much on computing as it is practiced today, with a glimpse into tomorrow, rather than a lengthy description of the past. Today's computer is the micro, whose techniques spread into the larger minicomputers, and threaten the old-style mainframe. This book is aimed at the buyer of today's computer, a buyer who is no longer a computer science graduate but a user to whom the computer is a tool rather than a study for its own sake. Here you will find up-to-date definitions and clear explanations of the new computing.

The dictionary has been set out in a form that should make it easy to apply. In each entry, words which are cross-referenced are shown in SMALL CAPITALS. Wherever possible, illustration has been by way of example, rather than by extended and formal academic definitions.

I must thank Ian Crofton and Edwin Moore of Collins Publishers for their unstinting effort in working this book into shape from the material on seven floppy disks, because, true to the topic, the text was produced on a BBC Micro using the Wordwise wordprocessor.

Ian R. Sinclair

A

abbreviations, *n.* shortened forms of commands. Some computers allow BASIC or other command RESERVED WORDS to be abbreviated. A very common example in BASIC is ? used in place of PRINT. Many machines allow a letter followed by a full stop to represent a keyword, such as L. for LIST. The problem with using abbreviations is that they are non-standardized, which can cause problems when changing to another machine.

abort, *vb.* to stop a RUN before it is completed. When the machine uses an INTERPRETED LANGUAGE, it may be possible to resume the run, even if data was being entered and was not saved. When the language is a COMPILED one, it is possible to resume the run only if some provision has been made in the program for this. In general, an abort routine must dump any data, and possibly SYSTEM VARIABLES, on to the disk before closing down.

ABS, *n.* a FUNCTION that removes the sign from a number. Thus ABS(-22) is 22. One use is to decide whether a given number is close to another. A test such as: IF ABS(TARGET - GUESS)<3 will work equally well for values of TARGET - GUESS of +1, +2, -1 or -2. See also ABSOLUTE VALUE.

absolute address, *n.* a method of specifying an address in memory. When each byte of the memory of a computer is numbered in sequence, the absolute address of a byte is the memory number which will allow access to that byte. The memory CHIPS are connected to a set of conductors called the ADDRESS BUS, and when these conductors carry an absolute address number (in binary form), then one byte of memory will be available for reading or writing. The absolute address is used in machine code programming. See also RELATIVE ADDRESSING.

absolute addressing, *n.* an ADDRESSING METHOD that makes use of

ABSOLUTE ADDRESS numbers. Also called *extended addressing*. This requires the absolute address number to be fed to the PROCESSOR, and this is usually done in reverse order, the lowest order byte first. A command which uses absolute addressing will be relatively slow to execute because of the number of reading steps that are required.

absolute value, *n.* the value of a number, ignoring any sign. For example, the absolute value of –6.7 is 6.7. See also ABS.

AC, *abbrev. for* alternating current, the type of electric current used for power transmission. The current flows in either direction alternately, and the direction reverses typically 100 times a second. This type of current cannot be used as a power supply for computers, and so the POWER SUPPLY UNIT has to convert to unidirectional current (*rectification*) and then to steady current (*smoothing*). Compare DC.

accent mark, *n.* the marks which are placed over or under letters in many languages. Typical accent marks are the grave, acute, and circumflex. A few computers contain CHARACTER GENERATORS for these marks, and many DOT-MATRIX printers can produce them on paper. Users of DAISYWHEEL printers can obtain accent marks only if the appropriate print-wheels are available.

acceptance testing, *n.* a scheme for checking that a computer system will perform as intended. A large computer system, whose cost may run to many hundreds of thousands of pounds, cannot simply be put in place and switched on. It is extensively tested with the type of program and data that will eventually be used with it. During the time of this testing, the operators of the machine will also undergo training in its use.

access, 1. *n.* the right of use of a computer and its files. This may require the entry of a PASSWORD if the machine is to be used by a selected number of operators. **2.** *vb.* (a) to gain connection to software; (b) to retrieve information from storage; (c) to place information in storage.

access control, *n.* a method, such as the use of a PASSWORD, which can be used to ensure that only a selected number of operators can use a computer system. A good access system should be proof against HACKERS, but many good systems can be rendered useless by carelessness. This includes using the initials of the operator as a password, leaving passwords written on scraps of paper, or using numbers like 12345.

access point, *n.* the part of a RECORD which is used to identify the record. Also called *access field, key field*. For example, in a name-and-address FILE, the access point might be the surname part of each record, so that any record could be identified by specifying the surname. See KEY, FIELD.

access time, *n.* the time that is needed to find data. To obtain access to a byte of the memory, the ABSOLUTE ADDRESS number has to be placed onto the conductors of the ADDRESS BUS. This can involve several steps of passing data to the PROCESSOR before the address can be assembled. For example, if the processor is an 8-bit type, then because an address uses 16 bits, two sets of data have to be read in order to pass an address number to the processor. These actions take time, and the time from issuing a command to gaining access to the byte is called the access time. Access time is important also in disk systems, where it means the time that elapses, on average, between requesting an input and getting the data. The delay in this case is caused mainly (when the disk runs continuously) by the time that is needed to position the disk READ/WRITE head correctly. For the smaller disk systems, the access time also includes the time that is needed to bring the disk up to operating speed.

accession number, *n.* a number which is attached to a RECORD to show the order of entry. Applies mainly to DISK files in which each record is assigned a sequential number when it is entered.

accumulator, *n.* the main register of a microprocessor. A microprocessor consists of a number of memory locations, called REGISTERS, which can be interconnected. The accumulator is the most important of these registers in which numbers can be manipulated. The term 'accumulator' comes from the fact that this register always accumulates the result of a series of arithmetic steps. When any arithmetic or logic action is carried out, one of the bytes is stored in the accumulator, and the result of the action is also stored in the accumulator. The terms such as 8-bit or 16-bit which are applied to a processor are related to the

most significant
bit

least significant
bit

7 6 5 4 3 2 1 0 ◄── bit position number

| 0 | 0 | 0 | 0 | 0 | 0 | 0 | 0 |

Accumulator clear (reset)

Action: load accumulator with byte 00101101 (hex 2D)

result: | 0 | 0 | 1 | 0 | 1 | 1 | 0 | 1 | byte stored in accumulator

Action: add byte 00011011

Addition: 00101101
00011011
result: | 0 | 1 | 0 | 0 | 1 | 0 | 0 | 0 | 01001000

Accumulator stores accumulated total

Fig. 1. **Accumulator.** The example shows an 8-bit accumulator. A byte can be loaded into the accumulator and another byte added, subtracted or logically compared. Whatever the action, the accumulator stores the end result (or accumulation) of these processes until a new accumulator action is carried out.

number of bits that can be stored in the accumulator. Some processor types use more than one accumulator. See Fig. 1.

accuracy, *n.* freedom from errors in data. For example, in a file dealing with people, accuracy would imply that no one has been recorded as being 190 years old, or being 69 feet tall. Accuracy in a data file depends on the correct entry of data by the user, but the programmer can often help by designing a program which checks for ridiculous entries. Don't confuse accuracy with PRECISION OF NUMBER, which could mean that age was recorded to the nearest minute. See also VALIDATION.

acoustic coupler, *n.* a method of transmitting data over telephone lines or radio links. To transmit computer data over telephone lines, the data must be converted into electrical tone signals, and sent at a comparatively low rate. If direct connection of electrical equipment to the telephone system is prohibited, an acoustic coupler converts the electrical signals into musical notes which are sent and received by the normal telephone microphone and earpiece. This is done by placing the hand-piece of the telephone over a pair of rubber cups, one of which contains a loudspeaker, the other containing a microphone. Problems of this arrangement include interference from other sounds, and inefficient coupling, both of which lead to data errors. A direct electrical connection to the telephone system is greatly preferable. See also MODEM.

action frame, *n.* a frame (or screenful) of information which requests or prompts some reply from the user. Applies particularly to computer assisted learning (CAL) programs in which each frame is designed to advance the user's knowledge of the topic, and the response is to a simple test question which will check that this part of the topic has been understood.

active file, *n.* a file which is open and in use. Data programs should be arranged so that a file is active only for as long as it needs to be and that any interruption (see ABORT) should close all active files. Failure to close files properly can cause loss of data, and result in disks containing data that cannot be accessed except by an expert programmer.

activity, *n.* the fraction of the total number of stored records which will be processed in a run. A file with low activity might indicate that many records are redundant.

activity loading, *n.* a method of organizing a file on a disk so that the records which are most often used can be most rapidly loaded.

ADA, *n.* a comparatively modern HIGH LEVEL-LANGUAGE developed for and used mainly for military computing. ADA is now becoming available for the smaller computers (IBM PC size), but requires large memory and disk capacity. The language is named after the first programmer, Ada, Countess of Lovelace who suggested to Charles Babbage several programming principles which remain valid to this day.

address, *n.* a reference number for a byte in the MEMORY. When this number, in BINARY form, is placed on the ADDRESS BUS, the byte of memory can be written to or read. Small 8-bit computers use address numbers 0 to 65535, but the more modern 16-bit machines can use a much larger range of address numbers.

addressability, *n.* the degree to which the PIXELS on a graphics screen can be *separately* controlled. Many graphics systems appear to control small single pixels, but in fact deal with pixels in groups. This is revealed when two lines of different colours cross on the screen with a large blob of colour where the lines meet. High addressability requires a very large amount of memory dedicated to graphics use.

addressing method, *n.* (in ASSEMBLY LANGUAGE and MACHINE CODE) the method by which an ADDRESS is obtained in the PROGRAM COUNTER in order to store or load a byte of data.

address bus, *n.* a set of connections which carry BINARY signals corresponding to ADDRESS numbers. For the older 8-bit microprocessors, 16 lines of address bus are used, allowing 2^{16} address numbers. The newer 16-bit microprocessors have either 20 or 24 lines of address bus, allowing much greater amounts of memory to be used easily. The term 'bus' (Latin *omnibus*, for all) is used because the lines are connected to the processor and to all of the memory chips. It is therefore possible to have two chips which can be activated by the same address signals, but to select one or the other by using another signal. In this way, memory can be extended by BANK-SWITCHING.

adventure game, *n.* a variety of game in which the screen describes situations and the user is challenged to escape and to find some object. This is done by using simple command words and phrases like LOOK LEFT, GO NORTH, PICK UP WAND, etc. The original adventure games were written by Scott Adams for a mainframe computer, and consisted of text only. Subsequent adventures have been biased to mythical kingdoms, with malignant dwarves, trolls and wizards featuring prominently. Nowadays, thanks to ingenious COMPACTING ALGORITHMS, adventure games can be obtained for microcomputers, often with graphics.

AI, *abbrev. for* artificial intelligence. At its simplest, the term means that a computer system can be programmed to adapt itself, in the sense that it analyses the reply to a question and will modify other questions in the light of that reply. This should not be confused with any sign of thought on the part of a computer, because the computer is still completely controlled by its programming. The *Turing test*, named after the computing genius Alan Turing, is often applied to AI systems. Briefly, this test consists of arranging for a human to communicate with a machine from a remote terminal. If, by looking at the machine's answers to his or her questions the human is unable to tell whether there is a human or a machine at the other end, then the machine is exhibiting artificial intelligence. One objective of work on AI is the development of systems that can work with NATURAL LANGUAGE, meaning the language that we speak and write as distinct from the artificial languages of programming. Another aspect of AI is the ability of the computer to search a DATABASE for the best possible reply to a question, because this has strong parallels with the way that we solve problems for ourselves. Another branch is the development of pattern-recognition systems which would allow a computer system a crude form of sight.

ALGOL, *n. acronym for* Algorithmic-Oriented Language. ALGOL was the first HIGH-LEVEL LANGUAGE to break away from using mathematical formula processing (see FORTRAN) and be aimed more at general problem solving. Later versions of ALGOL, such as ALGOL-68, are very useful and powerful languages, and the style of ALGOL-68 is also heavily reflected in PASCAL, C and other languages.

algorithm, *n.* a plan or routine for solving a problem. This might be a strategy for playing a game, a method of solving an equation, or a way of arranging data. The important point is that until an algorithm for a problem is available, the problem cannot be solved by using the computer. The algorithm is therefore the first step towards any computer program.

alphabetical order, *n.* the order of the letters of the alphabet from A to Z. Computers do not necessarily follow a strict alphabetical order when arranging words, because the computer ASCII codes distinguish between upper-case and lower-case characters, placing A before Z, and Z before a. For example, in a truly alphabetical index you might find the order *Ambiguous, ASCII, Attack*. The computer would normally arrange these words in the order *ASCII, Ambiguous, Attack* because the S is given a position ahead of *any* lower-case letter. A few computers allow the order to take consideration of upper and lower-case together.

alphanumeric, *adj.* (of a character set, code, file of data, etc.) consisting of a range of characters that includes all of the letters, upper and lower case, and digits. This excludes the PUNCTUATION MARKS and signs such as $ and %.

alternating current, see AC.

alternative mode, *n.* a form of multi-user application which allows two operators to share a single set of files. Also called *alternating mode*.

ALU, *abbrev. for* arithmetic and logic unit. This is a part of the microprocessor where the ARITHMETIC actions (usually addition and subtraction only) and LOGIC actions (such as AND, OR, XOR) are carried out. The result of any such action is placed in the ACCUMULATOR.

ambiguous filename, *n.* a filename in which an asterisk is substituted for a letter or group of letters. It is possible to make use of such filenames in most disk-operating systems. The substitution can allow a command to refer to more than one filename, so that the effect is ambiguous. For example, *DELETE X.* (BBC Micro example) would delete the files X.FIRST, X.SECOND, X.THIRD and so on. Very great care must be taken when using ambiguous filenames so that files are not unintentionally deleted.

ampersand, *n.* the & sign, which is used in some computer languages with special significance. For example, in the BBC Micro, the ampersand is used to mark a HEXADECIMAL number.

amplitude, *n.* the size of a signal, measured from the zero level to one peak. This can apply to an electrical, acoustic, or any other signal which is shaped like a wave. The amplitude of a sound signal is a measure of the loudness of the sound that is heard, and the amplitude of a light signal is a measure of the light brightness. Digital signals are of fixed amplitude, with a considerable margin allowed. For example, in a system which uses signals that are nominally zero volts for binary 0 and +5V for binary 1, levels of 0 to +1.2V may be read as binary zero, and levels of 3.5V to 5V read as binary 1. See Fig. 2.

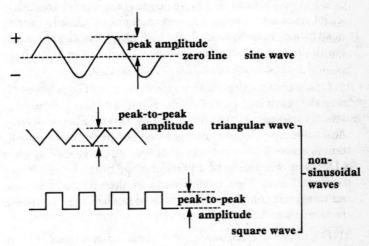

Fig. 2. **Amplitude.** The height of a wave. For the simplest shape of wave, the sine wave, the peak amplitude is measured from the centre (zero) line to one peak. For other wave shapes, it is more common to measure the peak-to-peak amplitude as illustrated.

analogue, *adj.* (of quantities) capable of representation by electrical voltage. An input quantity such as temperature, light brightness or sound volume can be represented by an electrical voltage whose amplitude is proportional to the amplitude of the input. By contrast, a DIGITAL representation would use a set of electrical signals to mean a number which measures the amplitude of the input.

analogue computer, *n.* a form of computer which deals with ANALOGUE signals of continually varying sizes. This type of computer was developed to a working extent before the digital type, and is still very useful. A crude example was the bombsight computer of World War II, which used inputs from the bomb-aiming telescope, the air-speed indicator, the altimeter, and other measuring units to operate the bomb release mechanism. This was done mechanically, but the later analogue computers used electronic methods, making use of a unit called the OPERATIONAL AMPLIFIER. The analogue computer is particularly useful when a system has a large number of continually varying inputs which must be processed at high speed to obtain an output. For this reason, the analogue computer is still favoured for many control tasks. Compare DIGITAL COMPUTER.

AND, *n.* a LOGIC action that compares two bits. If both bits are 1, then the result is 1, otherwise the result is 0. This is written as 1*1=1, meaning 1 AND 1 gives 1. In programming languages, the AND statement is used to connect two conditions. For example, the statement IF Name="Smith" AND Age <40 can be used to select records of one name and a particular age group by combining two conditions. These comparisons are described as BOOLEAN, meaning that either condition can be described as being true or false. See Fig. 3.

AND gate, *n.* an electronic circuit whose action carries out AND logic. A single AND gate would compare a number of inputs and give a single output which would be a logic 1 only when all of the inputs were also logic 1s. The AND gates of microprocessors are multiple gates, typically working with eight sets of two inputs and giving eight outputs (for an 8-bit microprocessor). The construction of the microprocessor itself incorporates AND gates, and LOGIC CIRCUITS can be constructed with such gates. A much more versatile system, however, uses *NAND* gates, in which the output is inverted so that the output is 0 if both inputs are 1. See Fig. 3.

angle, *n.* the difference in the direction of two straight lines. Computer functions such as SIN and COS which take an angle as their ARGUMENT normally require the angle to be in radians. A radian is the angle between two radii of a circle, when the segment length of the circle between the ends of the radii is equal to the radius (see Fig. 4 on page 12). A few computers can work with angles in degrees by using a DEG function. If the DEG function is not available, then the conversion is 1 radian = 57.295779 degrees or 1 degree = 0.0174532 radians.

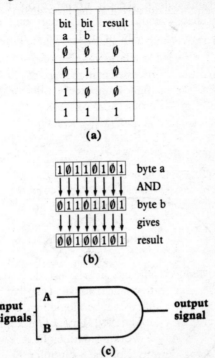

(a)

(b)

(c)

Fig. 3. **AND** and **AND-gate.** (a) A truth-table for the AND action, which shows all the possible results of ANDing two bits. When two complete bytes are ANDED, (b) the AND action is carried out on corresponding bits, bits in the same position in each byte. The result is put into the corresponding position in the result-byte. Each bit action is self-contained — there is no carry bit as there would be in an ADD or SUB action. (c) The symbol which represents an AND gate in an electronic circuit.

animation, *n.* making an object appear to move on the screen. This has to be done by drawing the object, waiting, wiping out the diagram, and then drawing in a slightly different position. If an INTERPRETED LANGUAGE is used for these actions, animation will inevitably be slow, and for this reason programs which

11

make use of fast animation inevitably use either compiled code or machine code. An alternative animation method is to prepare a set of diagrams which are all in background colour, and successively change each one to a foreground colour. Fast animation is possible by this method, even with an interpreted language.

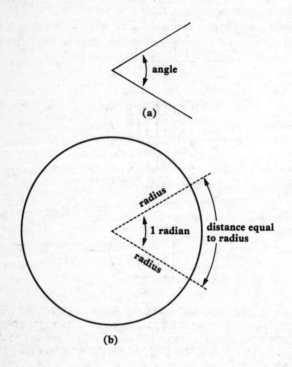

Fig. 4. **Angles.** Angle (a) is normally measured in degrees, with each degree equal to $\frac{1}{360}$ of a complete circle. The alternative angular measurement which is used in most programming languages, is the radian (b). The radian is the angle which is obtained by marking out the distance of a radius along the rim of a circle and then connecting the centre to each end of this line. The radian is the same size for any value of radius of the circle, and is approximately equal to 57.295779 degrees.

ANSI, *n. acronym for* the American National Standards Institute. ANSI has issued standardized specifications of many computing languages, notably COBOL. An ANSI BASIC standard exists, but has not been implemented by any major computer manufacturer to date.

APL, *abbrev. for* A Programming Language. This is the name of a language which uses symbols that are not available on the ordinary typewriter keyboard. The language is very compact, hard to read, and seldom seen on microcomputers. It was designed originally for use on IBM mainframes.

apostrophe, *n.* the ' sign, which is used to specify actions in many computer languages. Some varieties of BASIC use the apostrophe to force printing on to a new line. PASCAL uses the apostrophe to enclose words which are to be printed.

append, *vb.* to add to existing material; especially to add a FILE to an existing file by loading it in a particular way. In the case of program files, the term generally means that the new file is added to the end of the old one. Many WORD PROCESSORS allow text to be appended to the CURSOR, meaning that the new text will be inserted at the position in the old text which is indicated by the cursor.

Apple, *n. Trademark.* one of the first and certainly the most influential of the microcomputer manufacturers. Founded in 1976 by Steve Jobs and Steve Wozniak, using the family garage as a base and $100 capital, Apple computers were wildly successful. Because of excellent design principles, the early Apple-2 model is still useful, and later types such as Lisa and Macintosh have greatly affected the design of other machines and of software.

applications package, *n.* a set of programs which are dedicated to a particular purpose. A WORD PROCESSOR, a SPREADSHEET, or a DATABASE, are all applications packages. The significance of the word 'package' is that the programs often consist of several sections, and only one may be in the memory of the computer at a given time. A word processor, for example, may consist of a TEXT EDITOR, which deals with the entry of words, their display on the screen, and their storage in memory and on disk. The accompanying PRINT FORMATTER is concerned with the formatting of the text on to paper, and with any special codes that must be sent to the printer.

Many packages can be modified by the user so as to fit some special purpose, for example by putting in ACCENT MARKS for foreign language use.

approximation error, *n.* an error caused by ROUNDING a REAL NUMBER. See also PRECISION OF NUMBER.

arcade game, *n.* a type of game which features a fast-moving graphics display, and in which the user must manipulate keys or a joystick to shoot down a moving object, or objects. Arcade games are said to be very good for developing the reflexes, but they often appear to be paralysing to the brain. The graphics techniques which have been so greatly developed by designers of these games have gradually seeped into programs which are designed for business use, making many business programs more USER-FRIENDLY as a result.

architecture, *n.* the way in which hardware is constructed. The microprocessor architecture, for example, decides what registers are available and how data can be passed between them. The system architecture determines how efficiently the memory of a computer can be used and software run. The user of a computer seldom needs to worry about system architecture, but for the programmer and systems designer, this can be of considerable importance.

archive, *n.* any set of data that must be preserved over a long period. In general, magnetic storage (tape or disk) is not considered suitable for archives, and only punched paper tape has a proven long life for this purpose. Users of business programs on modern machines do not generally have the option of a paper tape system, and must rely on many BACKUP copies of disks and tapes for archival use. See also FATHER.

area search, *n.* a search for items of a specified type. The term is used in the context of filing records and means a search for a number of items which have something in common. For example, you might want to search through a set of files for the names of all males born in 1945. The area that is referred to in this example consists of the items 'male' and '1945'.

argument, *n.* the number upon which a FUNCTION operates. For example, the TAB function in BASIC needs to be followed by a number in brackets which controls where the CURSOR will be moved to. This number is then the argument of the TAB function. All of the arithmetic functions, such as LOG, SIN, COS, will need a suitable argument, and in many cases the possible range of values is limited. This may make it important to include VALIDATION for these values.

arithmetic, *n.* any action that involves elementary calculation with numbers. The main arithmetic operations are addition, subtraction, multiplication and division. To this, we usually attach evolution (raising to a power) and involution (taking a root). The microprocessor is generally capable only of adding and subtracting small binary numbers, and the mathematical actions of the computer are obtained by programming. For microcomputers, these programs form part of the ROM of the computer, and very often involve approximations. Larger machines can call upon arithmetic routines which exist on a disk, or which can be implemented by a COPROCESSOR which is specially designed to deal with arithmetic actions.

arithmetic capability, *n.* the ability of a word-processing program to carry out simple arithmetical actions. A word processor with arithmetic capability could, for example, be used to produce a balance sheet. The operator would type the main figures, but the totals would be produced by the computer, under the command of the program. Even a modest amount of arithmetic capability can be of very great use in a word processor, because it allows the computer to be used more efficiently. Integrated suites of programs deal with arithmetic by allowing data to be passed from one program to another. A SPREADSHEET might, for example, be used and its output passed to a word processor for incorporation into a report.

arithmetic functions, *n.* actions on numbers which are more complex than addition, subtraction, division and multiplication. These are programmed by KEYWORDS in combination with an

ARITHMETIC OPERATIONS

ARGUMENT. Typical arithmetic functions include LOG, SIN, ARCTAN. All of these function actions are programmed by processing the argument number in a loop that may be repeated many times. This can make such actions very slow by comparison with simple arithmetic. For some purposes, using a TABLE of values in memory can be very much more efficient than calculating quantities.

arithmetic operations, *n.* any operations of the type which carry out an action of arithmetic on numbers.

arithmetic operators, *n.* symbols such as $+$, $-$, $*$, $/$, and words such as DIV and MOD, which carry out an arithmetic action.

ARQ, *n.* an automatic request (for) data correction. In a signalling system which can detect transmitted data errors, the ARQ signal can be sent back to the transmitter when an error is detected. This signal can be used to force the transmitter to retransmit the dubious character or word.

array, *n.* a set of related values that uses one IDENTIFIER along with number subscripts (see SUBSCRIPTED VARIABLE). For example, if you wanted to store a set of names of class members, you would not use one string name for each member, but an array like Name$. Members of this array would be Name$(1), Name$(2), Name$(3), and so on. The number within the brackets is called the subscript number. This makes it very easy to find, for example, the 15th name, or to print the names in order of number, or to rearrange the names in alphabetical order.

Many computers require the DIMENSIONING of an array before using it. This means that you have to declare the maximum number that you will use, for example, DIM Name$(25). In some languages, arrays require the subscript number to be in square brackets. Most languages store an array so that the members are arranged in order, using one section of memory. Any attempt to change the dimensions of an array while it is in use will lead to an error message.

array processor, *n.* a type of computer that uses a large number of linked processors. This allows array data to be manipulated very rapidly, with one processor handling each part of the array.

artificial intelligence, *n.* see AI.

ASC, *n.* a statement in BASIC which finds the ASCII code of a letter or other character. Other languages use different statements for this purposes, for example, ORD in Pascal.

ascender, *n.* the part of a printed character which rises above the main body, as in the letters b, d, h, k. All printers can cater for ascenders, but a few DOT-MATRIX printers cannot print DESCENDERS.

ASCII, *n. acronym for* American Standard Code for Information Interchange (pronounced *ass-key*), a number code for letters, digits and other characters which has been standardized for computing use. In general, if a file is recorded as a set of ASCII codes, it can be read by other types of computer. The ASCII coding system makes it easy to convert between lower-case and upper-case letters, and between the stored form of a number and its ASCII code. A few computers use internal codes of their own, particularly for screen-display codes.

assemble, *n.* to convert from assembly language (or MNEMONIC) instructions into machine code. This saves the effort and errors that are involved in programming directly in machine code. It is much easier to follow a listing in assembly language than in machine code. For example, the meaning of the instruction ADD A,C (add a number into the accumulator from register C) is much easier to remember than 129, its machine code number equivalent.

assembler, *n.* a program that converts text in ASSEMBLY LANGUAGE into MACHINE CODE to be used by a computer. A *one-pass assembler* will convert the instructions into code in one run, but most types of assemblers require the assembly-language text to be scanned twice, sometimes three times. This means that LABELS which are used in place of numbers can be allocated on one pass, and the code assigned on the next.

assembly language, *n.* a language that uses word ABBREVIATIONS for actions that the microprocessor can carry out. A program in assembly language can be converted by an ASSEMBLER into number codes which the microprocessor will obey. Because these codes are commands direct to the microprocessor (the machine), these codes are called machine code, and their use results in very fast-running programs. Writing in assembly language demands a very detailed knowledge of the ARCHITECTURE of the microprocessor, and of the design of the computer in which it is used. See Fig. 5.

Z-80	6502	68000
LD A,C	LDA Start,X	LEA.L Data
CALL #BB5A	STA New,X	BSR.S Start
INC C	INX	BNE.S Mesg
DJNZ LOOP	CPX #Number	MOVEQ #16,D2
RET	BNE Loop	RTS
	RTS	

Fig. 5. **Assembly language.** This is a set of instructions in abbreviated form, called mnemonics, along with the numbers that they act on. The numbers may also be specified in symbolic form, as labels. Assembly language is specific to a microprocessor type, and the language conventions are laid down by the manufacturer of the microprocessor. The three examples show typical assembly language fragments for three microprocessors that are widely used in microcomputers.

assembly listing, *n.* a listing of ASSEMBLY LANGUAGE, often with the corresponding machine code and memory addresses printed out. This is the type of listing that is produced by an ASSEMBLER as it operates. The DEFAULT listing is to the screen, but most assemblers will optionally produce a listing to a printer. This is more useful, because it is easier to check a listing on paper than on the screen.

assignation, *n.* the action of making a letter or name (a VARIABLE name or IDENTIFIER) represent a number or a string of characters. For example, LET A$ = "NAME" (in BASIC) means that the symbols A$ now take the value of NAME wherever they are used. Some varieties of BASIC use LET to mean assignation, others omit this word. Another common symbol for assignation is := as used in Pascal and other high-level languages. Another option is to use '=' to mean assignment, and '==' to mean equality. BASIC is one of the few languages in which the '=' sign can be used for both actions.

asynchronous transmission, *n.* the sending of signals from a transmitter to a receiver at irregular intervals, rather than at 'clocked' times. To take a simple example, the signals from a keyboard to the computer are asynchronous, because the operator presses keys at irregular intervals. The signals from a disk system are normally closely timed synchronous signals, meaning that the time between signals is always the same.

A to D, *n.* a change from an ANALOGUE coding system to a DIGITAL coding system. Signals from measuring devices are usually analogue, meaning that they are quantities like electrical voltage which can take a range of values. Computers work with BINARY numbers, expressed by signals which are either of high value (1) or low (0). An *A to D converter* is a device which can change an analogue input into a digital output, so that each input value is represented by a binary number at the output. See also ANALOGUE COMPUTER, DIGITIZER. See Fig. 6 on page 20.

attached processor, *n.* an auxiliary microprocessor in a computer. The attached processor is a separate processor under the control of the main processor, and is used for auxiliary actions, usually as a NUMBER-CRUNCHER. See also COPROCESSOR.

attack, *n.* the start of a musical note or noise. The four sections of a note are called ATTACK, DECAY, SUSTAIN and RELEASE. The attack section deals with the rise in amplitude of sound from zero (at the start of a note) to its peak value. Instruments which are struck or plucked cause notes to have fast attacks, and explosions have very high attack rates.

attenuation, *n.* weakening or thinning. The term is applied to the decrease in AMPLITUDE of a signal as it is transmitted through space or along a line. If the attenuation is too great, the signal will have to be amplified before it can be used. Attenuation may be important if signals are being transmitted along long lines.

audio cassette, *n.* a cassette that is primarily intended for recording sound, and which will not be ideal for the recording of digital data. Home computers which use audio-cassette recorders for data storage are the only computing application for audio cassettes. In such computers, the digital data is converted into musical tones, with one tone representing 1 and another

AUDIO CASSETTE

representing 0. This makes the recording rate for data very much slower than that of a true digital recorder.

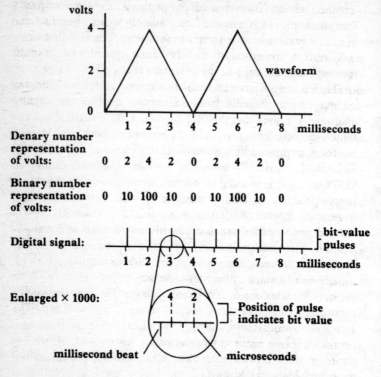

The time lapse between the millisecond clock beat and the pulse indicates the bit value (representing voltage); the shorter the time lapse, the greater the bit value. No pulse indicates a bit value of zero.

Fig. 6. **A to D.** A-to-D conversion simply illustrated. The wave is sampled at time intervals which are precisely controlled by clock pulses. At each clock pulse, the amplitude of the wave is measured and the measurement is converted to binary code. This is then used to create a digital signal in which the timing of the pulses relative to the clock pulses indicates the significance of each bit. The rate of sampling would be much greater than has been indicated here.

audio range, *n.* the frequency range of about 30Hz to 20kHz, which is the range of sound frequencies that can be heard. Many communication channels, such as telephones and tape recorders, can deal only with a limited part of this audio range, so that digital signals have to be sent in the form of musical notes.

audit trail, *n.* a method of checking the output of a program by tracing back the steps to the original input.

authentication, *n.* a routine which is used to check that the user of a system is entitled to do so. The procedure usually involves the verification of a PASSWORD.

authorization code, *n.* a combination of a PASSWORD and identity number which is used to establish the identity of a computer system user.

AUTO, *n.* a command used in many microcomputers to implement automatic line numbering. When the RETURN or ENTER key is pressed after typing a line, a new line number is automatically generated and placed on the screen. The AUTO command is useful only for computers that use BASIC, because most other languages do not employ numbered lines.

auto advance, *n.* the ability to move automatically to the next position. Auto advance as used in a SPREADSHEET means that the CURSOR will move to the next CELL when the RETURN or ENTER key is pressed.

autoboot, *vb.* to make a program run when the computer is switched on. This is used in some disk systems, when a special program (often called BOOT) can be loaded and run either at switch-on, or by pressing certain keys. This program can be used to INITIALIZE a system, such as setting the action of a FUNCTION KEY, or to load other programs from a disk.

automatic decimal alignment, *n.* a useful WORD PROCESSOR action that allows columns of numbers to be positioned so that all of the decimal points line up. This makes the presentation of items such as balance sheets much easier. The decimal points can, of course, be aligned manually by any word-processor system.

automatic letter writing, *n.* a system based on a WORD PROCESSOR in which a standard text can be produced, with names and addresses inserted from a MAILING LIST. Each copy then reproduces the standard text, but with names and other references from the mailing list.

automation, *n.* the replacement of human labour with machines, now generally computer-controlled. The positive aspects of automation include elimination of drudgery, raising of standards of workmanship (machineship?), and increased productivity, which should lead to higher living standards. Its undesirable aspects include unemployment, particularly for the lower-skilled, and the feeling that you are 'tied to a machine' if you work in an extensively automated environment.

autorepeat, *n.* the automatic repetition of key action. Most modern computers provide autorepeat on all keys, meaning that if any key is held down for more than a fraction of a second, its action repeats. The delay time can often be altered to suit the operator, and this is one item which might be set by an AUTOBOOT.

autostart, *n.* the automatic running of a program after loading. Some machines allow a program to be recorded in such a way that the program will start to run as soon as it has been loaded. Other machines permit a special command to be used to load and run a program. Automatic load-and-run is one method of deterring copying, because it can be combined with disabling the ESCAPE or BREAK key. This means that the program will run as soon as it has loaded, and cannot be stopped except by switching off the machine. Programs of this type are undesirable, because no BACKUP can be made, and no amendments can be patched in.

auxiliary equipment, *n.* parts of a computer system which are not directly controlled by the processor. This often refers to 'passive' objects like copyholders, computer workstands, disk-storage boxes and the like. Equipment which *is* controlled by the processor is referred to as PERIPHERAL.

availability, *n.* the fraction of the total active time during which a computer is available to the user. One of the problems of MULTI-USER systems is that the availability may be low for each user. This can lead to each user needing a long time to complete a program run, or having to wait too long for data to be accessed.

B

babble, *n.* interference between two channels that are transmitting data. Also called *crosstalk*.

background, *n.* the colour of the parts of the screen which are not occupied by TEXT or GRAPHICS. Also called *paper*. Some dialects of BASIC use a PAPER STATEMENT to change the background colour. Compare FOREGROUND.

background ROM, *n.* a ROM which can be switched in and out of use and is normally out of use when the computer is first switched on. Background ROMS are used for programs which are alternatives to the normal programming-language ROM. For example, if the normal ROM is a BASIC interpreter, a background ROM might be used for a word processor or a spreadsheet.

background task, *n.* (in a time-shared system) a routine which the computer will run when there is nothing with a higher priority. For example, the time intervals during the input of data from a keyboard allow for background tasks to be carried out.

backing store, *n.* a store for data which is not a working part of the computer's memory. A typical example is a DISK DRIVE. A backing store can be used to hold programs and data which can be read and used by the computer during the course of a main program.

backslash, *n.* the \ sign. It is used in some machines to mean INTEGER division.

backup, *n.* a spare copy of a program or data. Storage of data on magnetic materials has not been used for a long time, and is not totally trustworthy. Any valuable program or data should therefore be backed up, and many commercial users maintain two backups, which are renewed at regular intervals, using the grandfather, FATHER, son principle.

Backus-Naur form, *n.* a 'shorthand' method of writing the syntax of computer statements. See Fig. 7.

alternative

IF ‹expression› THEN ‹statement(s)› | ‹line number›

[ELSE ‹statement(s)›| ‹line number›]

optional   alternative

IF X=Y   THEN PRINT X

expression   statement

IF A$ = 'NO'   THEN 150

expression   line number

IF A$ = 'NO'   THEN 200 ELSE

expression   line number

IF A$ = 'YES'   PRINT 'COUNTING'

expression   statement

Fig. 7. **Backus-Naur form.** This is used to define and summarize the syntax of a language in written phrases. In this example, reserved words of the language are shown in capitals, and actions such as expressions and statements are placed between angled brackets. The slash sign means that what follows is an alternative, and square brackets are used to enclose a part that is optional. The illustration shows the syntax of the BASIC IF test, and the examples underneath show how the syntax is interpreted in the form of program lines. The symbols ? for optional and * for repetition are also used.

backward recovery, *n.* a method of recovering original data after a system failure. The partly-processed data is used in a routine which reverses the actions of the main program, so that the original data can be calculated.

bandwidth, *n.* the FREQUENCY range of signals. Bandwidths are measured in kilohertz (narrow band) or megahertz (broad band). Data transmission can be carried out on narrow-band channels only by using slow transmission rates; for fast transmissions, broad-band channels must be used. Bandwidth is important also in respect of VDU monitors. The television-type of video signal to a monitor has a very large bandwidth, and if the monitor cannot make use of this full bandwidth, characters will not be sufficiently clear on an 80 character-per-line display. The average bandwidth for a monitor is 18MHz, in contrast to the normal 5MHz for a TV receiver.

bank-switching, *n.* a way of making use of more memory than can normally be addressed. For example, the sixteen ADDRESS lines of an 8-bit microprocessor permit 64K of memory to be addressed. If another set of 64K of memory is present, it is possible to switch all of the address lines to this 'bank'. Rather elaborate FIRMWARE is needed if all of the memory is to be used as if it were one set, and a more common application is to keep one bank for ROM and possibly the screen RAM, with the other set used for programs and data.

bar code, *n.* a method of coding BINARY numbers as a set of thick and thin lines on paper. The system is used extensively in price and item codings on articles in supermarkets. Bar coding can also be used as a low cost way of printing, storing, and reading computer programs.

bar printer, *n.* a printer which uses type bars in the style of a typewriter.

base, *n.* the number which is represented by the column immediately to the left of the units column of a number system. In the conventional DENARY system, this column represents tens, so that the base of our numbers is ten. In a BINARY system, this column represents 2s, and in octal, 8. See Fig. 8 on page 27. In the HEXADECIMAL system, the column next to the units is the 16s column.

base address, *n.* a starting address for a BLOCK OF DATA. When a set of items of data is stored in the memory of a computer, it is often convenient to keep the data in order, and store it in a set of consecutive addresses. When this is done, the first of these addresses is known as the base address, because any other address can be found by adding to or subtracting from this number.

BASIC, *n. acronym for* Beginners All-purpose Symbolic Instruction Code, a computing language. Devised originally as a way of teaching computing, BASIC, which is loosely based on FORTRAN was invented at Dartmouth College, USA. It has since that time been greatly developed and enhanced to become a powerful and useful language. Its main handicaps are lack of standardization, and lack of structure.

batch processing, *n.* the processing of data which has been gathered earlier and recorded. Batch processing involves gathering data in the form of punched tape, magnetic tape or magnetic disks, and operating on all of the data in one program run. For example, if you want to arrange names in alphabetical order, you might enter all of the names into a disk file, and then use a sorting program. Compare REAL-TIME PROCESSING.

baud rate, *n.* the speed of serial data transmission. When data is transmitted along a line bit by bit, the rate of transmission is called the baud rate. The name comes from Baudot, the engineer who pioneered the Teleprinter in the 1860s. For most purposes, the baud rate is equal to the number of bits transmitted per second.

BBC, *abbrev. for* British Broadcasting Corporation. The BBC provided the specification of a microcomputer for educational use, particularly for use in a TV series. The specification was achieved by an Acorn machine, which was allowed to bear the name of BBC Microcomputer.

BCD, *abbrev. for* binary-coded decimal. In this number system, each digit of a number is written as a BINARY number, rather than converting the whole number. For example, 47 would be coded as 01000111, the binary codes for 4 and 7. Contrast this with 101111, which is the true binary code for 47. See Fig. 9.

BCPL, *n.* a HIGH-LEVEL LANGUAGE. BCPL was evolved (in 1967) from ALGOL, and is a very compact language, though rather lacking in data types. A development of BCPL, C, has added more flexibility, and has become very popular since its birth in 1972.

BCS, *abbrev. for* British Computer Society.

bead, *n.* a short routine that carries out one complete action. The term comes from the idea that a set of such routines can be combined ('threaded') together to make up a useful program. A language which is constructed around this principle is called a *threaded language*, of which FORTH is probably the best-known example.

Denary

10^4	10^3	10^2	10^1	10^0
or	or	or	or	or
10000	1000	100	10	1

e.g. 1467
$$= (1 \times 10^3) + (4 \times 10^2) + (6 \times 10^1) + (7 \times 10^0)$$
$$= 1000 + 400 + 60 + 7$$

Binary

2^4	2^3	2^2	2^1	2^0
or	or	or	or	or
16	8	4	2	1

e.g. 10101
$$= (1 \times 2^4) + 0 + (1 \times 2^2) + 0 + (1 \times 2^0)$$
$$= 16 + 4 + 1 = 21 \text{ in denary}$$

Fig. 8. **Base.** The denary and binary number systems.

Denary number =	147
Binary form of digits: (4-bit)	1 = 0001 4 = 0100 7 = 0111
BCD form is:	000101000111

number of bits = 4 × number of denary digits

True binary form of 147 is 10010011

Fig. 9. **BCD.** Each digit of a denary number is converted into a 4-bit binary number. This makes the binary representation of a number longer than its true binary counterpart, but actions such as arithmetic and screen display can be simpler. Real numbers can be represented in more precise form, but processing is slower than for binary numbers.

BECOMES SIGN

becomes sign, *n.* a sign used to indicate change of VARIABLE value. Many high-level languages distinguish between the sign =, which means exact equality, and := which means 'becomes'. For example, A=A+1 would be meaningless, but A:=A+1 means simply that the value of A is increased by 1. BASIC does not use a separate 'becomes' sign, though some DIALECTS insist on the word LET being used in this context.

beep, *n.* a tone of short duration, used to draw the attention of the operator. In some versions of BASIC, there is a BEEP STATEMENT which will produce this sound. See also PROMPT.

beginning of file (BOF), *n.* an entry which describes the file content; a form of index to the file.

bell character, *n.* the ASCII code 7. When the ASCII code was devised, the main printing PERIPHERAL was the TELETYPE, and the ASCII code 7 had the effect of ringing the bell on the teletype. The character has become known as the bell character even though the bell is no longer in use. On many computers, this character produces a BEEP.

(a)
```
1Ø FOR J = 1 TO 1ØØØØ
2Ø NEXT
```

(b)
```
1Ø FOR J = 1 TO 1ØØØØ
2Ø PRINT 'TEST'
3Ø NEXT
```

Fig. 10. **Benchmarks.** The illustration shows two possible benchmark programs for BASIC. (a) The first performs a loop which can be timed. The time depends on the machine clock rate and also on the way that the interpreter has been written. If an integer number can be specified for J, the loop will run much faster than if a floating-point number is used. (b) The second tests the speed of screen printing and scrolling. Different benchmarks are needed for other languages, and also for testing speed of disk access and filing.

benchmark, *n.* a short program which is intended to be used as a way of comparing one computer with another. It really only compares the implementation of the programming language.

Like all other over-simplified comparisons, it is seldom really useful except as a way of indicating how quickly various computers perform the benchmark! See Fig. 10.

bidirectional printing, *n.* printing in both directions. This is used by many DOT-MATRIX and DAISYWHEEL printers to achieve extra speed. One line of the text is printed left-to-right, and the next line right-to-left. This requires some memory and a considerable amount of FIRMWARE to be built into the printer.

BIM, *n. acronym for* Beginning of Information Mark. The name is given to a code which marks the start of a stream of data along a line or from a tape or disk.

binary, *adj.* of or relating to any system consisting of two components. In computing, the term always refers to the number system which uses digits 0 and 1. See BIT.

binary chop, *n.* a method of finding an item in an ORDERED LIST. A binary chop involves dividing a list into parts by slicing the list into two, then treating one such slice as a new list and slicing again. See also BINARY SEARCH.

binary-coded decimal, see BCD.

binary digit, see BIT.

binary fraction, *n.* a fraction which uses powers of 2 rather than powers of 10. The decimal fraction .123 means 1 tenth, 2 hundredths and 3 thousandths. Similarly, the binary fraction .101 means one half, no quarters, and one eighth. A REAL NUMBER (not an INTEGER) is stored in the memory of the computer as a binary fraction, and this is the cause of APPROXIMATION errors. See also PRECISION OF NUMBER.

binary search, *n.* a method of finding an entry in a list which is ordered in some way, such as in alphabetical order (see ORDERED LIST). In a binary search of such a list, the middle item would be compared with the item being searched for. If the two do not match, then the program decides in which half of the list the item must be held. This half is then selected, and the process is repeated until a match is obtained or until the last item is found not to match. The advantage of a binary search is that it can be very fast, even if the list of items is very large. The disadvantage is that the items must be in order.

binary tree, *n.* a form of TREE structure in which each branching consists of two branches only.

bit, *n.* either of the two digits 0 or 1, used in binary notation. Also called *binary digit*. A binary number consists of a collection of bits, often 8 bits. In a binary number such as 00110101, the BIT POSITION of each digit indicates its SIGNIFICANCE. The binary number 101, for example, means one 4, no 2s and 1 unit. The bit on the right-hand side of such a number is the *least-significant bit (lsb)*, because this position is used for units, which have the minimum value in the number. The bit on the left-hand side of the number is the *most-significant bit (msb)*, because this position is the position of maximum value. The msb is often used as a SIGN BIT. See also BYTE.

bit density, *n.* the density with which bits are packed, particularly on tape or disk. The usual measurement of bit density is the number of stored bits per inch of linear track.

bit-mapping, *n.* a form of MEMORY MAPPING in which the brightness and colour of each point on a screen is controlled by bits stored in memory addresses of the computer. See BLITTER.

bit position, *n.* the position of a BIT in a BYTE. In a byte of 8 bits, each bit is located in its own column when the byte is written as a binary number. The positions are numbered from zero (the units column, or LEAST SIGNIFICANT) bit to 7 (the 128s column, or most significant) bit. See MSB.

bit rate, *n.* the speed of transmission of data, expressed as the number of bits per second. This is often taken to be the same as BAUD RATE, for computing purposes.

bit-significant, *adj.* (of a byte) in which one or more BITS of the BYTE may be used to convey some meaning other than the number value in binary code. For example, testing bit 6 (see BIT POSITION) of an ASCII coded letter can distinguish between an upper-case and a lower-case letter.

bit-slice machine, *n.* a computer which uses a number of microprocessors each of which deals with a few bits only. Bit-slice units are microprocessors which exist in units of (usually) 4 bits, and which can be connected together to give the action of a processor of as many bits as is required for the design.

black box, *n.* literally a piece of machinery whose action is known but whose workings are not. Treating a piece of hardware or software as a 'black box' means that you know what outputs will be obtained for any given inputs, but that you do not know (or need to know) precisely how the outputs are obtained. The aim is to speed up understanding of a complete system by eliminating unnecessary detail.

blank string, *n.* a STRING quantity which contains nothing; used in routines which build up a string by starting with a blank string and then adding characters. Also called *empty string*.

bleed, *n.* (originally, in printing) the spreading out of ink from a printed character. This makes the outline of the character fuzzy and difficult to read, particularly for OPTICAL CHARACTER READERS. The term is also applied in graphics displays to a blob of colour which appears at the point where lines of different colour cross.

blitter, *n.* a bit-map image manipulator. A piece of hardware or software which carries out the action of transferring bytes from one part of memory to another. See also BLOCK TRANSFER, DIRECT ACCESS.

block, *n.***1.** a part of a computer system which carries out one set of actions. We might refer, for example, to the memory block or the input/output block. **2.** a piece of program which has a single start and a single end. This could be the main program or a PROCEDURE.

block diagram, *n.* a diagram of a system which shows the main units, but no details of any unit. A block diagram is the essential first step towards understanding how any system (not just a computer system) works. The block diagram is the HARDWARE engineer's equivalent of a FLOWCHART. See Fig. 11 on page 32.

block gap, *n.* an unrecorded piece of tape or disk. Also called *interblock gap, record gap*. The data is recorded in blocks or groups of, typically, 256 bytes, and there is an interval, the block gap, between blocks. Following such a gap, there may be a short HEADER which carries the filename and the next block number.

block of data, *n.* a set of data items that belong together. These might, for example, be the items of an array, or a piece of text.

BLOCK OPERATIONS

A block of data such as this would be stored in a continuous set of memory addresses.

block operations, *n.* the transfer of a complete set of words from one place to another in a document during word processing.

block transfer, *n.* the movement of a block of data from one place to another. Usually applied to data in memory being copied from one set of memory addresses to another set. See also BLITTER.

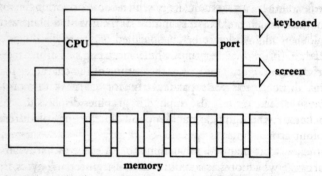

Fig. 11. **Block diagram.** The example shows units of a system in the form of blocks, with no details. The aim is to show how parts of a system are connected and how they relate to each other.

blow, *vb.* to record a PROM with data. This data will remain until the PROM is washed. See WASH PROM.

body, *n.* **1.** the main part of a program. **2.** the text that is held in a word processor.

boilerplate, *n.* a document that is assembled from standard pieces of text held in the memory of a WORD PROCESSOR.

bomb, *n.* a concealed fault which can cause a system crash. The term 'bug' is used of a fault that is present through oversight or accident, and 'bomb' is normally reserved to mean a fault that has been deliberately planted, often in order to conceal evidence of fraud.

bomb, *vb.* to CRASH with a FATAL ERROR.

Boolean, *adj.* (of a quantity) taking only two values which can be described as TRUE or FALSE. Several languages (not BASIC) possess a data type called Boolean.

boot, *vb.* to load in a starting program. Many large computers require most of the operating system to be loaded in from disk, and this action is called *booting up*. Some faults can cause this to happen again (a REBOOT), in which case all the data that was in the memory will be lost. Small computers contain their operating system in ROM, so that booting is not needed, though in some examples a disk operating system may need to be booted.

border, *n.* that part of the video screen which surrounds the main portion used for text or graphics. Some machines allow the colour of this border to be changed, or its size to be altered.

BPI, *abbrev. for* bits per inch, the measurement of RECORDING DENSITY.

BPS, *abbrev. for* bits per second, the measurement of rate of data transmission.

brackets, *n.* the signs ( ) which enclose words or numbers. Most computing languages use brackets with special meanings. Brackets can be used in arithmetic to enforce an order of carrying out actions; actions within brackets are carried out first. Another use is to enclose the ARGUMENT of a function. Brackets are also used to enclose the SUBSCRIPT number of an ARRAY. Some computer languages make use of the square and curly brackets as well as the ordinary (parenthesis) brackets.

branch, *n.* a point at which a program can take one of two paths.

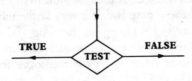

```
Pascal
        IF Answer = ('yes') THEN Proceed ELSE Errormesg
BASIC
   200  IF A = 2 THEN GOTO 100
   210  (this line is executed if A is not equal to 2)
```

Fig. 12. Branch. A test step must have one of two possible answers, true or false. The program then takes either branch according to the result of this test. The examples show typical branch steps in Pascal and in BASIC.

For example, if you see a message on the screen which reads: ANOTHER GAME (Y/N), then the program contains a branch. One route will be followed if you press the Y or y, another if you press the N or n. See Fig. 12.

breadboard, *n.* a temporary construction in electronics. *Breadboarding* means trying out an idea in a rough way. Careless connection to a breadboard circuit can cause considerable damage to a computer.

BREAK, *n.* a computer key which will stop program action.

breakpoint, *n.* a point at which a program will stop. By making the program stop at a selected point and printing the values of its variables, a fault can often be diagnosed. Breakpoints are used particularly often in assembly language program testing.

broadcast network, *n.* a NETWORK on which a user can transmit a PACKET of data that can be picked up and used by any other computer on the network. Normally, each packet carries an address code so that the packet can be intercepted by one other user.

BSI, *abbrev. for* the British Standards Institute, which draws up standards for materials, procedures and systems throughout the UK.

bubble memory, *n.* a form of memory which makes use of tiny artificially produced irregularities (bubbles) in a magnetic material. Each 'bubble' is used to indicate a binary 1, and the advantage of the system is that a very large number of bits can be stored in a very small space. Reading and writing are not straightforward, as both actions require the bubbles to be moved past a read/write head. A bubble memory, however, is NON-VOLATILE.

bubble sort, *n.* the simplest and least satisfactory way of sorting a LIST into order. In a bubble sort, each item on the list is compared with the following item, and if the two are in the wrong order, they are interchanged. The process is repeated until no exchanges have to be made on a run through the data. The bubble sort is very slow, sometimes taking hours to sort a few hundred string items, because the whole list has to be processed many times to allow an item at the end of the list, which belongs at the start, to 'bubble' its way to the start. The method is used only as a simple example of how a sort *can* be achieved. See SHELL SORT, QUICKSORT.

buffer, *n.* a piece of memory that is used for temporary storage. A buffer is often used in conjunction with a keyboard, so that if several keys are pressed in quick succession, all the codes can be dealt with in the correct order. A keyboard that is so equipped is described as having *N-key rollover*. Another use is in CASSETTE or DISK filing, when data is gathered up in a buffer until it can be transferred.

bug, *n.* a fault in a program. The act of removing the fault is called DEBUGGING, and the person who puts the bug in place is called a programmer.

built-in function, *n.* a program action which is part of the program code. Most languages contain routines for finding square roots, logarithms, and so on, and these are described as 'built-in functions'. Other functions have to be provided by the programmer in the form of DEFINED FUNCTIONS.

bulk storage, *n.* a system which allows large amounts of data to be stored, usually with rather slow access times. A disk drive is an example of a bulk storage system, also called a BACKING STORE.

bulk erase, *vb.* to wipe all signals from a tape. Tape is normally erased immediately prior to recording, but a bulk eraser can clear the whole of a tape without the need to wind the tape past a head. The principle is to set up an intense AC magnetic FIELD around the tape. Valuable disks and other tapes should be kept well clear of any bulk eraser.

bulletin board, *n.* a term used in ELECTRONIC MAIL to describe a message facility. Using a PASSWORD, you transmit your message to a host computer over the telephone lines, and the message is stored until the intended recipient, using his/her password, reads it. Bulletin board systems are vulnerable to HACKERS, and should not be used for confidential information. See also RING-BACK SYSTEM.

burner, *n.* a circuit that allows PROMS to be loaded with data. This usually involves applying voltages higher than normal, and repeatedly addressing each byte of the PROM with the correct data placed on the data terminals. See also BLOW, WASH PROM.

bus, *n.* a set of electrical conductors which carry related signals. For example, a DATA bus carries the set of signals for a character or other data item, and an ADDRESS BUS carries the signals that locate a byte in the memory. See Fig. 13.

byte, *n.* the unit of data or memory which is now universally taken to mean 8 BITS. One important feature of a byte is that a character in ASCII code needs only one byte for storage. This means that 16-bit computers often deal with ASCII-coded material no faster than 8-bit computers, because only one byte is being processed at a time.

The byte furthest to the right in a group of bytes is the *least-significant*, as it represents the number of ones, and can represent any denary number between 0 and 255 (i.e. 0 and $2^8 - 1$), e.g.:

binary 11111111 = denary $(1 \times 2^7) + (1 \times 2^6) + (1 \times 2^5) + (1 \times 2^4) + (1 \times 2^3) + (1 \times 2^2) + (1 \times 2^1) + (1 \times 2^0)$

$= 128 + 64 + 32 + 16 + 8 + 4 + 2 + 1$

$= 255 \times 1$

The least-significant byte is often stored in the memory as the first byte of the set.

The byte to the left of the least-significant byte represents the number of 256s (or 2^8s), and can represent any multiple of 256 between 256 and 65280 (i.e. 256^1 and $256^2 - 256$, or 256 and 256×255, or 2^8 and $2^{16} - 2^8$), e.g.:

binary 11111111 (in the position left of the least-significant bit) = denary $(1 \times 2^{15}) + (1 \times 2^{14}) + (1 \times 2^{13}) + (1 \times 2^{12}) + (1 \times 2^{11}) + (1 \times 2^{10}) + (1 \times 2^9) + (1 \times 2^8)$

$= 32,768 + 16,384 + 8192 + 4096 + 2048 + 1024 + 512 + 256$

$= (128 \times 256) + (64 \times 256) + (32 \times 256) + (16 \times 256) + (8 \times 256) + (4 \times 256) + (2 \times 256) + (1 \times 256)$

$= 65280$

$= 256 \times 255$

The byte to the left of this again represents the number of 65536s (or 2^{16}s), and can represent any multiple of 65536 between 65536 and 65536×65535 (i.e. 65536^1 and $65536^2 - 65536$, or 2^{16} and $2^{24} - 2^{16}$); and so on.

In a group of bytes, the *most-significant byte* is the leftmost byte, which represents the largest number of units, e.g.:

01110101   1111001   001011101   11011001

most-significant   least-significant
byte   byte

The most-significant byte is often stored in the memory as the last byte of the set.

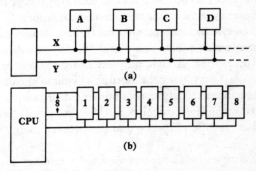

Fig. 13. **Bus.** A bus consists of a set of signal lines which are all connected to several devices. (a) A simple two-line bus, with lines X and Y connected to devices A, B, C and D. (b) The usual representation of a bus in a circuit diagram. In this example, the bus consists of 8 lines, with all 8 connected to each of the numbered devices. Buses like this are used for address signals that select memory, data signals for passing data to and from memory and ports, and for control signals that switch different sets of memory or ports on and off.

C

C, *n.* a HIGH-LEVEL computing language, derived from BCPL. The language is compact, so that a few short instruction words and symbols can control a large amount of computing action. The language is also tightly STRUCTURED, which means that it encourages the writing of logically designed programs. C is a flexible language which allows some liberties to be taken with DATA TYPES, though at the cost of relaxing error checking. These features make the language very attractive, and is widely used by professionals for writing OPERATING SYSTEMS, business software and games.

cache memory, *n.* a form of BUFFER memory. The word 'cache' usually implies that the memory can be accessed very rapidly, so that the user is unaware of the use of the memory.

CAD, *n. acronym for* Computer-Aided Design. This usually means a program which produces a visual output, or a diagram on a printer or plotter. Rough sketches can be made, using such devices as a LIGHT PEN or a MOUSE, and these sketches can be converted automatically to more precise diagrams, with lists of parts and quantities calculated. CAD programs need to be tailored to specific purposes, and can be very useful and time-saving.

CAL, *n. acronym for* Computer-Assisted Learning. The term is applied to any system in which the computer is used to provide practice, repetitive testing, visual simulations and other aids to learning. The full acceptance of CAL awaits the production of reliable voice synthesizers and voice recognition devices, so that the user can be freed completely from the use of the keyboard. See DIRECT VOICE INPUT.

CALL, *n.* a command word used on many machines as a way of running machine-code routines in the OPERATING SYSTEM during the action of a BASIC program. For example, CALL 23406 would cause the routine which started at address 23406 to run. Unless you understand the operating system thoroughly, you should not use commands of this type. Other words which are used for this purpose include SYS and USR.

calling, *n.* the requesting of connection to a remote terminal. A calling code is sent to the remote terminal so that it can be activated for the reception of data.

CAM, *n. acronym for* Computer-Aided Management. The term is applied to the use of a computer as a management tool by providing information, forecasts, visual simulations and data retrieval. The most important action, however, is usually communication.

Cambridge ring, *n.* a method of passing data round a group of computers. Also called *ring*. This is a form of LAN which as the name suggests was developed in Cambridge, and which is widely used in educational applications.

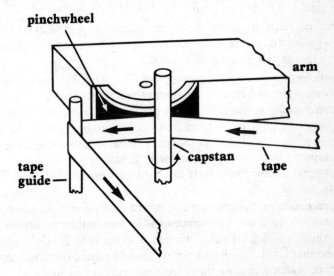

pinchwheel

arm

tape guide —

capstan

tape

Fig. 14. **Capstan.** The capstan spindle of a tape recorder is a round polished shaft which revolves at a steady speed. The tape is pinched between the capstan and the rubber pinchwheel, and this forces the tape also to move at a steady speed, pulling it past the record/replay head. Any irregularity in the capstan surface will cause the tape to run at an uneven speed.

caps, *abbrev. for* capital letters, also called UPPER CASE. Some implementations of programming languages insist on all instruction words being entered in upper case, others allow the choice of lower or upper case.

caps lock, *n.* the key that can make a keyboard provide either upper-case letters only, or a mixture of upper and lower case. A few older machines did not provide lower case from the keyboard, and the caps lock key was used only to select graphics. The key normally has a TOGGLE action (press for caps, press again for lower case), and should be provided with an indicator light.

capstan, *n.* the spindle of a cassette recorder which drives the tape along past the TAPEHEAD. Any dirt deposited, scratching, or distortion of the capstan will make the recorder unusable for loading or saving programs. See Fig. 14 on page 39.

card column, *n.* one of the eighty columns of a PUNCHED CARD. Each column can be located by the CARD PUNCH or CARD READER by means of a locating punch hole.

card feed, *n.* a device for automatically taking PUNCHED CARDS from a pile and feeding them into the CARD READER.

card punch, *n.* the device that marks PUNCHED CARDS. Under computer control, this grips the card, locates the correct column, and places punch marks in each column. This can be done in response to letters typed at the keyboard, or in response to a program action in which the card carries the output of the program.

card reader, *n.* the device that converts card punch hole positions into ASCII codes. The conversion is done either by electrical contacts which are made where a hole has been punched, or by beams of light which pass through holes to strike PHOTOSENSORS. The reader will sense the correct starting column, and read each byte, moving the card along, until it is ejected when all of the columns have been read.

carriage return, *n.* the action of moving to the left-hand side of a piece of paper. On the computer the RETURN key is normally used to declare the end of a reply or a command, so that the CURSOR returns to the left hand side on the next screen line. Some computers label this key as ENTER. The ASCII code for this action is 13.

carry, *n.* a digit that is generated in an addition or subtraction and which will affect the next part of the action. In binary code, for example, adding the numbers 1 and 1 will give the result 0, with a 1 carried to the next position, making 10. The microprocessor

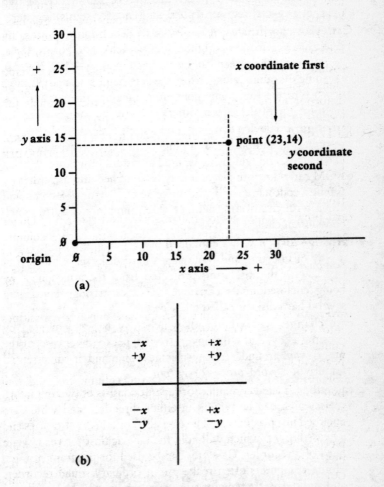

Fig. 15. **Cartesian coordinates.** (a) Two axes, X and Y, are specified, lying at right angles to each other. The position of a point is given in terms of the distance along each axis from a starting point which is called the origin. The bottom left-hand corner of the screen is often taken as the origin for graphics purposes. (b) Points in any other position can be specified by using negative values for X or Y distances.

stores each carry bit from the addition or subtraction of two bytes in a special register, called the FLAG, (or status) register.

Cartesian coordinates, *n.* a system of determining position by reference to two axes at right angles to each other. For example, a position on the screen can be referred to as X = 100, Y = 50, meaning 100 units along from the left-hand side and 50 units down fom the top. Sòme computers measure the Y DIRECTION from the top of the screen, others from the bottom. See Fig. 15.

cartridge, *n.* a device that plugs into a slot . There are two distinct meanings in computing. **1.** a plug-in memory board which can carry ROMs, and which can be used as instant programs. When a ROM cartridge is in place, it may be switched into use either by typing a code name, or by the use of a CALL SYS or USR command along with an ADDRESS number. **2.** A miniature cassette which contains an endless loop of tape. See also FLOPPY TAPE.

cartridge disk, *n.* a disk contained in a removable casing. This is a way of inserting and removing a hard disk (see WINCHESTER DISK), with the disk itself protected from the atmosphere by being enclosed in its cartridge. A disk cartridge containing several hard disks is called a *disk pack*.

case change, *n.* a command, which may be implemented by pressing a key, that will convert from upper to lower case, or the other way around. A case-change command is an essential feature of a word-processor system.

cassette, *n.* a rigid container for tape. It consists of two miniature reels which can be wound in either direction, and which are enclosed in a plastic case. The case also contains TAPE GUIDES and a PRESSURE PAD which will hold the tape against the read/write head of a recorder. Cassettes can be used for program storage. Home computers often make use of ordinary sound recorders and audio cassette tape for storage, a system which is much less satisfactory than a specially designed digital cassette system using special tape.

CAT, *abbrev. for* catalogue, a directory command which is used in many disk systems, and a few tape systems, to provide a list of all the FILES on a disk or tape.

catalogue of disk, *n.* a list of FILES on the disk. The form of the listing should show the FILENAME, type and approximate length for each file. The catalogue is usually obtained by typing the command word DIR or CAT.

catastrophic error, see FATAL ERROR.

CD ROM, see COMPACT DISC.

cell, *n.* **1.** in a SPREADSHEET type of program, a unit position on the screen which will contain a number or a word. Each cell of the spreadsheet is located by numbering its row and its column. **2.** a unit of memory, storing one byte, and with a unique ADDRESS number.

centring, *n.* the placing of a word or phrase in the middle of a printed line during word processing.

Centronics interface, *n.* a universally accepted INTERFACE for printers. This is the type of interface which is referred to as *parallel*, meaning that one line is used for each bit of a byte, along with lines for synchronizing signals. The standard was devised by the printer manufacturer Centronics Inc., and it is normal to find that any computer which uses the Centronics interface will match to any printer that uses this interface.

CHAIN, *n.* **1.** in some computing languages, a command that forces a program to halt and then load and run another program and make use of the results. The extra program uses variable values from the main program, does *not* replace the original, and is deleted after it has run. **2.** on some small machines, a command that loads and runs a program, deleting any other program that was previously present.

chain search, *n.* a SEQUENTIAL search through items. This involves items such as RECORDS which can contain POINTERS to other items, until the required item or the end of the list is reached. A typical example of chain searching is found in information services of the TELETEXT type, so that if you look up 'travel', you find references to road, rail, sea, and air. Looking up 'air' then produces a list of airports, and so on. Chain searching is acceptable if the computer carries out the search automatically, but can be very slow if each item has to be selected manually.

channel, *n.* a path for data. Also called *stream*. Several operating systems use fixed channels which are identified by number so that, for example, PRINT#0 means print on screen, PRINT#8 means print on paper, and PRINT#9 means store on tape or disk. The use of channels in this way makes it possible to have commands such as PRINT#X, in which the VARIABLE X can be assigned (see ASSIGNATION) with numbers that will cause the data to be directed in different ways.

character, *n.* any letter, digit, punctuation mark, or graphics symbol which is represented by one ASCII code number. This excludes codes for actions, such as line feed or carriage return, which are represented by code numbers in the range 0 to 31.

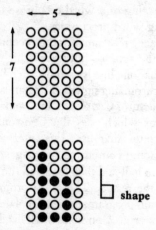

Fig. 16. **Character block.** This consists of the group of dots from which any character shape can be obtained. On the screen, these dots are lit, but on paper, each dot is inked.

character block, *n.* the set of dots that can be used to make up a character. A screen display of the usual VDU type uses a dot of light which scans across and down the screen. The shape of a character is obtained by brightening the dot in the required places as it moves across the screen. Each character is therefore built up from dots, and the pattern of dots that is available at each character position is called the character block. This is specified as the number of dots across the character and the number down.

A typical block is 15×9 dots, but DOT-MATRIX printers often use fewer dots, sometimes only 7×5. See Fig. 16.

character code, *n.* a number which represents a CHARACTER. Usually the number will be one of the ASCII set, but some computers use different INTERNAL CODES.

character generator, *n.* a ROM-based circuit which converts codes. When the input to a character generator is a valid ASCII code, the output will be a set of numbers which will cause the VDU to illuminate the correct pattern of dots in the CHARACTER BLOCK.

character recognition, *n.* automatic conversion from character shape to ASCII code. This is carried out by a photosensor which can be moved across a line of print and which will 'read' and convert each character into ASCII code. Character recognition can be a very elaborate and expensive process, especially if the device has to be able to read any kind of character, as, for example, post-code readers. Character recognition devices are now obtainable in simplified form for reading typed characters. See OPTICAL CHARACTER READER, GRID.

character set, *n.* the complete set of coded characters, both text and graphics, which can be printed on the screen by a computer. The larger the character set, the more versatile the computer is likely to be in providing visual data from simple programs.

chart recorder, *n.* a form of automatic graph-drawing device. A roll of paper is moved at a constant speed, and a pen touching the paper is moved across the width of the paper by an input voltage. See also X-Y PLOTTER. The important difference between the chart recorder and the X-Y plotter is that the computer controls only the up-and-down movement of the pen of a chart recorder.

check bit, *n.* a bit used as a method of error detection. If one bit of a byte (or any other group of bits) is not used for data, it can be used to check that the remaining bits are valid. This is usually done by PARITY checks. The use of a check bit allows each byte to be checked, and can be used to signal which byte may contain an error.

checksum, *n.* a programming method that is used to minimize data errors when data is transferred. The data consists internally of a stream of numbers, which are summed. The final total is compared with another total which is also read in. If the two disagree, there has been a read error, but the method cannot show where. A variation on this is to read data in small blocks, with a checksum for each block. In this way, the block which contains the fault can be located. Checksums are particularly important in routines that save and load data on tape or disk. See also CRC.

chip, *n.* the form of electronic CIRCUIT module used for computer construction. An electronic circuit which has been formed on to one small piece of SILICON or other SEMICONDUCTOR material by photographic printing, etching and the condensation of semiconductor vapours.

circuit, *n.* the path of an electric current. The circuits of computers are ELECTRONIC circuits, in which the current passes through semiconductor devices.

circuit board, *n.* a plastic or laminated board which carries a carefully-planned network of copper strips. See also CIRCUIT CARD. Printed circuit boards (PCBs) replaced hand-wired circuits in the 1950s because of their much greater reliability.

circuit card, *n.* the insulating board on which an electronics circuit is constructed. Circuit cards are fabricated from an insulator such as resin-impregnated paper or glass-fibre which has been coated with metal. Using photographic techniques, patterns of connections are printed on the metal surface, and the unused metal is etched away with acids. The board is then drilled to allow the connecting pins of the ICs and other electronic components to be inserted and soldered to the metal strips. A complete circuit card is often fabricated with a set of EDGE CONNECTORS so that the whole board can be easily plugged into or out of the computer. This makes for easy repairs, and also for easy expansion of a computer which has been designed in this form. See also CIRCUIT BOARD.

circular file, *n.* a file with no beginning or end consisting of a list of items, each of which contains a POINTER to the next item. Also called *ring*. The 'last' item in the list carries a pointer to the 'first' item, so that the list can be searched indefinitely from any starting position.

clean machine, *n.* a computer which uses the minimum of ROM, to BOOT its OPERATING SYSTEM in from a disk. A clean machine will also need to load its operating LANGUAGE from disk. The advantages include the ability to make the best use of memory for different types of languages, and the ability to alter both language and operating system as required. The disadvantages include the time needed to start the system, and the vulnerability to CORRUPTION.

clear variable, *vb.* to make the value of a variable blank or zero. In the normal operation of a computer, all variables that are used in a program are cleared at the start of a run. For actions such as chaining (see CHAIN), however, variable values may have to be retained so that they can be used by more than one program. During a program run, a variable will retain any value that is assigned to it unless it is cleared or reassigned. The exception is the use of 'local' variables, which are used only in SUBPROGRAMS and cleared immediately the subprogram ends.

clock, *n.* a circuit that issues signals at regular intervals. Each action of a microprocessor is set into motion by an electrical pulse, and the speed of processing depends on the rate of these pulses, called the clock-rate. The pulses are generated by a circuit which is called the 'clock'. A typical clock speed for a small computer is four million pulses per second, but much higher clock speeds are used for mini and mainframe machines.

CLOSE, *n.* a command used in many computing LANGUAGES to mean that a disk or tape FILE is at an end. When a file is being recorded, the command usually causes the recording of any data that remains in a BUFFER and then the recording of an END OF FILE code on to the disk or tape.

closed loop, *n.* a type of electronic control circuit, in which any deviation from the desired output is amplified and used to correct the output. This type of control is also known as negative FEEDBACK. Closed-loop circuits are used to a large extent in motor-speed controls, for example for DISK DRIVES.

closed user group (CUG), *n.* a restricted number of intercommunicating computer users. Any computer owner can connect via a MODEM to public telephone lines, and hence to any other modems. Databases such as PRESTEL and MICRONET are available only to users who have paid fees, and who have been issued with pass codes. A closed user group is vulnerable to HACKERS unless the password system is a good one.

CLS, *n.* a command in most varieties of BASIC denoting the clear screen action.

cluster, *n.* a group of TERMINALS which operate together. A system which consists of a central processor with several remote terminals is often arranged so that each terminal will provide an identical display, and this group of terminals constitutes a 'cluster'.

CMOS, *abbrev. for* complementary metal-oxide semiconductor, a form of construction for ICs which requires very low power inputs, and is now being extensively used both for microprocessors and for memories. See also NMOS, PMOS.

coaxial cable, *n.* a cable consisting of one central conductor which is surrounded with an insulator and then with the other conductor. Often shortened to *coax*. In this way, the outer conductor prevents interference from reaching the inner. Coax cable is used for TV signals, including the aerial leads for domestic TV, and also for high speed data links.

COBOL, *n. acronym for* Common Business-Oriented Language. It was one of the first high-level languages which was not intended for mathematical or scientific use. COBOL is a clumsy language, which needs large amounts of memory, but it has the advantage of using terms that look reasonably like English language words.

code, *n.* the use of one symbol or set of symbols to represent something else. The most important code for microcomputing purposes is ASCII which uses numbers to represent characters. See also EBDIC, GRAY CODE.

code conversion, *n.* the conversion of one code into another. Computers which use INTERNAL CODES for screen displays may carry out conversion from the ASCII codes which are used to store data in memory. The form of an ASCII code may also have to be converted. One very common example is conversion between

ASCII codes on parallel lines and serial ASCII codes on a single line.

coding sheet, *n.* a printed paper form for writing a program. The paper is ruled into rows and columns so that the programmer can check how, for example, the text will look on the screen. Coding sheets are not really necessary with modern programming languages and TERMINALS, but were widely used in the days of PUNCHED CARDS and TELETYPES.

cold start, *n.* the clearing of computer memory and the starting of the operating system. A cold start is usually performed when a microcomputer is first switched on. If, due to a fault, a cold start is performed during operation, all data and programs in the memory will be lost. Compare WARM START. See also BOOT, REBOOT.

collision detection, *n.* the reporting of the coincidence of two events. In SPRITE graphics, a signal can be issued when two sprites overlap, so that the program can make use of this signal in some way. The programmer might, for example, want to detect when a graphics 'shell' shape hit a 'warship' shape, and use this collision to operate an explosion sound and the removal of both objects from the screen. In a NETWORK, collision detection is a system which is used to make sure that the shared lines are free when a computer requests to send signals.

colon, *n.* the : symbol, which is used in several computing LANGUAGES. In Pascal, for example, the colon is used to separate a word or number from a FIELD number which decides how the item will be printed. For example, (WRITE(NR:7:2) will print the value of variable NR with a total of 7 characters (including decimal point) and with two digits following the decimal point. In many dialects of BASIC, the colon is used to separate STATEMENTS on the same line (a MULTI-STATEMENT LINE).

colour displays, *n.* VIDEO output signals which will produce colour displays on colour monitors or TV receivers. This has led to a number of commands being added to BASIC for the purpose of colour control. Unfortunately, there is no standard set of commands. Many programming languages have no colour instructions, and users of these languages must insert MACHINE CODE sections to carry out such actions.

colour monitor, *n.* a MONITOR which is fitted with a colour CRT. The highest RESOLUTION is obtained when separate red, green and blue signals can be used, and a monitor with such an input is termed an RGB monitor. When the signals are combined into one, cabling is easier, but the resolution is poorer. This system, which applies also to video recorders, is called COMPOSITE VIDEO. The lowest resolution is obtained when the composite signal is in turn modulated (see MODULATION) on to a TV channel frequency and used to feed a TV receiver. If the monitor is used extensively for word processing with 80 characters per line, then a monochrome monitor which uses an amber display is considerably less tiring on the eyes of the user than a colour monitor.

column, *n.* a preset horizontal position. The VDU screen has character positions which are vertically aligned in columns, usually either 80 or 40 per screen width. Printers follow the same scheme, but can usually select a wider range of column numbers. The position of any character on the screen or on paper can be determined by using the column number and the row number. See also ROWS AND COLUMNS.

combiner, *n.* a device used to connect to more than one signal without switching. A very common use in home computing is in the lead to a TV receiver. This allows the use of both computer and TV signals without the need for plugging and unplugging leads. Combiners can also be used in data channels to allow data from more than one source to flow down a common line.

comma, *n.* the , symbol which is used as a SEPARATOR or print MODIFIER in most computing languages. BASIC uses the comma to cause printed material to appear in columns. Pascal uses the comma simply to separate items that are to be printed, with no spacing effect.

command, *n.* a direct instruction to the computer. The word is normally used to mean a computer instruction that is obeyed at once, as distinct from an INSTRUCTION or STATEMENT in a PROGRAM which is obeyed when the program is run. The words 'command' and 'instruction' are often used interchangeably, however.

command language, *n.* a form of simplified computing LAN-GUAGE which is itself part of a PROGRAM. Many programs such as DATABASES, WORD PROCESSORS and SPREADSHEETS require the operator to be able to enter sets of commands that will modify the output of the program. This requires the use of a command language which is specific to the program. A very elaborate command language can make a program very flexible, but may also make it difficult to use until the user has had a lot of experience with the program.

compact disc, *n.* A method of storing DIGITAL data. Also called *laser disc*. The form of compact disc that is used for audio or video recording uses a LASER to burn small pits in a metal surface. These pits represent digital signals which are used to code the AMPLITUDE of the audio or video signal. This digital recording is ideal for storing computer data. Such devices, *CD ROMS*, are used for permanent storage of data external to the computer, in the way that a ROM or PROM would be used internally. The drawback is that access to data is not as fast as can be obtained from RAM, but very large amounts of data can be stored and the rate of transfer can be very high.

compacting algorithm, *n.* a method of storing data in com-pressed form. Also called *data compacting*. Some computing LANGUAGES have such ALGORITHMS built in, so that an array can be specified as being a PACKED STRUCTURE, meaning that the data is stored as compactly as possible. Compacting is particularly important when the computing language makes inefficient use of memory. The techniques are also important where a program makes a lot of use of text.

companding, *n.* a combination of COMPRESSING and EXPANDING.

comparing strings, *n.* the action of determining the relative order of sets of ASCII codes. In BASIC, a STRING of characters can be compared for order by using the mathematical symbols $=<$ and $>$. The comparison is done by using the ASCII codes for the letters. Many other languages do not use strings, using in their place arrays of character codes, but the comparison methods can still be carried out.

compatibility, *n.* the ability of devices to work together. A computer made by one manufacturer may not work with a printer or disk drive made by another manufacturer. Lack of compatibility of this type restricts the users choice of peripherals, and often makes it necessary to replace all of the computer equipment when any item is to be upgraded. Lack of compatibility is caused in a few examples by lack of standardization, but is more usually due to a manufacturer's belief that no other manufacturer should be involved with his product.

compile, *vb.* to convert a COMPILED LANGUAGE into MACHINE CODE, using a COMPILER.

compiled language, *n.* a language which is completely converted into MACHINE CODE before use. A program which is written in a HIGH-LEVEL LANGUAGE will consist only of ASCII codes for the STATEMENTS of that language. This form of program cannot be run until it is compiled or interpreted. Compiling consists of translating the program instructions into machine code that the microprocessor of the computer can use. See COMPILER, INTERPRETER.

compiler, *n.* a program that compiles instructions. A compiler will convert a text program (a set of instructions, usually in ASCII codes) of a high-level language into MACHINE CODE. Many compilers do not compile fully; they generate an intermediate code or INTERNAL LANGUAGE (such as Pascal P-CODE), and then interpret this code (see INTERPRETER). A program which is compiled fully (to native machine code) can run very much faster than an interpreted program.

complement, see NEGATION.

composite video, *n.* video signals from the computer which combine coded colour signals with the normal monochrome signal. Composite video signals can be recorded on video recorders, and can be used by several types of monitors, including TV studio monitors. The RESOLUTION, however, is not so good as can be obtained using RGB monitors.

compound statement, *n.* a group of statements that is treated by the computer as one statement. In Pascal, for example, such a statement starts with BEGIN; and continues until the END; mark, with everything between being treated as one statement.

compressing, *n.* the packing of anything into a limited space. Data can often be compressed or compacted so as to fit into the minimum possible memory space. See also COMPANDING.

computer, *n.* a device that will manipulate data. See ANALOGUE COMPUTER, DIGITAL COMPUTER.

computer bureau, *n.* a form of computer hiring organization. The bureau owns or rents a computer, and hires out time and programming assistance to users.

computer graphics, *n.* the visual representation of patterns (see GRAPHICS) on the VDU screen. Anything that can be drawn on paper can be drawn on the VDU screen. The difference is that the computer-graphics patterns are programmed, can be erased and changed almost instantly, and can be manipulated in ways that are impossible with images on paper or on film. Computer graphics are closely associated with computer games, but their more important roles are in simulations (such as flight simulators for pilot training) and in CAD.

computer literacy, *n.* the understanding of the applications of computers. This does not necessarily require knowledge of how computers work or how they are programmed.

computing power, *n.* the relative speed of computing. One computer is described as being more powerful than another if it can handle more work at a faster speed. This, however, is by no means easy to measure, because a computer which is fast on one type of task may be slow on another type of work. BENCHMARKS are sometimes used as comparisons, but these are often misleading and seldom useful.

concatenation, *n.* the joining of STRINGS. For example, if one string is HOLIDAY and another is TIME, then concatenating the strings in that order would give HOLIDAYTIME.

conditional, *n.* anything depending on the result of a test. In many languages, the word IF is used to form the test, so that a statement like: IF Number>100 THEN Makeroom will cause the procedure Makeroom to run conditional on the value of variable Number. If

Number is greater than 100, then Makeroom runs, but if Number is less than 100 or equal to 100, then Makeroom does not run.

configuration, *n.* the arrangment of some feature of the computer system. For example, a screen configuration may be 80 characters per line and 25 lines per frame; a disk drive may use a configuration of 40 tracks, single sided, double density. Operating systems such as CP/M can be modified to suit the configurations of individual computer systems.

connector, *n.* anything that joins one item to another. In HARDWARE, a connector means an electrical plug and socket, usually for data transmission. See also MALE CONNECTOR, FEMALE CONNECTOR. In software, a connector is a word such as AND, OR, NOT which is used to connect conditions. For example, the instruction: IF N1 = 5 AND N2<100 THEN OUTLINE would carry out the PROCEDURE called OUTLINE only if both conditions were true. The word AND is the connector between the conditions.

console, *n.* an old-fashioned term for a combination of keyboard and screen, with no computing action. The term TERMINAL is also used, but this often implies some computing actions as well.

constant, *n.* a quantity whose value is not changed in the course of a program. In BASIC, there is no specific constant data type, and variables can be used. In Pascal and other languages, a number or a STRING can be defined as a constant.

constant length field, *n.* a specification of number of characters for data. When a RANDOM-ACCESS FILE is in use, programming is greatly simplified if each item of data is of a known number of characters. If, for example, all names are of 50 characters and all addresses of 80 characters, then a RECORD that consists of name and address will contain 130 characters, and the start of the next record will be 130 characters beyond the start of the current record. Data items which are shorter than the specified 'field' length can be padded with blanks, items which are longer can be dealt with by TRUNCATION.

contiguous graphics, *n.* shapes which touch each other. VDU CHARACTER BLOCKS are arranged so that each text character has a space at one side and underneath. This allows text to be printed on the screen without the letters touching each other. When graphics characters are used, however, it is usually easier to make satisfactory diagrams if adjacent characters do touch each other. See Fig. 17. Compare SEPARATED GRAPHICS.

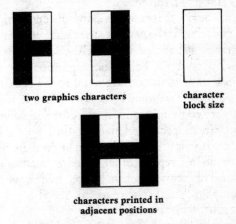

two graphics characters

character
block size

characters printed in
adjacent positions

Fig. 17. **Contiguous graphics.** These characters use the whole width and height of a character block. When printed in adjacent positions, the characters will touch and merge, making it easier to produce patterns.

continuous stationery, *n.* paper intended for use by a printer. The paper consists of a continuous sheet, perforated at lengths of 28 cm.(11″) or alternatively 30.5 cm.(12″) and usually TRACTOR-FED. Another form of continuous stationery is TELETYPE roll, which is much cheaper to use. The alternative to continuous stationery is single sheets. For high-speed work, this requires an expensive single-sheet feeder for the printer.

contrast, *n.* the difference between light and dark. On a VDU screen, the contrast should be made variable so as to allow for differences in the lighting of rooms. Some screens use coloured or neutral-density optical filters to improve contrast, so that the screen looks very dark when the VDU is switched off. Contrast of black lettering on white paper is often important when OPTICAL CHARACTER RECOGNITION is being used.

control character, *n.* a character whose ASCII code is outside the range of codes that produce shapes on the screen. The purpose of a control character is to produce some effect like clearing the screen or moving the CURSOR. These codes differ from one computer to another although some, like codes 13, 10, 8, and 9 are practically standardized.

converter, *n.* a device that converts data from one form to another. A typical converter is the PAPER-TAPE reader, which converts the punch marks on paper tape into ASCII-coded electrical signals.

coordinates, *n.* systems of defining position by the use of numbers. See CARTESIAN COORDINATES, POLAR COORDINATES.

coprocessor, *n.* an additional MICROPROCESSOR for auxiliary actions. A very common requirement is for a separate processor that can undertake specialized mathematical work which would otherwise greatly slow down the action of the main processor. A coprocessor of this type is often called a NUMBER CRUNCHER. Another form of coprocessor can be used to deal with display of text and graphics, another with sound. See also BLITTER, VIDEO INTERFACE CHIP, SOUND CHIP.

copy, *n.* **1.** text ready for a printer. **2.** to make a duplicate of a file on disk or on tape.

copy protection, *n.* any system that makes a tape or disk difficult to copy. This inevitably makes it difficult to BACKUP, and so makes the program risky to use. The use of copy-protection methods is highly undesirable, and has been forced on manufacturers by the problem of software PIRACY. Since any copy-protection method can be broken by a proficient programmer (or HACKER), these habits penalize the honest user who needs a backup, but have no effect on the professional pirates who stand to gain a large sum by their activities.

copyright notice, *n.* a warning of copyright. This takes the form of a statement which is part of a program and is usually printed on the screen at the start of the program. It reminds the user that the program is copyright, and that taking copies for any purpose other than for BACKUP is illegal. The user is sometimes asked in addition to sign and return a pledge of observance of copyright.

core memory, *n.* a form of magnetic memory. Each bit of a stored byte of data is stored in a separate tiny ring of magnetic material, which is threaded by a set of wires. The value of a bit is represented by the direction of magnetization in the core, which is altered both by writing (recording) and by reading. Because reading reverses the state of a core, each read must be followed by rewriting. The process is clumsy, and the store requires a lot of space and is expensive to construct. The speed of operation, however, can be very much higher than can be achieved by other methods, so that core stores are necessarily used on the largest and fastest computers. See Fig. 18. See also MAGNETIC CORE.

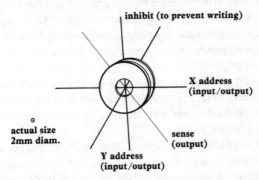

Fig. 18. **Core memory.** A magnetic core memory element. Each magnetic ring is threaded by four wires. Two are used to address the core, and will also write a '1' data bit. One is used to prevent writing a '1', and the sense line detects an output when a core that stores a '1' is read.

core program, *n.* the outline set of steps in a TOP-DOWN designed program. This core, which may be a LINEAR or a LOOPING PROGRAM, consists of all the main steps, which may be in the form of PROCEDURE names, or SUBROUTINE calls. The whole action should therefore be evident by looking at this core, which may consist of only a few steps, as for example:

```
10 Setup
20 Entry
30 Process
40 Record
50 Askmore
60 END
```

CORRUPTION

Some languages allow a program to be constructed with this core at the start, others require the core to be placed at the end. Most DIALECTS of BASIC do not allow the use of PROCEDURES that can be called by name, and can use only SUBROUTINES.

corruption, *n.* the unwanted changing of data, either in the memory or during replay from disk or tape. If the corruption affects only text which is in ASCII codes, it can be edited out, but corruption of other codes may be impossible to correct. If any part of memory which is used by the operating system becomes corrupted, the computer may LOCKUP or REBOOT. Computers which keep their whole operating system in RAM are more liable to corruption problems than those which use an operating system in ROM.

counter, *n.* a variable that is used to keep a running count of actions or items. The counter variable will be INCREMENTED or DECREMENTED each time an action is performed or an item entered. See also FOR.

CP/M, *abbrev. for* control, program, monitor. CP/M was the first 'universal' disk-based operating system for microcomputers, devised in 1973. The original CP/M applied only to computers which used the 8080 MICROPROCESSOR chip, and was later adapted to the very popular Z-80 microprocessor.

CP/M is stored mainly on disk, and provides routines for using the screen, printer and disk system. As the name suggests, it has routines for controlling the computer's action, for programming (in machine code) and for monitoring the working of programs. A computer which uses CP/M must use the 8080 or Z-80 microprocessor, and the memory of the machine must be arranged in a particular way, with certain addresses reserved. The machine must contain a small amount of code in ROM which will be used to BOOT the main CP/M system. Many developments of CP/M exist, in particular for the later types of microprocessor such as the 8088 and 8086. See also MP/M.

CPU, *abbrev. for* central processing unit. In large computers, this may consist of a circuit that contains a number of chips, but for microcomputers, the CPU is almost invariably a single chip, the microprocessor. Some computers, however, use more than one microprocessor, usually so that one can service the screen actions and the other performs the main computing actions. Another option is the use of a 'slave' NUMBER CRUNCHER, or COPROCESSOR, which is reserved for mathematical routines. In large machines, the CPU may consist of a complete CIRCUIT CARD, or even more than one card, particularly if BIT-SLICE MACHINE techniques are used.

crash, 1. *n*. an undesired end to a program, often brought about by a SOFTWARE fault. Also called *program crash*. Some computers will store a program unchanged after a crash, and allow easy recovery. Others crash very completely, corrupting the RAM, and need to be REBOOTED before they can be used again. A crash can come about as a result of a badly-designed program, but may also be caused by fluctuations of mains supply voltage, strong radiated signals, the effect of incorrectly connected PERIPHERALS, or partial failure of memory. See also FATAL ERROR. **2**. *vb*. to end a program unintentionally.

Cray-1, *n. Trademark*. one of the world's most powerful computers, of which some thirty are built each year. Also called *supercomputer*. The most obvious feature is its circular shape, which is intended to reduce the distance over which data signals have to travel. At the computing speeds which are used in this machine, even the time for an electrical signal to cover the distance of one metre (a fraction of a NANOSECOND) is significant. Other supercomputers in this class are the CRAY-2 and the Cyber.

critical path, *n*. the route which takes the least time. In any process which consists of many actions, some actions will take very much more time than others. The critical path is the combination and arrangement of actions which takes the least time, and *critical path analysis* means trying to find this sequence in a scientific way. The main feature of critical path analysis is to try to arrange long tasks so that they can be performed in parallel with other tasks rather then in sequence. This may require substantial redesigning of the tasks themselves.

cross compiler, *n*. a COMPILER that will generate code for a microprocessor which is *not* the one that is used in the compiling machine. For example, if your computer uses a Z-80 microprocessor, a cross compiler for 6502 would allow you to produce code which could be used by a 6502 microprocessor. Cross compilers are much used by games designers, who can take advantage of the facilities of very large computers to design games which will run on small machines.

CRC, *abbrev. for* cyclic redundancy check. This is a method (related to the CHECKSUM) for detecting errors in transmitted data. It is particularly useful for data stored on tape or on disk.

CRT, *abbrev. for* cathode-ray tube, the display device used in most monitors and TV receivers. Alternatives, such as LCD display screens, are being used for portable computers, but the CRT still predominates for larger displays. It has the particular advantage of being a large bright display which can be used in dark places. Its disadvantages include fragile construction (using glass), large bulk, and the requirement for high electrical voltages. It is also less easy to INTERFACE with computer signals than other devices.

CTRL, *abbrev. for* control key. This key is used on most computers, but the action varies. One common use is to allow actions to be performed without the need for extra keys. This is done by pressing the CTRL key along with a letter key. For example, on the PC machine, holding down CTRL along with C will terminate an action. The use of a CTRL key is assumed in CP/M and MS-DOS actions. The CTRL key on most computers generates the ASCII code 29.

current address, *n.* the memory address that is currently in use. For a MACHINE CODE program stored in memory, the current address is the address of the byte which is being acted on. This current address is stored in the PROGRAM COUNTER register of the microprocessor.

cursor, *n.* the screen position indicator, a marker which is placed on the display screen to show where text will appear when you type. The cursor often consists of a flashing block or dash. Several computers allow the cursor to be switched on or off.

cursor-control keys, *n.* the keys that will cause cursor movement. These keys are usually marked with arrows which show in which direction the cursor will move when a key is pressed. Many computers dispense with these keys, using only a delete or backspace key for left movement, and the spacebar for right movement.

cybernetics, *n.* the study of thought processes. Cybernetics as a study dates from the discovery of the principles of machine control by negative FEEDBACK. The action of a CLOSED-LOOP system mimics in many ways the control action of the brain and nervous system, and the similarities have led to researchers explaining such actions in terms borrowed from electronics. This has been a very fruitful method both for the design of ROBOT mechanisms and for deeper understanding of the action of the human brain.

cycle, *n.* a set of repeating actions. See also CLOCK.

cycle time, *n.* the time that is needed for a complete cycle of actions.

D

daisywheel, *n.* the PRINTHEAD of one type of printer mechanism. Type characters are moulded on the end of short flexible stalks which are arranged around a hub like the petals of a daisy. The printer action consists of rotating the daisywheel so as to select the correct character, and then hitting the back of the typeblock with a miniature hammer so as to press the type against the ribbon and the paper. See Fig. 19 on page 62.

data, *n.* anything that the computer can work with. This could be numbers of any kind, text characters, positions on a diagram, and so on. Whatever the 'raw' data happens to be, it is always converted into BINARY number form for use by the computer. This causes no problems for TEXT data and INTEGER numbers, but REAL NUMBERS generally have to be stored in the form of a binary approximation, because only a few real numbers can be represented as an exact BINARY FRACTION. The computer

DATABASE

depends on valid data being fed to it, and ridiculous errors can result if the program does not make some form of check on data that is entered from the keyboard. See also DATA VALIDATION.

database, *n.* a collection of data items which are used frequently by programs. A database of any size would be kept on a disk, probably on several disks. For example, a firm might keep a database which consisted of the name, address, phone number and state of account for each customer. This database would then be used extensively each day, and would be continually updated.

The database disks are precious, and several copies of each disk must be kept in reserve (see FATHER). In addition, the state of the database should be printed out to paper at frequent intervals.

data capture, *n.* any method that converts raw (not recorded) data into the form of numbers that the computer can use, and includes the keyboard itself and OPTICAL CHARACTER READER devices. In computers which are used to control manufacturing processes, the data may be obtained from measuring instruments, using

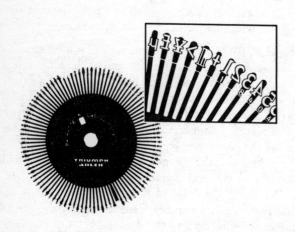

Fig. 19. **Daisywheel.** A single embossed character is carried at the end of each stalk.

DIGITIZERS to convert to BINARY form. Data capture in such a case is entirely automatic and does not depend on a human operator.

data compacting, see COMPACTING ALGORITHM.

data processing, *n.* the arrangement of data into a form that will be more useful. This could mean solving mathematical problems, arranging names into alphabetical order, or displaying data in such a way as to show relationships. The use of a computer allows data processing to be carried out much more rapidly than by other methods. In addition, much more complex and tedious operations can be carried out, like searching through large amounts of data for given items. The results of data processing actions are only as useful as the validity of the data itself, however. If the data is suspect, the results are not to be trusted. See GARBAGE.

data security, *n.* any system of keeping data confidential. Where confidential data, such as personal and medical records, must be processed, several security steps will be needed to avoid leakage of information. These include PASSWORD access to data, with passwords issued to a restricted number of users, frequent changes of password, with alarm systems to detect an incorrect password, and random checks on the use of TERMINALS. Passwords should never be simple (such as initials of the user), but should be capable of being memorized without writing down. A data system which is intended to be secure should *never* be connected to public telephone lines.

data structure, *n.* a set of related data items which the computer can use like one single item. In several languages, for example, there is a data structure which is called a RECORD. A record for an addressbook application might contain data on name, address, age, telephone number and hobbies for each entry. The computer would then manipulate all this data for one entry as one piece, rather than as a number of separate items.

data type, *n.* the kind of data that can be used. Most dialects of BASIC possess only three data types, INTEGER number, REAL NUMBER and STRING. Other languages use many more, such as BOOLEAN, CHARACTER, RECORD, FILE, etc. The greater the number of data types, in general, the easier it should be to devise good data-handling programs. Some languages, however, take the opposite view that flexibility in the use of variables is more important than a large number of variable types. See Fig. 20.

data validation, *n.* a check on entered data. Any data that is entered from a keyboard by a human operator is liable to contain mistakes. These mistakes may be trivial, such as the misspelling of an address. Others may be unimportant for a human operator, who will automatically correct the mistake, but important for the computer. In general, at any point in a program where a keyboard entry is made, the program should contain routines which will check the validity of the entry. Some mistakes, such as a date of 30th February, can easily be trapped and lead to the request for the date to be entered again. Other errors, such as an age of 100 instead of 10, are not so simple to trap. The main problems arise when there is no hard and fast rule that can be applied. In some cases, the only form of validation which can be used is to print the data, and ask the user to check it.

Simple BASIC	Extended BASIC
integer	integer
real	single-precision
string	double-precision
array	string
	array

Pascal	C
integer	integer
word	char
char	floating point
Boolean	double-precision
real	array
array	structure
record	pointer
list	
file	
pointer	
set	

Fig. 20. **Data types.** Data types for a few languages. The data types of number and character are primary data types, the others represent groupings of these types into compound data types.

D-base, *n. Trademark.* the name of a popular database program. The program has existed in several versions, most notably D-base 2 and D-base 3. The most important feature is the provision of a specialized programming language which allows the user to create a version of the program for his/her own use. This makes the program very versatile, though difficult to use without help (in the form of guidebooks) and experience.

DC, *abbrev. for* direct current. This form of electrical supply uses a steady voltage, such as is supplied from a battery. Computer systems require DC supplies at low voltage, and a POWER SUPPLY UNIT is needed to convert the mains AC into this form.

deadlock, *n.* a conflict between programs. This may occur in a system that allows two programs to run at the same time. A deadlock occurs when both programs require to use a printer, modem, or other peripheral at the same time. The OPERATING SYSTEM should include a method of avoiding deadlock by assigning PRIORITY.

debugging, *n.* the process of removing errors from programs. This can be very difficult for large and complicated programs, and most long programs are never made completely bug-free. This is because it is never possible to think of every possible fault that could exist. A program can be considered as being reasonably debugged if it never crashes or loses data because of an incorrect entry or because of an unusual set of commands.

Debugging starts with checking that the program will run from start to finish with simple data. It must then be tested with data that is on the verge of acceptability – the maximum and minimum amounts that can be used. It must also be tested with unacceptable entries, to test the DATA VALIDATION steps. The outputs from the program have to be checked for accuracy, and this means operating with genuine data for which an independently calculated output is available. The more complicated the program, the longer this testing takes, and the easier it is to overlook a particular set of items which can cause trouble.

decay, *n.* the fading of a sound. As applied to computer sound commands, the term denotes the part of a sound ENVELOPE in which the amplitude decreases after the initial rise or ATTACK. The decay is followed by the SUSTAIN and the RELEASE sections.

decimal, *n.* a method of writing a fraction, using an unwritten denominator of a power of 10. The decimal 0.3 means $\frac{3}{10}$, the decimal 0.56 means $\frac{56}{100}$ and so on. In this way, the position of each digit indicates its significance, just as it does for numbers greater than 1. See also DENARY.

deck, *n.* a set of cards. The cards of a computing deck are PUNCHED CARDS which carry data.

declare, *vb.* to assign a type. This action specifies to the computer that a 'name' represents a particular TYPE of variable, such as INTEGER, REAL NUMBER etc. Languages such as PASCAL require that each variable name that will be used should be predeclared (see PREDECLARATION), meaning that its type is specified before it is used. The principle is not much used in BASIC.

decoder, *n.* a device that changes data from coded form to clear (or normal) form. A BCD to BINARY decoder, for example, will transform numbers that are stored in BCD form into normal binary form that the computer can use.

decrement, *n.* a reduction in the value of a number, usually by one. A decrement action is an essential part of a LOOP which is used in counting, the other essential being an INCREMENT action. In BASIC, the FOR ... NEXT loop can be modified by the instruction STEP to allow for increments or decrements of any size. In PASCAL, the loop forms are FOR A TO B DO and FOR A DOWNTO B DO. The first is an increment, the second a decrement, with a step of one in each case. Both increment and decrement actions are also present in machine-code form, represented by the assembly language commands INC and DEC.

dedicated, *adj.* (of any part of a computer system) designed for one task only. A dedicated word processor, for example, can be used only for word processing, despite the fact that it contains the same circuits as a computer, and differs only in FIRMWARE. The personal computer has replaced many of the dedicated machines which used to be available.

default, *n.* a decision that is taken if not countermanded. Your computer, for example, may when you switch it on use a screen pattern of 40 characters per line, 24 lines per frame, white text on black background. These are default settings, and you can change them by issuing various commands. Many programs that allow you a wide choice of actions will also provide sensible default values if you fail to make some or any of the choices.

defensive programming, *n.* programming that allows for contingencies under the reasonable assumption that if something *can* go wrong, it will. A common example of defensive programming is to test for the end of a count with an action like: IF N%>100 rather than using: IF N% = 100. The thinking behind this is that if the count is interfered with and the value of N% changed, the value of N% might never be exactly equal to 100, but by testing for N% greater than 100, the action would be more certain to stop. The use of defensive programming can save a considerable amount of time spent on DEBUGGING.

defined function, *n.* an action, very often on numbers, that can be designed by the programmer rather than being provided as part of the operating LANGUAGE. A defined function must return a number or a string for further processing; it does not by itself carry out any visible action. The definition of the function must include a name or IDENTIFIER, the action of the function, and (in most languages), the type of value that will be returned. The function can then be 'called' by using its name, just as if it were one of the built-in functions. In PASCAL, for example, we can define a function:

```
FUNCTION AREA (diam:real):real;
BEGIN;
AREA:=PI*SQR(DIAM/2);
END;
```

which calculates the area of a circle whose diameter is represented by the real number variable DIAM. If, in a later part of the program, we needed to print the area of a circle whose diameter was represented by the variable D, then we would use:

```
WRITE(AREA(D));
```

DEFINITION

– using the name of the function to call up the action, and supplying the PARAMETER D. The parameter DIAM exists only within the function; it is LOCAL.

definition, *n.* the fineness of detail in an image. For example, a screen definition of 640 × 320 means that dot sizes are being used which are of width equal to $\frac{1}{640}$ of the screen width and of height equal to $\frac{1}{320}$ of the screen height. This corresponds to a total possible dot number of 204,800 in a complete screen, and would require a large amount of memory reserved for display purposes. This would be classed as a high–definition display. Low–definition displays require much less memory, but can display only coarse patterns. A good test of definition is to draw a diagonal line and inspect the size of the 'steps' that make up the diagonal. The word is also applied to the act of specifying a variable type as REAL, INTEGER, CHARACTER, etc.

degradation, *n.* the smoothing out of the shape of a signal's electrical pulses. This form of CORRUPTION makes the number of pulses difficult to count, and hinders data interpretation. Degradation inevitably occurs when data is transmitted along lines or by radio waves, but it can also be caused by overloading output terminals with too many peripherals. See Fig. 21.

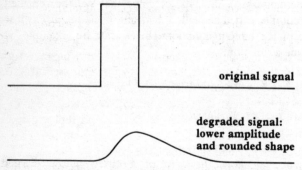

original signal

degraded signal: lower amplitude and rounded shape

Fig. 21. **Degradation.** Degradation of a digital signal. This can be caused when a digital signal is sent down a long cable. The degraded signal will cause data errors unless the correct waveshape can be regenerated. This is why it is unwise to add extension leads to disk drives and to parallel printers.

delay line, *n.* a method of delaying an electrical signal deliberately. The main use of a delay line is to ensure that signals which have been transmitted along different paths arrive together. This use of a delay line is particularly important for colour VDU signals.

delimiter, *n.* a separating character, usually a PUNCTUATION MARK, which is used to show a boundary between an instruction word and text or other ARGUMENT. In BASIC, for example, INVERTED COMMAS are used to show where a STRING begins and ends. PASCAL takes the combination of brackets and asterisks to indicate a remark, such as (*REMARK*). Many WORD PROCESSORS use the full stop as a form of delimiter, relying on the principle that a word does not normally start with a full stop, so that commands such as .CP or .HM can be put into text. When the text is printed, these commands are taken as instructions to the printer, and the command letters are *not* printed.

demand processing, *n.* the processing of data as soon as it is INPUT. The data may be stored in an input BUFFER so that it can be completely assembled, but the only delay will be the time needed to fill the buffer. See also REAL TIME.

demodulation, *n.* the action of decoding a modulated signal. The term has two main meanings in computing. **1.** the conversion of signals in the form of audio tones back to digital signals, an action carried out by the receiving MODEM **2.** The extraction of a VIDEO signal from a UHF carrier in a TV receiver. See MODULATION.

denary, *n.* the scale-of-ten numbering system which we normally use. In this system, the least-significant digit (see BIT), on the right-hand side of a number, can be 0 to 9. The next column to the left represents tens, the next represents hundreds, and so on. This form of numbering is Arabic in origin, and replaced the older Roman system. The same form of arrangement into columns is used by BINARY and HEXADECIMAL scales.

density, *n.* the degree of the packing of data bits, particularly on a disk.

descender, *n.* the part of a character which lies below the base line. LOWER-CASE characters such as p,q,y and g all have portions which descend below the normal writing line level. These descenders can be printed only if sufficient space is left between lines, and the

CHARACTER BLOCK is of the correct size. A few CRT displays, and some printers, do not permit descenders, and these letters are therefore poorly formed and difficult to read. This is unimportant if only UPPER-CASE displays are used.

descriptor, *n.* a KEYWORD or identification codeword. This might mean the filename, a program name, or any word that is used as a code for a file. See also IDENTIFIER.

destructive readout, *n.* a readout that destroys data. Some forms of storage systems retain data only until the data is read, and the reading action destroys the data. If the data is to be retained, it must be rewritten after reading. Destructive readout was a feature of early electrostatic storage systems, and is still used to read CORE MEMORY.

device, *n.* any active part of a computer system. The name is usually reserved for PERIPHERALS, such as keyboard, screen, printer, disk drive and so on, that are part of the electronics of the computer system.

DFS, *abbrev. for* disk-filing system, an operating system for managing a disk drive or set of drives for the purposes of data filing. The DFS should make the action of the disk system TRANSPARENT to the user unless a manual action like changing disks is needed. In other words, the user does not have to specify which SECTOR and TRACK of a disk is to be used, nor how the data is to be stored on the disk. See also DOS.

diagnostic, *n.* a checking routine or program which allows you to check and report on any faults in the computer or its OPERATING SYSTEM. Some very large and elaborate programs may contain their own diagnostic system, and many computers are arranged to run a simple diagnostic program (testing RAM) each time the machine is switched on.

dialect, *n.* a non-standard version of a computing LANGUAGE. Many languages are very closely standardized, and the only variations that exist have been created to allow a particular machine to run the language. Other languages, notably BASIC, consist almost exclusively of dialects, with no manufacturer using a 'standard' version. The MICROSOFT version of BASIC is often taken as a de facto standard, but there is also an ANSI specification. The problem is that standardization halts progress on the development of a language. Languages which are rigidly standardized often have rather short periods of popularity before being replaced by another language which is in reality little more than a dialect of the original. See also ENHANCEMENT.

dialup, *n.* a method of connecting to a remote computer. If the remote computer is permanently connected to a MODEM which in turn is permanently plugged into the telephone lines, then the computer can be dialled up just as a telephone can be dialled up. Data on such a system is never totally secure from HACKERS unless very well designed PASSWORD systems are used. A useful safeguard is to use a form of RING-BACK system, in which the initial call places the caller's telephone number into memory, and prints this out. The caller is then asked to terminate the call, and the remote computer then calls back. In this way, anyone who uses the system has his telephone number noted and can be traced later.

digit, *n.* literally means 'finger', and denotes a unit of counting. The DENARY counting scale uses ten digits (0 to 9) and the BINARY scale uses the two digits, 0 and 1. The HEXADECIMAL scale uses 15 digits, with letters A, B, C, D, E, and F added to the normal range of 0 to 9.

digital, *adj.* (of quantities) making use of digits. This normally means making use of BINARY digits, and refers to any system in which data is coded in the form of binary numbers.

digital computer, *n.* a computer that carries out its tasks by working with numbers in the form of BINARY coded electrical signals. This distinguishes it from the ANALOGUE COMPUTER which works with electrical voltages which are not in binary coded form.

digitize, *vb.* to change into BINARY coded form. Any type of signal can be digitized by measuring the AMPLITUDE of the signal and converting this number into binary form. The process may have to be repeated at frequent intervals if the signal changes amplitude. Digitization is comparatively simple for signals that change comparatively slowly, but needs very high SAMPLING

RATES if the signal is a rapidly-changing one, such as a VIDEO signal.

digitizer, *n.* a device that changes information into digital form. A VIDEO digitizer, for example, will change a TV camera image into a set of numbers which can be stored, recalled, and used to display and manipulate the image. Digitizers for signals of this type make use of HARDWARE rather than SOFTWARE because of the operating speeds that are required.

dimensioning, *n.* the act of declaring an ARRAY size stating how many members of the array in a program must be allowed for. You are not forced to use this number, but you must not exceed it. In BASIC, for example, DIM A$(25) means that you can use items A$(0) to A$(25), a total of 26 items, but you cannot use A$(26) or higher.

A similar scheme is followed in other languages, usually at the point where a name is declared (see DECLARE). This method allows array members to be stored in consecutive memory positions, making access to and manipulation of items much easier. The dimensioning action will reserve enough memory for the items, and if there is not enough memory in the computer, this will be signalled at the dimensioning stage, rather than when the machine is nearly full of data. This method of allocating memory can cause GARBAGE COLLECTION problems when STRING arrays are in use.

DIN, *n. acronym for* Deutsche Industrie Norm, the German Industry Standard. In computing, this normally denotes a type of plug and socket that is used for some signal connections. Commonly encountered DIN plugs and sockets can use 3, 5, or 7 pins, and have a 'key and slot' arrangement to ensure that the plug can be inserted only one way round. The sockets were originally used in audio applications, and are found only on the smaller sizes of computers. The use of flat-pin connectors with ribbon cable is more common for interconnections.

direct access, *n.* access to memory without making use of the CPU of the computer. Also called DMA (direct memory access). Most small computers do not permit any form of direct access, because it is simpler to use the main MICROPROCESSOR to control all access to memory. If direct access is to be used, some method of control is still needed. See also BLITTER.

direct mode, *n.* the passing of COMMANDS to the OPERATING SYSTEM without the use of a program. Certain commands, such as RUN, SAVE, and LOAD are nearly always used in direct mode by typing the command words (and any ARGUMENTS such as filenames) on the keyboard, then pressing the RETURN key. Interpreted languages like BASIC permit a much wider range of direct mode commands than do compiled languages (see INTERPRETER, COMPILE). In some DIALECTS of BASIC, practically every BASIC RESERVED WORD can be used as a direct command. This makes it very easy to learn the SYNTAX of the word by trying it out.

directory, *n.* a list of files on tape or disk. Also called *catalogue of disk*. Many disk-operating systems require the typing of the command DIR to obtain a disk catalogue. The word is also used to mean an EXTENSION character which is added to FILENAMES. For example, the BBC machine will use by default a directory letter of $ for files. If you save a file called MYFIL, this appears in the catalogue as $.MYFIL, though it is not normally printed on screen in this form. If the extension is specified in the filename, and is not $, then it *does* appear in the catalogue. CP/M places these extensions following the filenames.

direct voice input, *n.* the control of a computer by voice. This is the aim of several research programs, but though some degree of success has been achieved, the enormous variation in human speech patterns makes true direct voice input for anything other than a few control words exceedingly difficult to achieve, particularly in English. See also SPEECH RECOGNITION, SPEECH SYNTHESIS.

disable interrupt, *vb.* to prevent interruption of the microprocessor action. In many computer designs, the action of the CPU is interrupted at regular intervals, typically 50 times per second, to scan the keyboard or to service the screen display. This interruption may have to be disabled when the CPU needs to carry out tasks which depend on precise timing, such as tape or disk access. This is why, on small computers, you often see a screen go blank, or a keyboard become ineffective, when a

DISASSEMBLER

program is being saved or loaded. In addition, much of the keyboard will be disabled when a program runs, apart from steps in the program when an input is called for. If the keyboard contains a BREAK or ESCAPE key, then this may still be active, though it can normally be disabled by a machine code routine.

disassembler, *n.* a program which carries out a DISASSEMBLY action. The results may be listed on the screen, or on paper. Some disassemblers will also record a disassembly listing in a form that can be used by an ASSEMBLER. See Fig. 22.

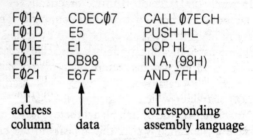

F∅1A	CDEC∅7	CALL ∅7ECH
F∅1D	E5	PUSH HL
F∅1E	E1	POP HL
F∅1F	DB98	IN A, (98H)
F∅21	E67F	AND 7FH

address
column   data

corresponding
assembly language

Fig. 22. **Disassembler.** Typical output from a disassembler. This shows address numbers, data, and the corresponding assembler mnemonics. Some labelling disassemblers will substitute artificial label names such as A001, A002, ... Z009, for addresses to make the disassembly clearer. Many disassemblers make no provision for stored data bytes within a program, and will interpret these as instructions.

disassembly, *n.* the analysis of a set of machine-code bytes into assembly-language instructions (see ASSEMBLE). A disassembler program is essential if you want to find out how the operating system of your computer works, or to analyse any program that is written in machine code. Since both instructions and data are normally present in a program, a disassembly will often interpret data as if it were program instructions in MACHINE CODE. This can be avoided if the programmer can detect the data areas, and notify them to the disassembler before a run. A well-designed DISASSEMBLER program can produce an output which is almost identical to the original SOURCE CODE in ASSEMBLY LANGUAGE.

disc, see DISK.

disk, *n.* a method of data storage. Sometimes spelt *disc*. Disks can be FLOPPY or hard (see WINCHESTER DISK). In a DISK DRIVE, the disk is spun at about 300 revolutions per minute, and a READ/WRITE HEAD head is put into contact with the surface in order to read or write magnetic signals. The position of the head is gauged by the position of the outer TRACK of the disk, and also from a SECTORING HOLE. The important difference between disk storage and tape storage is that every part of the disk surface can be reached by the head in a very short time. The access, in other words, is RANDOM rather than SEQUENTIAL.

The older standard sizes of floppy disks are 8″ and 5¼″; the smaller size is sometimes known as a diskette. More recent developments are smaller disks which use a rigid plastic case that offers greater protection to the disk. The standard size for these smaller disks is 3½″, though some 3″ disks have also appeared. These disks, though smaller, use closer packing of data to achieve large storage sizes, comparable with the storage on 8″ disks. Unfortunately, at the time of writing, only 8″ floppy disks used a standardized format. This means that it is not usually possible to interchange other disks between machines of different makes.

Hard or WINCHESTER disks are rigid, spin at higher speeds, and use a head that floats very close to the disk surface. Recent 'Bernouilli drives' have achieved even closer spacings. Hard disks were originally obtained in large sizes only, but smaller versions ('miniwinnies') have subsequently appeared. Such a disk has to be kept in a dust-free atmosphere, and the disk is very often built into the drive. The alternative to the built-in disk is the use of a CARTRIDGE DISK, with the disk drives kept in an air-conditioned space. See also DENSITY, TRACK, SECTOR, HARD SECTORING, SOFT SECTORING.

disk crash, *n.* a failure of a disk drive, usually with damage to the disk. A typical disk crash might be caused by a speck of grit on a disk, which becomes wedged between the disk head and the surface, causing the disk surface to be scratched. This will remove magnetic coating, and result in massive loss of data. When disks are intensively used, disk surfaces should be kept clean, and head-cleaning disks used at regular intervals.

If a disk drive crashes with no damage to a disk, it is usually possible to restore normal operation. One common cause of frequent crashes, with no permanent disk damage, is operating a disk drive too close to a video monitor, or any other device which emits strong magnetic radiation. The steel casing of a disk drive does *not* protect the drive against magnetic fields, and it can even make the drive more susceptible to such interference.

disk doctor, *n.* a program that allows you to investigate directly what is stored on a disk. The disk content can be displayed in hex (see HEXADECIMAL) on the screen, or complete disk sectors can be copied into the memory. Several such programs allow you also to modify the content of a disk. This can lead to a disk becoming unreadable in normal use, and is the basis of one method of COPY PROTECTION. Disk editing of this kind can also be used to recover data from a disk that has become corrupted. The use of a disk doctor may be the only way of recovering valuable data following a DISK CRASH.

disk drive, *n.* an assembly that contains the mechanisms for spinning a disk and moving a READ/WRITE HEAD over the surface. Often shortened to *drive*. Disk drives may contain an operating system (see DOS), often with a MICROPROCESSOR controller chip of its own, which will ensure that the disk spins when required and that the head locates the correct part of the surface. More commonly, the disk drive contains the hardware for disk control, and the operating system resides in the computer itself. See also DFS.

disk pack, see CARTRIDGE DISK.

displacement, *n.* the distance in computing from a fixed point. In ASSEMBLY LANGUAGE, a displacement byte means one which is added to an ADDRESS number in order to obtain a new address which will then be used. In graphics instructions, displacement numbers are used to specify position relative to a point.

distortion, *n.* a change of the shape of a signal. See DEGRADATION.

distributed logic, *n.* a system in which the logic actions are not confined to the central processor. See also DISTRIBUTED PROCESSING.

distributed processing, *n.* a system that uses several processor units in different places. This is an alternative to a system which places all the processing in one central unit, with DUMB TERMINALS that have no processing action.

DIV, *n.* an instruction word for integer division. The result of using, for example 7DIV2 would be 3, the integer result.

DMA, see direct memory access.

DMS, *n. acronym for* DATABASE Management System. This is the part of a database program that maintains the organization of the database, as distinct from the part that carries out input/output and searching through the records. An efficient management system will, for example, organize the data to take up the least amount of space on each disk, allow space vacated by deleted records to be reused, and treat DOUBLE-SIDED DISKS as if they were one large single side.

document reader, *n.* a method of reading by computer. This is a form of OPTICAL CHARACTER READER which can deal, often automatically, with complete documents, translating each printed character into ASCII code and transmitting this to the computer. Document readers can never produce ASCII code which is completely free from errors, but given a good clean manuscript, the results need very little correction.

documentation, *n.* the paperwork that accompanies a piece of hardware or software. When this paperwork has been prepared by professional authors, it is clear, comprehensive, and allows you to find quickly and easily for yourself what to do in order to get the best from the computer or the program. Only too often, however, the documentation is prepared too early in the course of the design of the project, and is written by engineers. As authors, engineers have the advantage of knowing everything about the system, but the disadvantage of believing that nothing needs to be explained for the user.

dollar sign, *n.* the $ used extensively in BASIC, to signal that a STRING variable is being used. Some languages use the dollar sign to indicate that a hex number (see HEXADECIMAL) follows, others do not use the sign at all.

DOS, *n. acronym for* Disk-Operating System. This refers to the FIRMWARE which carries out the actions of controlling the disk drive or drives, selecting correct TRACKS and SECTORS and avoiding accidental CORRUPTION. CP/M is one example of a disk-operating system which is used by a large number of computers, another is MS-DOS. Disk-operating systems such as CP/M and MS-DOS offer a considerable number of 'utilities' in addition to the actions of disk-drive control. Many manufacturers devise their own DOS in order to avoid paying royalties for the use of standard systems, and to restrict access to programs. This very often has the opposite effect, because users tend to select programs that they want to run, and then look for a machine which will run these programs. In any case, users of business programs will want to select machines that can run a large number of programs, and this nowadays restricts the choice to CP/M, MS-DOS and a very few other systems. See also DFS.

dot command, *n.* a command that consists of a full stop followed by letters. Used in some older types of word processor programs for EMBEDDED COMMANDS. More modern word processor programs have been written for machines which make use of PROGRAMMABLE KEYS, so that the dot commands can be dispensed with. See also DELIMITER.

dot-matrix, *n.* a method of making patterns visible, particularly for characters on screen or on paper. A dot-matrix screen display allows a rectangle of closely-spaced dots, often 7 across by 9 deep, to be controlled. By lighting a pattern of dots, a character shape is displayed. The same principle is used in printers in which a matrix of tiny needles can be fired selectively at a ribbon which is placed between the needles and the paper. Screen displays are always of the dot-matrix type, but alternative methods of printing on paper are available. See also CHARACTER BLOCK, MATRIX PRINTER.

double-density, *n.* disk recording in which the number of bytes recorded per sector of disk is double the normal amount, typically 512 bytes per sector in place of 256. Double-density recording obviously doubles the storage capacity of a disk, but requires a higher standard of head alignment, cleanliness, and smoothness of disk surface. Quadruple density is attainable, and is used on the small size disks in order to pack a large amount of data on to each disk.

double-sided disk, *n.* a disk with usable recording surfaces on each side. All disks are manufactured with magnetic coating on each side, but on test some disks fail to FORMAT correctly on one side, and are sold as single-sided disks. Double-sided disks can be used by disk drives that have two READ/WRITE heads, one on each side of the disk. Some disk operating systems (see DOS) treat such drives as separate units, others as being equivalent to a drive with one large disk. A few disks are made in such a form that they can be turned over to allow both sides to be used in a single-sided drive. See also FLOPPY DISK.

double word, *n.* data that uses 4 bytes. A WORD means 2 bytes, equal to 16 bits, hence a double word is 4 bytes. The term is used in particular on 16-bit machines.

download, *vb.* to transfer data to or from a computer along a line which may be a telephone line, a radio link, a network or any other type of link.

down time, *n.* the time during which a computer is out of action for repair or maintenance. One of the advantages of microcomputers is that they often have zero down time during their useful life. Another advantage is that a microcomputer is easily replacable, so that a machine which is down can be replaced by a spare, with little loss of time. For a large computer system, down time can represent an enormous loss of income, and the user will normally maintain both an insurance policy and a maintenance contract to offset these losses.

downward compatibility, *n.* the ability of a complex system to work along with a simple one. If the large computer in an office can use a program which is also usable by a small portable machine, the program is said to have 'downward compatibility'. This should allow data to be handled by both systems, and passed between them. Downward compatibility is an attribute of microprocessor families such as the Motorola 68000 series which exist in several levels of complexity. Compare UPWARD COMPATIBILITY.

DRAW, *n.* a graphics instruction in many versions of BASIC which cater for HIGH-RESOLUTION GRAPHICS. The simplest variety of DRAW is followed by two sets of COORDINATES, and the effect of the instruction is to draw a straight line between the two points. Variations on the instruction allow for control of the line colour, for drawing from the cursor position to any other point, and even for drawing arcs, circles and ellipses.

drive, see DISK DRIVE.

driver, *n.* a program routine which is used to carry out some interfacing action (see INTERFACE). For example, a printer driver is the routine that is used to control the feeding of signals to a printer. Most computers come equipped with suitable driver routines, but for unorthodox applications, the user may have to write such routines in MACHINE CODE. Many machines allow such user-written driver programs to be inserted into their own printer routines if necessary.

drop-in, *n.* a piece of dirt adhering to a disk or tape surface. This will prevent recording on that part of the surface, so corrupting the recording. See also DROPOUT.

dropout, *n.* a type of failure of magnetic recording medium. A dropout on a tape or disk denotes a small piece of material which does not magnetize correctly. Since no signals can be recorded on a dropout, this can lead to loss of data. The problem is particularly difficult on audio recording tape used by small computers, because such tape is not normally checked (in a FORMATTING action) by these computers before recording. Digital tape is normally certified as being free from dropouts, but can be used with success only with suitable digital mechanisms. On disks, if the dropout exists when a disk is new, it will be detected during formatting, and the disk can be returned. A dropout which develops later, however, will nearly always lead to loss of data, though recovery is sometimes possible using a DISK-DOCTOR program. The possibility of dropouts makes it important to keep BACKUPS of all data, and to avoid the use of programs which cannot be backed up because of COPY PROTECTION. See also DROP-IN.

drum printer, *n.* a form of LINE PRINTER. The mechanism consists of a drum on which a full set of characters is embossed around a drum in each column position.

dual processor, *n.* a computer that uses two microprocessors. At one time, the use of dual processors was fairly common (as in the 'Superbrain', for example), because it could allow the use of fast processors such as the 6502 and 6809, along with a Z-80 which needed to be present so as to permit the use of CP/M. This system is still used (as in the Commodore 128), but dual processor use nowadays is more often aimed at faster and more efficient processing. The main object is to relieve the main processor of the tasks of memory management, graphics displays, and, sometimes, advanced mathematical functions. See also COPROCESSOR.

dumb terminal, *n.* a TERMINAL with no processing ability. A dumb terminal allows VDU output from a computer, and keyboard input, but possesses no processing ability apart from the ability to send and receive signals. Compare INTELLIGENT TERMINAL.

dump, *vb.* to cause output of data in either of two ways. **1.** to record a program or data on tape or disk. **2.** to display a machine code program in HEXADECIMAL characters on the screen or to a printer. This type of dump action is often called *hex-dump*.

duplex, *n.* the two-way transmission of data. A duplex link allows you to transmit and receive information without any external switching actions being required. Compare SIMPLEX.

Dvorak keyboard, *n.* a non-QWERTY type of key arrangement. The normal arrangement of typewriter keys is very inefficient, and was originally designed to force typists to operate slowly, so avoiding jamming the type bars of early machines. The reason for the layout has long since disappeared, but because it had become standardized, it remains in use despite all of its faults. The Dvorak keyboard, like the MALTRON, is an attempt to design a keyboard which is easier and much faster to use with less training. These keyboards can be specified for a few machines to special order, or as a later add-on.

dynamic allocation, *n.* the allocation of memory as and when required. This is a system of allocation of memory for storage of data that does not use fixed memory locations. Many BASIC interpreters, for example, store the variable values that a program uses just beyond the last byte of the program text. This means that all variable values become unavailable if the program is edited in any way, because a new storage area is now in use. By contrast, when an ARRAY is declared, fixed memory places are allocated and reserved for the items of the array.

dynamic RAM, *n.* one form of RAM memory. This is a form of construction of memory which is very cheap and comparatively simple to manufacture in large memory sizes. Its disadvantage is that the data is retained for only a very short time unless a 'refreshing' pulse is applied to the memory at intervals of, typically, one thousandth of a second. Some MICROPROCESSORS, notably the Z-80, contain circuitry which will generate these REFRESH signals automatically. Dynamic RAM is being superseded by new and improved versions of STATIC RAM.

E

EBCDIC, *n. acronym for* Extended Binary Coded Decimal Interchange Code for information exchange, a code which uses all 8 bits in each byte, unlike ASCII which uses only 7 bits. The EBCDIC code can be used for transmitting data from one computer to another. It is not in general use for small computers, but is extensively used in communications equipment.

echo, *n.* the appearance on the VDU of the character corresponding to the key pressed on the keyboard. This sometimes implies that if you are using your computer to communicate with another one, each character that you type will be displayed twice, because the remote computer is also echoing back over the line. See ECHO CHECK.

echo check, *n.* the checking on screen of the accuracy of data transmission. Each transmitted character is returned ('echoed') to be displayed on the sending terminal, so that any corruption that has been caused by the transmission system will be visible to the sender as well as to the receiver. See ECHO.

edge card, *n.* a CIRCUIT CARD which is fitted with an EDGE CONNECTOR. An edge card offers a cheap, simple and convenient way of adding facilities (such as additional graphics capabilities, extra memory, communications facilities) to a computer. A computer, such as the early APPLE-2, which can use extra edge cards, is almost infinitely expandable, and does not readily become out of date. See also MOTHERBOARD.

edge connector, *n.* a way of making contact to an edge card. The chips of a computer system are mounted on CIRCUIT BOARDS from which connections have to be made to other boards, and to the keyboard and other devices. The cheapest way of making these connections is to shape part of the board like a tongue, and arrange connecting strips on it, often on each side. A suitable plug can then grip the board and make connection. These connections can be unreliable, are fragile, and can break if the plug is disconnected and reconnected too often. A much better method makes use of sockets soldered to the board which can be replaced if they make poor contacts. Edge connectors are satisfactory if they are used for edge cards which are seldom removed, and which can be supported on a MOTHERBOARD.

edit, *vb.* to change, delete or amend the text of a program or the data that a program uses. For program editing, computers use either line editing or screen editing.

In line editing a line is placed on the screen by a command such as EDIT 90, and the CURSOR is moved along the line. Pressing command letters (such as I for insert) will allow the actions of insertion, deletion and replacement to be carried out.

Screen editing is a more versatile system in which anything that appears on the screen can be edited simply by moving the cursor to the required place and typing. Typing causes insertion, and a DELETE key is used if text is to be removed. Pressing the RETURN or ENTER key terminates either type of editing.

editor, *n.* a program which edits text. A word processor consists of a text editor and print FORMATTER. The editor portion is concerned with the entry, deletion, amendment, and repositioning of words in the text. This is the portion of the word processor which is being used until the text is recorded on disk or printed out.

EDP, *abbrev. for* electronic data processing. This is the main action of all digital computers. It consists of the fundamental actions of data entry, storage, rearrangement and display.

EEPROM, *n. acronym for* Electrically Erasable Programmable Read-Only Memory, a form of EPROM chip in which the erasure is carried out by electric pulses rather then by ultra-violet light. To date, EEPROMS have not proved suitable for large-scale use in computers because of unreliable, slow operation, and high prices.

effective time, *n.* the time for which a piece of equipment operates. This is not necessarily equal to the time for which the equipment is switched on. On machines that are fitted with 8″ disk drives, the drives spin continually, but where the smaller drives are used, the drives run only when data is being read or written. The effective time might, for example, be recorded by a clock which was driven by the power supply to the disk drives. The reading of time from this clock would then be used to decide when maintenance of the disk drives was needed. Effective time measurement is also used for other mechanical items, such as cooling fans, but not generally for equipment that uses only semiconductor electronics, since their life is indefinite, and maintenance negligible.

eight-inch drive, *n.* the former standard size of disk drive. It had the very considerable advantage that the format of all 8-inch disks was standardized (by IBM), so that a disk made on one machine could be played on any other. Many computer users feel that the wholesale adoption of the smaller disks with no established standards represented a considerable backward step in terms of the easy interchange of data. Even for different machines which use CP/M, it is not possible to interchange disks unless the disk standards are identical.

eighty-track disk, *n.* a disk which has been formatted to use 80 rather than 40 tracks of data (see FORMAT). The width of the disk that is used for recording is the same, so 80-track operation means that the HEAD-OF-DISK DRIVE has to be moved in smaller steps, packing the tracks closer together. Some DISK DRIVES can be switched for either 40- or 80-track operation, and software can be written to allow an 80-track drive to read or write 40-track disks. The advantage of 80-track operation is that more data can be recorded on the disk, and the combination of 80-track and DOUBLE DENSITY allows still more packing, of the order of 800 Kbyte on each side of the disk.

eighty-column screen display, *n.* a screen display that allows up to 80 characters per screen or printer line. Business systems for microcomputers normally use 80 (sometimes 132) columns across the screen, which requires a very high standard of display MONITOR. Home computers which utilize a domestic TV as a display device can use only up to 40-column screen displays, because a domestic TV cannot display 80 columns clearly. Even small computers which use COLOUR MONITORS cannot provide clear 80-column displays, which is why many home computers that are claimed to be suitable for business use are, in fact, not really suitable for serious work over long periods. Even business machines are not always perfect in this respect, and some CHARACTER BLOCKS are too small to allow good character shape.

elastic banding, *n.* the movement in high-resolution graphics of a line drawn from a specified point on the screen to another point. Also called *rubber banding*. This second point can be moved around the screen by using the CURSOR CONTROL KEYS or a JOYSTICK, and the line length will expand or contract as if the line were made of elastic material. This makes the alteration of diagrams very much easier than it would be if lines had to be rubbed out and redrawn, so that elastic banding is much used in computer-assisted drawing packages. See Fig. 23. See also CAD.

elastic buffer, *n.* a buffer that can hold a variable amount of data. Most computer systems use buffers of fixed size, such as 256 or 512 bytes. The use of an elastic buffer requires an operating system which can ensure that the buffer does not expand to an extent which will cause overwriting of other data in the memory.

electronics, *n.* the science and technology of the development of

ELECTRONIC MAIL

devices and circuits in which electron flow is directly controlled.
electronic mail, *n.* a system for delivering messages by DOWN-
LOADING text from computers along telephone wires. An
electronic mailbox consists of a BACKING STORE on a large
computer which will store messages until the user requests
delivery along the line. An elaborate system of PASSWORDS is
needed if the MAILBOX messages are to be secure from HACKERS.

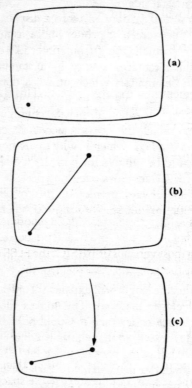

Fig. 23. **Elastic banding.** (a) A point is selected on the
screen. (b) When a new point is selected, a line is automatically drawn between the first point and the new point. (c) As
the new point is moved, the line is redrawn continually,
erasing the old line. This gives the appearance of a line whch
can expand and contract like an elastic band.

electrostatic printer, *n.* a system of printing that uses black paper coated with a thin metal film. The printing head is of the DOT-MATRIX type, using a set of sharp spikes. When a high voltage is placed between the metal coating and a spike, the resulting spark will vaporize the metal, leaving the black paper exposed. The system is simple, but suffers from the disadvantages that special paper is needed, only one copy is made, and the paper retains fingerprints and will mark other papers.

elimination factor, *n.* the fraction of data that is not used. When a database is searched for specified items, such as the number of red-headed males between 20 and 40, the fraction of the database that does not answer this specification is the elimination factor.

ELSE, *n.* a statement of alternative action. This is used in many languages to form an alternative in an IF test. For example, you could have a line that read:

```
IF Number/10 = INT(Number/10) THEN Countit ELSE Printit
```

which will cause the procedure Countit to run if the variable Number equals any multiple of ten, but otherwise the procedure Printit will run. Early versions of BASIC did not include the ELSE statement, so that tests very often had to be made in rather clumsy ways. In most versions of BASIC, the ELSE statement has to be placed on the same program line as the IF test. In other languages, the ELSE statement can follow on another line, providing that there is no end-of-line marker character preceding the ELSE.

embedded blank, *n.* a space character embedded in text. This is necessary in a word processor of the POST-FORMATTED type which formats text as it is printed, rather than showing the formatting on the screen. On the screen, the space character is visible, but it is printed as a blank. The purpose of this is to avoid breaking groups of words. For example, if you were typing a phrase which included the assembly language command LD A,02, you would not wish the LD to be printed at the end of a line with the A,02 on the next line. By putting an embedded blank between the D and the A, this breaking can be avoided, because the complete LD A,02 will be treated as one word by the formatting program.

embedded command, *n.* a term in word processing for coded instructions which allow the text on the screen to be manipulated, for example, centred, printed in bold face or indented. An embedded command consists of codes that will not cause printing, but that will be passed to the formatting portion (see FORMAT) of the word processor, or directly to the printer in order to cause the effects that are needed.

For most printers, embedded commands must start with the ASCII ESC code of 27, and be followed by whatever codes that particular printer needs. The problem with embedded codes is that different printers do not use identical codes, so that the code which gives bold type on one printer may cause a new page to be taken on another. Some word processors allow you to set up a CONFIGURATION program which will insert the correct codes for a particular printer.

empty string, see BLANK STRING.

emulator, *n.* a program that allows a computer or microprocessor to carry out a set of instructions which are designed for another one. Programs that are termed IBMulators are those which allow a machine to run IBM software. Machines which are sold for educational use should be provided with BBC-emulators so that they can run software which was initially written for the BBC machine.

encoder, *n.* a program or system that converts computer data into some code system other than the normal one, or any device that converts data into computer-usable form. A position encoder, for example, will convert the angular position of a shaft into numbers that can be used by a computer in a control system. See also DIGITIZER, OPTICAL DISK, DECODER.

encryption, *n.* the coding of data so that it cannot be easily understood if intercepted. Any confidential data which has to be sent over public telephone lines or along radio links should be encrypted (see SCRAMBLING).

end of file, *n.* a marker byte that indicates where the data of one FILE ends. Also called *EOF marker*. This marker is usually put in place when a disk file is closed. It will be used when the disk is read to indicate that no more data is to be read from the disk. If the file is left open, no marker is put in, and the file may be impossible to read except with the aid of a DISK DOCTOR. A few disk operating systems allow the end-of-file mark to be deleted so that a file can be opened for further writing.

endless loop, *n.* **1.** a piece of program that repeats until the machine is interrupted or switched off, consisting of a loop which has no ending condition, and which therefore cannot terminate normally. **2.** a piece of tape which has had its ends spliced together and which will return to any position simply by winding in one direction.

enhancement, *n.* the addition of features to a system. Programming LANGUAGES are designed to be run on mainframe machines, which have in general lagged behind microcomputers in the provision of facilities such as colour displays, sound generation, graphics, and USER-FRIENDLY interfaces. Such facilities have to be provided by using special programs rather than as part of the normal computing language.

Most computing languages, therefore, do not contain any statements that control these features of computing, and statements that will exercise such control have to be added as enhancements. The exception to this rule is BASIC, and a new version of BASIC seems to appear each time a new microcomputer is launched. This has led to other languages, notably C and PASCAL, being made available in enhanced versions so as to make use of features of machines which could otherwise be used only by MACHINE CODE programmers, or with the help of specialized programs.

ENTER, *n.* an alternative term for the RETURN key. The term is a better one in the sense that it describes the action better than the word 'return'.

enumerated type, *n.* a DATA TYPE that can be represented by a position number. This is not used in BASIC, but in Pascal and other languages you can create data types which can consist of members like ACE, TWO, THREE, FOUR, ... and so on. The machine encodes this type of list simply as 0, 1, 2, 3, ..., using the position in the list as a code number. It is this number which is stored in the memory to represent the item.

envelope, *n.* the shape of a graph of sound amplitude or frequency plotted against time. A musical note or sound does not consist of one sound wave, but of a whole set of waves. In addition, the waves are not of identical amplitudes, and the usual pattern is for the amplitude to increase sharply for the first few waves, then to decrease, settle to a fixed level, and finally die away. The shape of the amplitude envelope of a musical instrument is always complex, but it can be approximated by using a four-section envelope. The sections are labelled as ATTACK, DECAY, and RELEASE. See Fig. 24.

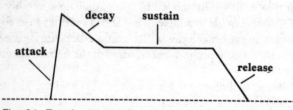

Fig. 24. **Envelopes.** (a) A typical sound envelope which shows how the amplitude of the many waves that make up one note changes during the time of the note. (b) Sound envelope shapes are complex, but can be simulated well by using the ADSR model. This shows the top half of the symmetrical envelope, and uses only four straight line sections.

The precise shape of the amplitude envelope determines to a considerable extent how the note will sound to your ears. Percussive notes, such as piano notes, drums and explosions, have high attacks and rapid decays. Instruments, such as string instruments that are bowed, have a long sustain, as do wind instruments. For good sound synthesis, both the waveform shape and the envelope must be controlled.

The pitch or frequency envelope is used to control effects like vibrato (variation of pitch) in musical notes, and is used to a considerable extent also in special sound effects.

EOF marker, see END OF FILE.

EPROM, *n. acronym for* Erasable Programmable Read-Only Memory, a form of read-only memory (ROM) chip that can be programmed with data (including program bytes) by writing the data repeatedly while higher than normal electrical voltages are applied to the chip. The data is secure until a cover is removed from a thin quartz window in the chip, and ultraviolet light shone into the chip. The use of EPROMs is a very convenient way of supplying a program for a machine which can make use of plug-in EPROMs. To put a program into an EPROM, you need only a BURNER that can be connected to your computer, and such devices are available for any computer which can make use of EPROMs.

Early versions of machines which will eventually use an operating system in ROM are very often supplied with the system in EPROM, which allows for new versions to be brought out as each new bug is found. In theory, the manufacturer should offer a free upgrade of an EPROM when a final version is ready, but you may have to spend a lot of money to obtain your 'free' upgrade. If in doubt, buy an older model which is bug-free. See also PROM.

Epson, *n. Trademark.* a very well-established make of dot-matrix printer, which can print graphics as well as text. Many other makes of dot-matrix printers use the same control codes as the Epson, and are said to be 'Epson-compatible'.

erasable storage, *n.* any storage which can be overwritten (see OVERWRITE). RAM, for example, will store data for as long as

91

power is applied to the memory, or until other data is written in to the memory. A disk will similarly store data until more data is stored in the same sectors, and a tape cassette can also be written with new data. Only digital tape recorders can be relied on to overwrite tape successfully. If audio cassettes are to be reused, they should be subjected to BULK ERASE first.

erase, *n.* to delete errors or data. Erasing a disk often simply involves removing the CATALOGUE OF DISK entry for a file, and the file data itself is not changed until some other file is recorded in its place. Erasing a tape means demagnetizing the tape, so that data is completely removed (see BULK ERASE). Erasing text on the screen is done by means of a DELETE or BACKSPACE key, and the action consists of replacing bytes in the screen memory by the ASCII code for a blank space.

error, *n.* a mistake of some kind. FATAL ERRORS will have the effect of stopping the program. As this can cause loss of data, the program should be written in such a way that either fatal errors cannot occur, or an ERROR MESSAGE is delivered before a fatal error can be committed.

error message, *n.* a message on the screen which signals an error in the program or in the data. If this is a FATAL ERROR it will *always* stop the computer from executing the program, and this can often lead to loss of data, either because data has not been recorded, or because disk files are left open. A non-fatal error can be dealt with by programming which will deal with the error without stopping the program. For example, a misspelling of an entered name is a non-fatal error, which is easy to correct. By contrast, pressing the BREAK key will cause the computer to stop unless the action of the key has been disabled.

ESC, see ESCAPE KEY.

escape key, *n.* the key that is labelled ESC or ESCAPE in some computers. This usually generates ASCII code 27, and in some computers does no more than this. If a programmer wants to make use of the key, then a program must be designed to detect this code and act upon it. In other machines, the escape key will cause a program run to be halted, and it should be possible to disable this action if the key is likely to be struck by accident.

Some machines allow the escape key to cause a halt only when it is pressed along with other keys (such as CTRL and SHIFT), so that an accidental halt is unlikely, and this is a better use of this key. On some machines which use BASIC with an INTERPRETER, pressing the escape key once will halt the program, and pressing any other key will allow the program to continue its action.

Ethernet, *n. Trademark.* a form of LOCAL AREA NETWORK. This is the system that was developed by Rank-Xerox for use with office computers and other equipment.

even parity, see PARITY.

exclusive OR (XOR), *n.* a logic comparison. The action compares two bits, and gives a result of 1 only if the bits that are being compared are different. Thus 1 XOR 0 gives 1, and 0 XOR 1 gives 1, but 1 XOR 1 gives 0 and 0 XOR 0 gives 0. When bytes are XORed together, the XOR action is carried out between bits in identical positions. In other words, bit 0 of one byte is XORed with bit 0 of the other byte, bit 1 of the first byte with bit 1 of the other byte, and so on. If a byte is XORed with another 'key' byte, the result can be used as a code. If this 'code' byte is then XORed with the same 'key', the original byte is obtained again. XOR is therefore extensively used in PASSWORD systems. See Fig. 25 on page 94.

execute, *vb.* to carry out a program. In BASIC, this requires typing the RUN command and pressing ENTER or RETURN, thus causing the BASIC interpreter to start work on the byte which is stored in the first address of the BASIC code area of memory. In machine code, execution is started by placing the address of the first byte of code into the PROGRAM COUNTER register of the microprocessor. For compiled languages, RUN (or R) has the effect of supplying this address to the program counter, so that the action closely resembles the execution of machine code.

execution address, *n.* the address of the start of a MACHINE CODE program. A machine-code program will have its first instruction byte stored at some address, which is known as the execution address. This address must be put into the PROGRAM-COUNTER register of the microprocessor in order to run the machine-code program. If this is commanded from BASIC, it is done by the

EXECUTION ADDRESS

CALL, USR or SYS commands, according to the version of BASIC that is being used.

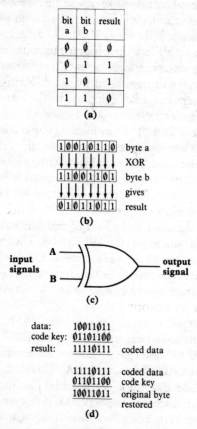

Fig. 25. **Exclusive OR (XOR).** (a) A truth-table for the XOR action, which shows all the possible results of XORing two bits. (b) When two complete bytes are XORed, the XOR action is carried out on corresponding bits, that is bits in the same position in each byte. The result is put into the corresponding position in the result-byte. Each bit action is self-contained — there is no carry bit as there would be in an ADD or SUB action. (c) The symbol which represents an XOR gate in an electronic circuit.

Some machine-code programs start with a block of data, and the execution address is not the same as the starting address. Machine-code programs that are recorded on tape or disk usually carry the starting address, the ending address, and the execution address on the tape. These addresses are used to place the bytes of machine code into the correct parts of memory, and the execution address can also be used to make the program start automatically. For this reason, machine code is more secure from illegal copying than BASIC, because the first action of an autostarting machine code can be to disable any keys that would allow the user to stop and examine the program bytes. It is often possible, however, to load such a program into an alternative set of memory addresses so that the autostart routine cannot run.

exit, *n.* a way out of a program. The word is sometimes used unnecessarily as a verb in a program menu, for example: PRESS 5 TO EXIT PROGRAM.

EXP, *n.* a number function which is used for finding a power of the number 'e', the exponential function. The power has to be supplied as an argument to EXP, so that EXP(5) means 'e' to the power 5. The exponential function is the series $1 + \frac{1}{1!} + \frac{1}{2!} + \frac{1}{3!} \ldots$ with an approximate value of 2.718.

expanding, *n.* the restoring of the normal coding arrangement. See COMPANDING.

expansion slot, *n.* a connector that carries all of the MICROPRO-CESSOR signals and that can be used to connect additional boards for the computer. This can allow additional memory or additional facilities (speech synthesizers, high-resolution graphics) to be added without the need to place additional boards within the computer. The expansion slot should be covered when no connector is plugged in, because accidental contact of metal objects to the expansion slot pins could cause damage to the computer.

expert system, *n.* the use of the computer to collect and use human expertise. The study of expert systems is one aspect of artificial intelligence (AI) research. The principle is that if all the experience and learning of several humans can be stored in a summarized form in a database, with a suitable management program, then this expertise can be tapped, made use of, and even extended by non-expert operators.

The reason for the involvement of AI in what might appear to be just a database application is that a lot of human experience and expertise cannot simply be summed into simple rules or examples; unless some attempt at summary is made, the database becomes too bulky to use. The main use of expert systems to date has been in trials of a medical diagnosis scheme. The results of this appear to indicate than many patients are happier to reveal all of their symptoms to a computer than to a doctor. The main advantage of the system has been to 'pre-screen' patients, so that the doctor can act more efficiently.

exponent, *n.* the part of a number in STANDARD FORM which represents the power of ten. For example, if a number is written as 2.45E5 then the number 5 is the exponent, the power of ten by which 2.45 is to be multiplied, giving 245000. In binary form, the exponent represents a power of 2. See also MANTISSA.

expression, *n.* a set of arithmetic or mathematical actions that will result in a number. For example, A+B*C is an expression which will yield a number when variables A, B, and C have been assigned with number values. Many program statements that require number arguments will also accept variables or expressions. The use of expressions allows a program action to be governed by a formula.

extended BASIC, *n.* any DIALECT of BASIC which contains more than the bare minimum of the language. Nowadays practically all versions of BASIC are extended, but the language has, because of this, become non-standard. MSX BASIC was an attempt to fix a standard, but it has not been outstandingly successful, though the implementation of the language was a good one. The tendency in recent years has been to extend other languages, rather than to standardize further.

extended addressing, see ABSOLUTE ADDRESSING.

extended filename, *n.* a disk filename in which the disk drive number and a DIRECTORY letter or other entry is included. Also called *extension*. For example, the filename for a BBC file of :0.F.TEST would refer to the file called TEST which is on drive 0 and uses directory F. In CP/M and other operating systems, files carry a suffix like .BAS or .COM which denotes file type (BASIC, machine code, text, etc.).

extending serial file, *n.* the adding of data to a SERIAL FILE. A serial file on tape or on disk consists of a list of items, one after another. This type of file can normally be amended or extended only by reading it in, making changes or alterations, and then recording the whole of the file again. For a large file, this can be very time-consuming, and RANDOM ACCESS filing is preferable.

extension, see EXTENDED FILENAME.

external memory, *n.* memory that is external to the computer. This generally means RAM or ROM which is connected by means of an EXPANSION SLOT, as distinct from internal memory, or the storage which can be obtained by using a disk drive. If external memory can be used, the machine can be expanded without any need to break seals and open the case.

external sort, *n.* a sorting routine which uses as its data a FILE on disk, and which uses the disk as part of its memory during sorting. This type of sorting routine is essential if very large lists have to be sorted, or if the memory of the computer is inadequate. Unless the machine can use a very efficient sorting ALGORITHM, and can access disk data quickly, an external sort can be very slow.

F

facsimile transmission (fax), *n.* a method of transmitting documents. Electromechanical systems have been in use for many years, particularly in connection with newspaper photographs, and can be expected to die out when standards for modern computer-controlled equipment are established.

fail-safe system, *n.* a system that resists human errors. As the name suggests, a fail-safe system is one that will fail in a way that causes least damage to system data. In computing terms, it means that any error that will stop a program should first of all cause a program to run that will save all data on a disk, and close all disk files.

FALSE, *n.* one of the two BOOLEAN values, the other being TRUE. In many languages, true is represented by 0 and false by –1. Languages which do not have a Boolean variable type must assign a variable with values for true or false.

false code, *n.* code that contains impossible values. The normal range of ASCII printing codes is 32 to 127, and many systems are programmed to treat any byte outside this range as false code. Another example of false code is found in a DISASSEMBLY of MACHINE CODE. In any machine-code program, data bytes, such as ASCII codes for messages, will be mixed with machine-code instructions. Some of these data bytes will be the same as valid machine-code bytes, others will not. Those which are not will be treated as false code by the disassembler, and some indication of this will be shown on the listing.

fanfold, *n.* a continuous strip of paper that is perforated at intervals (usually 28cm/11″ intervals) so that it can be folded in alternate directions into a neat pile. Many programs are arranged so that they will not print on the perforated part of the paper, allowing the paper to be separated ('burst') into separate sheets. Fanfold paper can also be supplied with vertical perforations that allow the sprocket hole strip to be removed. See also TELETYPE ROLL.

fast-access, *adj.* (of a computer memory) being capable of reading or writing rapidly. As applied to modern microcomputers, implies an access time of the order of 100 NANOSECONDS or less. Access times for very large computers can be much lower than this.

fatal error, *n.* an error that stops the execution of a program, with loss of data Also called *catastrophic error.* If the OPERATING SYSTEM and LANGUAGE are not in ROM, an error of this type may cause a REBOOT. Such errors are less of a problem when an interpreted language is used, because it is then usually possible to resume the program. See also CRASH, RERUN POINT.

father, *n.* the file that preceded the latest copy. Business users of files normally keep three copies, the 'father', *son*, and *grandfather* files. The son file is a recent copy, which is currently in use. The father file was copied from the grandfather, and the son file has been copied from the father. After the son file has been in use for some time, a new recording will be made. This will be the new son file, and the other files will be renamed, with the former grandfather file scrapped. This scheme ensures good file BACKUP, and can be easily maintained.

faulty sector, *n.* a common DISK error message caused by a defective part of the magnetic surface. If the faulty SECTOR is caused in manufacturing, the disk will not FORMAT correctly, and can be returned. A faulty sector which develops during use may be due to mishandling, and can cause loss of data.

Faulty sector messages may be caused by the presence of strong magnetic fields near the disk drive, as for example, from a MONITOR. A disk which has a faulty sector should not be used again, and it may be necessary to recover the data with a DISK DOCTOR if no BACKUP disk is available. See also DROP-IN, DROPOUT.

fax, see FACSIMILE TRANSMISSION.

feedback, *n.* short for negative feedback, a form of correction in a system. A negative feedback signal is a sample of the output of a system which is used to correct an input. The term has more applicability to analogue computing than to digital computing. The word feedback is sometimes loosely used to mean acknowledgement.

feeder, *n.* a cable that supplies signals to a number of units. The term BUS is more often used in computing.

female connector, *n.* the socket connector of a cable, or the socket on a computer. Compare also MALE CONNECTOR.

FET, see FIELD-EFFECT TRANSISTOR.

FF, *abbrev. for* form feed. The form feed ASCII code, 12, will cause most printers to advance the paper to the top of the next FANFOLD sheet. This is possible only if the paper has been correctly loaded initially, and the paper length corresponds to the length setting of the printer. Some computers are arranged so that if the FF character is sent to the screen memory, the screen will be cleared.

field, *n.* a unit of a RECORD. For example, if your record is of customers, the name would be one field, the address another and so on. A collection of fields for one data entry constitutes a record. For a RANDOM-ACCESS FILE, you may have to cut or pad each field to a specified length. See also FRAME.

field–effect transistor (FET), *n.* a SEMICONDUCTOR electronic device that uses electric fields to control electric currents. The distinguishing feature of a FET is that virtually no power is required to control electric current, and the device is very easy to fabricate in integrated circuit IC form. Field-effect transistors are therefore the basis of all the ICs that are used in microcomputing.

field flyback, *n.* a term in TV and VDU technology to describe the return of the scanning beam to the top of the screen.

fielding, *n.* the arranging for text or numbers to occupy the correct positions on the screen, or on paper.

FIFO, *n. acronym for* First-In, First-Out, a type of memory system.

fifth generation, *n.* the next generation of computers. These computers have been designed with the aid of and as a result of experience with the present fourth generation of computers. The (rumoured) features of these fifth-generation computers include PARALLEL PROCESSING, in which actions are performed simultaneously rather than in sequence. This can have an enormous effect in increasing speed of operation. This will have to be matched by new computing languages, and these are said to be in course of development from PROLOG.

file, *n.* a collection of data that can be recorded. A program is one type of file, and the data that it uses is another type of file. The main file types, however, are ASCII and BINARY. The important difference is that a file in ASCII code is much easier to transmit from one machine to another of a different type. Many disk systems record text and all SOURCE CODE programs in ASCII codes. For the sake of economy in memory, many small machines record BASIC programs in non-ASCII coded form, using codes called TOKENS in place of the ASCII codes for command or instruction words. In these, and in many other applications, numbers are also very often coded in binary form rather than as a set of ASCII codes. The advantage of using binary coding for numbers is that a fixed number of bytes can then be used for numbers of any size, so making RANDOM-ACCESS filing easier.

file conversion, *n.* the transferring of file data from one form to another. You might, for example, want to read an old file from PAPER TAPE and store it on a disk. This will require a file conversion, a program which can read from the paper tape and save on disk.

filename, *n.* the reference name which is given to a file when it is recorded. This, also known as the file DESCRIPTOR or IDENTIFIER, allows a tape or disk system to locate the correct file. In some languages, programs are given a filename which need not necessarily be the same as the disk filename. See also EXTENDED FILENAME.

FILL, see PAINT.

filter, *n.* **1.** in computing, a section of a program which selectively removes data. For example, a program file can be put through a 'filter' to remove spaces or REM statements. Similarly, a set of ASCII codes can be filtered to remove any non-ASCII codes, or to remove any code that is preceded by the ASCII 27 character. **2.** in sound synthesis, an electrical circuit that modifies the shape of the waveform. **3.** in electronics, a device that selectively passes or blocks certain frequencies.

fine-tune, *vb.* to make final small adjustments in order to get the best results. Used mainly in the context of a TV receiver, which needs a fine-tuning adjustment for the optimum display of colour and reception of sound. Sometimes also used to refer to small adjustments in the final version of a program.

firmware, *n.* the software, usually of the operating system, which is on ROM. Since it is on ROM which cannot be altered, it is neither completely SOFT nor HARD, and is therefore referred to as firm. Firmware on EPROM must be regarded as rather less firm than the ROM form!

fixed field, *n.* a FIELD in a RECORD that consists of a fixed number of characters, so allowing a RANDOM-ACCESS FILE to be used. If the number of characters in each field of a RECORD can be fixed, then the number of characters in the whole record is also fixed. This allows any record to be located by counting characters, and is the basis of random access to any field of any record.

fixed point, *n.* a way of manipulating numbers in which the position of the decimal point is fixed. Seldom used on microcomputers except in the form of FIELDING commands for displaying numbers. A few early machines, however, could operate on numbers only in fixed-point form. The alternative system became known as FLOATING POINT.

flag, *n.* a bit or byte that is used to indicate some event. Also called *status bit*. The term usually denotes a byte in the flag (or status) REGISTER of the microprocessor. These 'flags' are used to signal the presence of a carry, a negative number, zero in a register and so on. The flags are, in fact, bits in the register which may be 1 (flag set) or 0 (flag reset). In higher-level languages, a flag variable may be used to switch different parts of a program into action. Such a flag variable is usually of the BOOLEAN type, which can be either TRUE or FALSE.

flashing, *n.* the blinking on and off of characters on a VDU SCREEN. Many display systems allow characters to be flashed, meaning that they can be displayed in two colours alternating at a fixed interval. This allows programmers to draw the attention of the user to the need for some action, such as replacing a disk.

flat-bed plotter, *n.* a computer-controlled drawing machine. This consists of a flat plate on which a paper sheet can be laid. A pair of arms attached to a trolley are computer-controlled and can place the trolley at any part of the paper. A pen attached to the trolley can be raised or lowered so as to contact the paper. Then, under computer control, this device can draw pictures. If several pens of different colours can be controlled, then the pictures can be drawn in colour.

flicker, *n.* a noticable alternation of light and dark on a SCREEN. The standard television picture flickers at a rate of 50 times a second, and this is not particularly noticeable under normal viewing conditions. On a bright display which is very close to the operator, however, flicker at this rate can be very tiring to the eye, leading to eye irritation and headaches. Displays which use higher repetition rates are not compatible with TV outputs, but can be much less tiring to use.

flippy, *n.* a flip-over disk. The usual form of floppy disk is single or double-sided, but the double-sided type is intended to be used by a pair of read/write heads, one on each side of the disk. The second side cannot normally be used on a single-sided drive simply by turning the disk over. A disk which is designed to be used in a single-sided drive in this way is called a flippy. These disks are very uncommon in the 5¼" size, though the flippy technique is used on the miniature 3" type of disks.

floating point, *n.* a system of manipulating and displaying numbers in which the number of figures which follows the decimal point is as many as the quantity needs, subject to the maximum number of digits that the computer will print for a number. This allows the computer, for example, to print results like 2.36 and 5.014 rather than, perhaps, 2.360000 or 5.01. Most floating-point arithmetic routines will also accept numbers in STANDARD FORM, and the numbers are manipulated in binary standard form. See also REAL NUMBERS, FIXED POINT, ZERO COMPRESSION.

floppy disk, *n.* a thin plastic DISK coated with magnetic material and enclosed in a plastic jacket. Despite the name, floppy disks should *not* be bent, because this can loosen the magnetic coating. See DISK, WINCHESTER DISK.

floppy tape, *n.* an attempt to create a tape system which is controlled in the same way as a disk system. Also called *stringy floppy*. Floppy tape cartridges use an endless loop of narrow thin tape, which is prone to jamming and breakage, as well as allowing rather slow access to data.

flowchart, *n.* a method of designing programs which uses standardized shapes to represent computing actions in visual terms. The standard action shapes include terminal, process, in/out, decision, and junction. Flowcharts were very fashionable

FLUTTER

many years ago, when computing was taught mainly to those who would become professional programmers.

Other methods, such as WARNIER-ORR diagrams are preferred by a growing number of programmers today, and some programmers maintain that using TOP-DOWN methods with a language like PASCAL or MODULA-2 eliminates the need for flowcharts altogether. See Fig. 26.

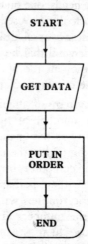

Fig. 26. **Flowchart.** As the name suggests, the aim is to show the order of computing actions in a procedural program.

flutter, *n.* the rapid fluctuation of tape speed, which may be caused by failure of the speed–controller circuits, or by a damaged CAPSTAN spindle. The effect on data recordings is usually to cause CORRUPTION, so that the tape cannot be read. If the flutter exists only on the machine that is being used to read the tape, this can be substituted. If the tape was created with a faulty drive, however, it is very difficult to recover the data. Compare WOW.

flyback, *n.* the return of a scanning electron beam. A TV picture is built up by a beam of electrons which is focused to a point on the screen and made to SCAN across and down the screen. The rate of scanning across is much greater than the rate of scanning down, so that the beam traces out a pattern of parallel lines. At the end of each line, the beam returns rapidly to its starting position on the left-hand side of the screen. This action is called the *line flyback*. When all the lines of a screen have been scanned, the beam returns to the top of the screen, and this action is called the field (or frame) flyback. During these flyback times, the beam is cut off so that no trace is made on the screen.

The importance of flyback is that it occurs at regular intervals. If the ANIMATION of fast graphics is not synchronized to the flyback events, then animation will appear jerky, and some parts of the animated pattern will not be visible because they have occurred in a flyback time.

footer, *n.* a message that appears at the foot of each page of printed text. Typical footer items include title, chapter number, page number, etc.

footprint, *n.* the amount of space that a computer, plus essential PERIPHERALS, will take up on a desk. A machine with a large footprint may need a desk to itself. The word applies only to microcomputers, because larger machines will need floor space rather than desk space.

FOR, *n.* the word that marks the start of a loop action. In several languages FOR signals the start of a loop which runs for a determined number of times. Following FOR there has to be a variable assignment with a range of numbers which will decide how often the loop will run. In BASIC, the usual syntax is:

```
FOR N=1 TO 10
(Actions)
NEXT
```

in which all of the actions between FOR and NEXT will be carried out, in this example, ten times. In Pascal, the loop actions are contained between the words BEGIN; and END; which follow a construction such as FOR N:=1 TO 10 DO;.

forbidden operation, *n.* an action avoided by the operating system because it will corrupt data or cause a reboot. A typical forbidden operation is redimensioning of an array while the array is in use. This would cause the allocation of RAM to be changed, corrupting any data that has already been stored.

foreground, *n.* any pattern that is seen on the screen. The normal screen colour when the screen is cleared is the BACKGROUND colour. The colour of text or graphics drawn on the screen is foreground. If the two colours are identical, then nothing is visible, so it is possible to draw patterns which cannot be seen until the foreground colour is changed. The significance of this is that drawing can be a slow operation, but change of foreground colour can be very rapid. See also INK, PAPER.

format, 1. *n.* (a) the configuration of a screen display as number of columns and rows; (b) the precise syntax of an instruction, showing use of words and separators; (c) the way in which data is organized on a disk in TRACKS and SECTORS. **2.** *vb.* to prepare a new disk for use by magnetically marking out the surface so that it is divided into TRACKS and SECTORS, with the boundaries indicated. This is accompanied by testing the disk, so that bytes are written and read again on all of the working surface. Any failure to read a byte correctly will be reported as a formatting error. Some formatting programs will then continually attempt to reformat this sector until successful or until the operator intervenes. A disk which will not format correctly, or which formats only after a subsequent attempt, should be returned to the manufacturer. Persistent failure to format any disks in a drive indicates a drive fault, though this problem can also be caused by strong magnetic fields such as exist around a VDU MONITOR or TV receiver.

formatter, *n.* a formatting program, usually in machine code, which will FORMAT a new disk.

form feed, see FF.

form letter, *n.* a standard letter. In word processing, the term denotes a letter of standard text which will need only a name and address to be added. This can be done from the keyboard, but is more likely to be carried out using a MAILING LIST. See also BOILERPLATE.

formula, *n.* a method of arriving at a result through an expression of rules for finding a quantity, usually but not necessarily a numerical quantity. The items in the formula consist of CONSTANTS and of VARIABLES, and the formula can be evaluated only when values have been assigned to all of the variables.

formula portability, *n.* a specialized SPREADSHEET action. When the figure in one CELL of a spreadsheet has been calculated by applying a formula to figures in other cells, it may be possible to apply this same formula to other sets of cells without retyping the formula. If this can be done, then the formula is 'portable'.

FORTH, *n.* a LANGUAGE of intermediate level which uses a small number of very brief INSTRUCTION words. The main feature of the language is that it can be extended by the user, who can then write a program in the form of a list of instruction words. The language is designed to compile easily, and was originally developed for machine-control use. It is widely used in ROBOTICS, but its disadvantage is that it is a 'write-only' language, meaning that a program written by anyone else is very difficult to follow. See also THREADED LANGUAGE, BEAD.

FORTRAN, *n.* one of the very early high-level languages, very popular in the 50s and 60s. Short for *formula translation*. It is predominantly a language for mathematical, scientific and engineering programs, but its general principles have been absorbed into BASIC, and any former FORTRAN programmer will find BASIC very easy to learn.

forty-track disk, *n.* a disk which has been formatted (see FORMAT) so as to use forty tracks of data. See also EIGHTY-TRACK DISK, DISK.

forward reference, *n.* a reference to something in a program that has not yet been established and which is defined later in the program. For example, if you have in a BASIC program the line:

```
100 GOSUB 5000
```

this is a forward reference to a line which the machine has not yet come to. In Pascal and several other languages, forward references are avoided by defining all constants, variables, functions and procedures in advance of the main program that uses them, thus enabling the program to be compiled more easily. If an unavoidable forward reference has to be made, it must be followed by the word FORWARD so that the COMPILER can search for the reference.

frame, *n.* the vertical dimension of the VDU display. The word FIELD is also used in TV technology. The difference arises because a TV display consists of a picture, the frame, built up from two sets of fields. One field consists of the odd-numbered screen lines, the other of the even-numbered lines. See also TV, RASTER.

frame flyback, *n.* the point in a TV display at which the scanning returns to the top of the screen so that a completely new picture is built up. This is done 25 (UK) or 30 (US) times per second. See also FLYBACK, RASTER.

Framework, *n. Trademark.* a suite of programs by Ashton-Tate (authors of D-BASE). This consists of WORD PROCESSOR, SPREAD-SHEET, DATABASE and GRAPHICS generator, all of which are controlled by a COMMAND LANGUAGE in which each instruction must start with the @ symbol. The suite is designed for microcomputers in the IBM PC class, with fairly large memory space.

FRE, *n.* a function that is used in some varieties of BASIC to find the amount of free memory that is available. This permits programs to be written so that the user can be warned if entering further data would result in an Out of Memory error. This could be important, because the Out of Memory error is a FATAL ERROR which causes the program to stop.

frequency, *n.* the number of times per second that something happens. Used to measure the pitch of a sound, or the rate of a CLOCK pulse generator. See also HERTZ.

friction feed, *n.* a method of feeding paper into a printer. The term is applied to a printer action in which unsprocketed paper is gripped between two rollers. Useful for single sheets, and for single-ply roll, but not for two-ply rolls, because the sheets tend to slide sideways over each other, causing unequal margins. See also SPROCKET HOLES.

Friday!, *n. Trademark.* a database package by Ashton-Tate, intended as a lower-level alternative to D-BASE 2. Friday! is MENU-DRIVEN, and uses fixed-format, fixed-length RECORDS which allow only short pieces of text. One outstanding feature is the ability to return quickly and easily to the main menu at any stage.

front end, *n.* the part of a computer that deals with inputs and outputs. This includes screen, keyboard, and peripherals like disk drives which pass data to and from the processor stage of the computer. All the actions of the front end of the computer are slow, and designs which separate the front end from the rest of the machine, using a separate FRONT-END PROCESSOR allow greater efficiency.

front-end processor, *n.* a system that deals with peripherals. In microcomputers, the front-end processor is a microprocessor which handles all of the front-end actions. In larger computing systems, the front-end processor is a complete computer which deals mainly with networking and with line communications.

function, *n.* a computer action that acts on data to produce other data. A number function will act on a number to produce another number. For example the BASIC statement INT(24.6) will produce 24, the integer part of 24.6. A string function acts on a string of characters to produce either a number or a string. For example, in BASIC, LEN(X$) will give a number equal to the number of characters in the string X$, and LEFT$(X$,3) will give a string which contains the first three characters of X$. Many languages do not make any use of string functions, because there is no string data type as such. Instead, an array of character codes is manipulated directly by way of character functions.

function key, *n.* a key which is used to start an action, as distinct from making a character appear on the screen. Keys of this type include the RETURN or ENTER key, and the ESC or BREAK keys. Several machines also provide function keys which are programmable, see PROGRAMMABLE KEY.

functional unit, *n.* a part of the computer system that carries out a clearly defined task.

fuse, *n.* a method of preventing electrical overload by providing an easily-melted link in the circuit. Most microcomputers and peripherals should be protected by a 3A fuse rather then by the 13A type which is commonly supplied in plugs. In addition to the fuse in the plug, equipment will also use fuses on the low-voltage supplies. These fuses will be internal, located on the printed circuit boards of the computer, usually in the POWER SUPPLY UNIT. Any fuse failure should be investigated; because fuses do not wear out, their failure is normally due to either the failure of another part of the circuit, or overloading.

fuzzy, *n.* anything in computing that is indeterminate. Many database programs allow you to make a 'fuzzy search' or 'fuzzy specification'. This would permit you, for example, to specify a word like SMITH, and get answers on SMYTHE as well, because the search allows similar sounding names to be checked. Fuzzy action deals in similarities and probabilities, and is very difficult to program, but is an essential part of AI(artificial intelligence), because humans can make considerable use of this type of logic.

G

gap, *n.* a space between groups of data. Usually applied to tape recording, in which the data is grouped into BLOCKS. Each block starts with a HEADER which contains the FILENAME and some information on the block, such as the number of bytes in the block. A short part of the tape is then left unrecorded between blocks, and this is referred to as the gap, or *interblock gap*. The presence of this gap allows time for the computer to check the block data, and to stop the tape if an error is found. If the tape system is well designed, it may be possible to rewind to the previous gap, and try to load the faulty block again. See Fig. 27.

garbage, *n.* meaningless computing data. No matter how well written a program may be, unless the data is valid, the program cannot produce useful results. The motto of all computer users is 'garbage in, garbage out' (GIGO). The name is also applied to bytes which appear in RAM memory at switch on. These bytes are caused by random switching of the memory units, and are meaningless. The initializing actions of the computer will clear this form of garbage (see INITIALIZE). Garbage may also be left in memory when one program has replaced another.

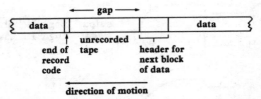

Fig. 27. **Gap.** A gap (interblock gap) in tape data. This allows the data to be recorded in blocks, and makes it possible to rewind the tape to a gap and reload an individual block if an error occurs.

garbage collection, *n.* the reallocation of memory. Computers which use BASIC generally allow strings to be of any size up to 255 characters. Each time a string name is reassigned, however, a new piece of memory is selected for the storage of that string. When a program which reassigns string names (a string-sort, for example) runs, the memory may fill with unused string characters and a 'garbage collection' routine in the operating system runs automatically to reallocate the memory. This can take a considerable time, during which the computer appears to have locked up.

The problem can be avoided by deliberately causing garbage collection at regular intervals, by defining strings as of fixed length, or by swapping POINTERS instead of strings. The problem is confined to BASIC programs on certain machines, and does not greatly affect other languages.

gate, *n.* a LOGIC device for computing actions. A gate is an electronic circuit which will give a 1 output only when the inputs fulfil certain conditions. The standard logic varieties are AND, OR and XOR, but many gates are manufactured with inverse outputs, so that the types NAND and NOR are more common than AND or OR. The logic actions of the computer are due to the use of gate circuits within the microprocessor or CPU.

GEM

Large computers use gate circuits which are supplied in separate IC form, using techniques that allow very fast operation. See Fig. 28.

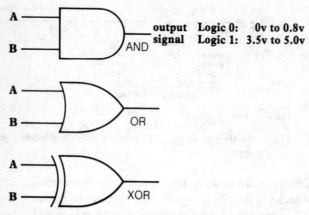

Fig. 28. **Gates.** Electrical gates in IC form carry out the arithmetic and logic actions of the computer. The gates respond to digital logic signals which are presented simultaneously at the inputs, and the results appear almost instantaneously at the outputs. The examples show typical signal voltage levels. For actions, see AND, OR, XOR.

GEM, *n. Trademark. acronym for* Graphics Environmental Manager. This is a program by Digital Research which allows the IBM computer, its clones, and several other machines to operate with a WIMP system similar to that used on the Apple Macintosh. See also USER-FRIENDLY.

generation, *n.* a level of MAINFRAME computer development. The first generation of computers used electronic valves, the second used transistors, and the third used early types of ICs. At the time of writing, the fourth generation of computers is being used to design the FIFTH GENERATION.

GET, *n.* an instruction word in BASIC which gets a character code from the keyboard.

giga, *n. prefix.* denoting a thousand million, or (US) billion.

GIGO, *n. acronym for* Garbage In, Garbage Out. See GARBAGE.

global, *adj.* of or relating to anything in computing that extends over the whole system. A global PARAMETER is one whose value is maintained in all parts of a program in which it is used. The opposite is a LOCAL parameter. In word processing, a global search and replace means that every occurrence of a word will be found and the word will be replaced by another specified word. The alternative is a selective SEARCH AND REPLACE action, in which the operator is notified each time the search word is found and asked if it is to be replaced.

golf ball, *n.* a form of typewriter head and action. Introduced by IBM, the golf-ball typewriter was one of the first to place all of the type on a single moving head. This avoided the action of moving the carriage of the typewriter, and greatly advanced the design of electric typewriters. The IBM machine became known as the golf ball because of the shape of the printhead. Some alternative designs used miniature barrels or thimble shapes. The DAISYWHEEL is now in wider use because of the simpler pattern of movement that is needed to operate the wheel.

GOSUB, *n.* an instruction word used in BASIC to mean that a subroutine is to be run. The line number at which the subroutine starts must follow the GOSUB instruction word.

GOTO, *n.* an instruction that forces the computer to jump from one instruction to another which is not the normal following instruction. Found in nearly all languages, but usually in conjunction with a 'label' which indicates where the program must jump to.

In BASIC, GOTO can be used with a line number, allowing a jump to be taken to any point in the program without marking that point. This is a good way of making a program unreadable and often unworkable.

grandfather, *n.* the oldest backup file copy, see FATHER.

graph, *n.* a method of displaying number relationships visually. This is usually done by plotting distances which are proportional to numbers. One number is plotted horizontally and the other vertically, so that the intersection is a dot on the screen or the paper. The data can thus be displayed as a set of points that can be joined to form a graph line.

Denary	4-bit Gray code	4-bit Binary
0	0000	0000
1	0001	0001
2	0011	0010
3	0010	0011
4	0110	0100
5	0111	0101
6	0101	0110
7	0100	0111
8	1100	1000
9	1101	1001
10	1111	1010
11	1110	1011
12	1010	1100

Fig. 29. **Gray code.** Gray code compared with binary code. The important feature of Gray code is that each number differs by only one bit from the preceding or following number, unlike binary code. Gray code, used in some digitizers, needs to be converted to binary for the purposes of arithmetic.

graphics, diagrams which are produced on the screen or, less commonly, on a printer. All computers have some amount of graphics capability, but nowadays most feature *high-resolution graphics*, in which the detail of the diagrams can be considerably finer than was possible in early systems. High-resolution graphics, however, requires a lot of RAM memory and may even make it impossible to use a long program that utilizes the graphics. Some designs overcome this by using a separate part of the memory for the screen display. Modern microcomputers feature high-resolution graphics in colour, and matching colour printers can now be obtained.

graphics tablet, *n.* a method of digitizing a diagram through a network of contacts or tiny pressure switches that INTERFACE to the computer. Also called *graphics pad*. See DIGITIZE. A piece of paper which carries a diagram is placed on the tablet, and a pen or stylus is used to press on the lines of the diagram, tracing out these lines. As the pen presses on the tablet, the lines appear on the screen.

The SOFTWARE which allows the tablet to operate is usually devised so that the position coordinates of each point can be memorized, allowing the pattern to be reproduced. Once the pattern has been digitized in this way, it can be manipulated by other graphics programs.

Gray code, *n.* an alternative form of BINARY code. The Gray code uses the digits 0 and 1, but in a different pattern, not following the 8-4-2-1 weighting of columns of conventional binary code. The particular advantage of Gray code is that when the number changes by one unit, only one digit in the Gray code will change. The code is used mainly by mechanical position ENCODERS, and not as a computer code. See Fig. 29.

grey scale, *n.* the number of discernible shades of grey between black and white on a VDU screen. The larger the grey scale, the better the picture quality. A good grey scale is important in computer use only if very advanced graphics are to be used. Most graphics systems on small computers use only a very small grey scale.

grid, *n.* a pattern that can be used for gauging shape and size. In character readers, the shape of a character can be assessed by placing a grid (or matrix) over it and measuring the intensity of print in each part of the grid. See also OPTICAL CHARACTER READER.

gulp, *n.* a term that is sometimes used to denote a group of bytes. See also NIBBLE, WORD.

H

hacker, *n.* a skilled computer user. The term originally denoted a very skilled programmer, particularly one skilled in MACHINE CODE and with a good knowledge of the machine and its OPERATING SYSTEM. The name arose from the fact that a good programmer could always 'hack' an unsatisfactory system around until it worked. The term later came to denote a user whose main interest is in defeating PASSWORD systems, particularly on ELECTRONIC MAIL systems. The term has thus acquired a pejorative sense, meaning one who deliberately and sometimes criminally interferes with data which is available through telephone lines. The activities of such hackers have led to considerable efforts to tighten up the security of transmitted data.

half-duplex, *n.* a communications system. A half-duplex system allows communication in either direction, but not at the same time. See SIMPLEX, DUPLEX.

Hamming code, *n.* a method of detecting and correcting transmission errors in data. Named after its inventor, the code uses CHECK BITS and CHECKSUMS to detect errors in data that has been transmitted. The system is complex, and is used mainly in TELETEXT systems.

handler, *n.* a part of the OPERATING SYSTEM designed to control the action of a PERIPHERAL like a tape or disk drive. The screen, printer and keyboard also have handlers. See also DRIVER.

handshake, *n.* a method in data transmission for stopping data from being sent until it can be processed. This is particularly true if data is being sent to a slow-acting device like a printer or a modem. A *handshake signal,* carried on a separate line, is one that is used to signal ready or not-ready for data. When the printer contains no BUFFER memory, this may mean that a computer is unavailable for use until the whole of a printing run has been completed.

Some systems allow 'spooling': the data which is to be sent to the printer is recorded on disk, and fed in small batches from disk to printer, thus making use of the microprocessor of the computer at times when it is not otherwise engaged (see SPOOL).

hard, *adj.* (of a part of a computer system) being in visible and solid form, as distinct from program instructions, which are SOFT or 'firm'. See HARDWARE, SOFTWARE, FIRMWARE.

hard copy, *n.* a copy of a program listing or data on paper as distinct from on the screen. For commercial programs, all outputs are hard copy, with the screen used only for messages to the operator. Compare READOUT.

hard disk, see WINCHESTER DISK.

hard sectoring, *n.* a system of permanent SECTOR allocation. This is a system of disk FORMATTING, not used for microcomputers, in which disks can be supplied ready-formatted with the sectors always marked out mechanically in the same way. The marking is done by a set of holes near the hub of the disk, with each hole marking the start of a sector. Each hole can be detected in the drive by passing a beam of light through the hole to a PHOTOSENSOR. See Fig. 30. Compare SOFT SECTORING.

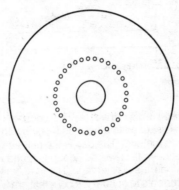

Fig. 30. **Hard sectoring.** A hard-sectored 8″ disk has typically 33 holes around the sectoring circle. Of these, one is an index hole, and the other 32 indicate the sector positions. A few types of disks have the sectoring holes around the outside rim. Most modern disk systems use soft-sectoring.

hardware, *n.* the mechanically visible parts of the computer, such as keyboard, printed circuit boards, chips, connectors, etc. See also SOFTWARE, FIRMWARE.

hard wiring, *n.* connection with wires rather than by using metal strips on boards. Hard wiring implies that the connections are made by hand, though automated methods are normally used. In computers, hard wiring will be found mainly on connections between units. A lot of hard wiring in a new machine may indicate that the design is not finalized. Hard wiring may also be needed to carry out modifications to a circuit.

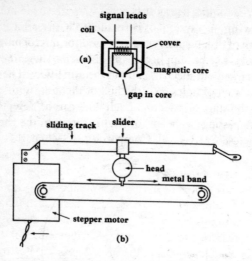

Fig. 31. **Head-of-disk drive.** (a) This consists of a magnetic core which is shaped to a (rounded) point, with a tiny gap in the magnetic material. The gap is the part across which an intense magnetic field will be generated, and it touches, or almost touches, the disk surface. The read/write signals are electrical currents to or from the coils that are wound around the magnetic material. The whole head is moved radially across the disk surface in steps by mechanisms such as the metal band shown in (b).

```
2400 Hz tone — 5 seconds
synchronizing byte
Filename bytes ( 1 to 10 characters)
end of filename marker
Load address of file (4 bytes)
Execution address of file (4 bytes)
Block number (2 bytes)                      header
Data block length (2 bytes)
Block flag (1 byte)
4 bytes spare
CRC for header (2 bytes)
Data (0 to 256 bytes)
CRC on data (2 bytes)
```

Fig. 32. **Header.** A typical tape header, in this example for the BBC Micro. The header contains all the essential information on the data that will follow. Any corruption of the header will cause misreading of the file, and an error message.

hashing, *n.* a method for extracting a reference code number for data. For example, a set of names could be 'hash coded' by adding up the ASCII codes for the first three letters. The resulting number is then used as a reference for locating the name in a file. In any reasonably simple hash–code system, different names may give the same hash codes. This is dealt with by storing the names in sequence following the code. In general, a hashing system of filing data can lead to considerable reduction in the time that is needed to find a given entry. Methods for hashing can be found in books that deal with programming techniques.

hashmark, *n.* the # mark used in the US as a symbol for number. Sometimes called *pound sign* (US). In computing languages, the hashmark often precedes reference numbers, as in Channel #3, and in instructions such as CLOSE #3. In some varieties of BASIC, the hashmark is used to distinguish a variable name for a number which is in 'double-precision' form, to a precision of 15 figures, for example.

head-of-disk drive, *n.* the data reading or writing device, an assembly of wire coils and shaped metal which will convert electrical signals to magnetic signals and vice versa. When electrical signals are applied to a head and the magnetic–disk surface is spun in close contact with the head, the disk will be magnetized in a pattern that represents the electrical signals. Conversely, if a magnetized disk track is spun close to the head, the coils will have electrical signals generated in them which correspond to the magnetic signals on the disk. The same head can therefore be used both for recording data signals on to the disk and for reading back these signals. See Fig. 31.

header, *n.* a set of signals at the start of the recording of a file on disk or tape. The header usually contains the file name and numbers for the file length and its position in memory at the time of recording. The header can also contain bytes that assist in protection systems. On replay, the header allows the program to be identified and placed correctly in memory. See also BLOCK, GAP. See Fig. 32.

Hertz, *n.* the unit of FREQUENCY. A frequency of one Hertz means that the action is carried out once per second. The unit of Hertz

119

HEURISTIC

Denary	Binary	Hex
Ø	ØØØØ	ØØ
1	ØØØ1	Ø1
2	ØØ1Ø	Ø2
3	ØØ11	Ø3
4	Ø1ØØ	Ø4
5	Ø1Ø1	Ø5
6	Ø11Ø	Ø6
7	Ø111	Ø7
8	1ØØØ	Ø8
9	1ØØ1	Ø9
10	1Ø1Ø	ØA
11	1Ø11	ØB
12	11ØØ	ØC
13	11Ø1	ØD
14	111Ø	ØE
15	1111	ØF

Hex-to-binary conversion:
Convert each hex digit into 4 binary bits, using table above.

Example: 6E = Ø11Ø 111Ø
  '6' 'E'

Binary-to-hex conversion:
Split off binary digits into groups of four starting at least significant bit. Convert each group to hex.

Example: 1Ø ! 11Ø1 ! Ø11Ø
  2 | D | 6
= 2D6 hex

Fig. 33. **Hexadecimal.** The hexadecimal (hex) scale of numbers. This is used by machine-code and assembly language programmers, and is also produced by disassemblers.

is therefore 1/seconds. For the rates that are used in computing, the units of kilohertz (kHz), equal to one thousand hertz, and megahertz (MHz), equal to one million hertz, are more appropriate.

heuristic, *adj.* (of learning) being based on experience, particularly by trial and error. A heuristic program is one that can 'learn' from the response of a user, meaning that the program can modify itself. The subject is of particular importance in the study of AI, artificial intelligence.

hexadecimal, *n.* a number system that uses 16 as a base, often abbreviated to 'hex'. The digits 0 to 9 have to be supplemented by letters A to F to represent the numbers 10 to 15. In this scale, a number like 2A means $2 \times 16 + 10 = 42$ in DENARY. The system is used extensively by MACHINE CODE and ASSEMBLY LANGUAGE programmers because one byte can be represented by just two hex digits, and an ADDRESS for an 8-bit microprocessor by just four digits. In addition, the command codes of MICROPROCESSORS are always listed in hex, and it is only in this code that relationships between codes are obvious. See Fig. 33.

hex dump, *n.* a display, usually on the screen, of the bytes of a program or block of data, in hex code. This type of display is useful only for a MACHINE CODE programmer. The CP/M operating system includes a hex-dump UTILITY.

hex pad, *n.* a hexadecimal keyboard that contains digits 0 to 9 and letters A to F. Early microcomputers used a hex pad in place of a full keyboard, because the machines were intended to be programmed only in machine code. A few devices that are intended for teaching machine-code programming still use hex pads.

hidden lines, *n.* **1.** lines of a diagram that are invisible. **2.** in perspective drawing, lines that cannot be seen because they are masked by the near surface of the drawn object. Graphics programs can often be arranged to draw in these lines in dotted form. **3.** lines that have been drawn on the screen in BACKGROUND colour, and which will not become visible until the colours are switched.

hierarchical classification, *n.* an arrangement of data in order of importance. The classification starts with the most important headings, and each of these can lead to a number of less important headings, and so on. The important feature of this TREE structure is that the order is of relative importance, rather than by features such as alphabetical order, numerical size, etc.

high density, *n.* tightly packed storage. The term usually denotes the packing of stored data bits on a disk, measured in terms of bits per linear inch of track. See also DOUBLE DENSITY, QUAD DENSITY.

high frequency, *n.* a fast rate of repetition of signal waveforms. See FREQUENCY.

high-level language, *n.* a language that allows you to program without having to know about the microprocessor actions that actually carry out the program actions. LOW-LEVEL LANGUAGES such as machine code and assembler require considerable knowledge of the microprocessor and how it is connected into the computer, along with other details of the computer ARCHITECTURE. In a high-level language, an operating system takes care of the HOUSEKEEPING actions, leaving the programmer free to concentrate on the actions that the program is intended to achieve. The program (or SOURCE CODE) itself is written in terms that are closer to NATURAL LANGUAGE than assembler.

There are two main types of high-level languages, classed as PROCEDURAL or LOGICAL. In a procedural language, the programmer defines a list of actions (procedures) that will carry out the action that is needed. Most high-level languages are of this type. The logical languages allow the programmer to specify the rules that are needed to solve a problem, and the relationships between any quantities that are involved. This approach requires much more effort in the specification and writing of the language, but provides the programmer with much more powerful methods. PROLOG is the best known example of this type of language, which forms the basis of the languages being developed for FIFTH GENERATION computers.

A further classification of the IMPLEMENTATION of high-level languages is as compiled or interpreted (see COMPILE, INTERPRETER).

high-resolution graphics (HRG), *n.* graphics that permit advanced diagrammatic commands. The use of a screen for text demands at most 80 columns and up to 30 rows, corresponding to 2400 screen locations at most, enabling only very coarse diagrams to be made. In a high-resolution graphics system, the number of controllable points is greatly increased.

In general, a number of controllable points greater than 30,000 can be taken as corresponding to HRG. When so many points are available, the computer needs some HIGH-LEVEL LANGUAGE instructions that can allow the creation of diagrams. These instructions may be built into the normal programming language, or they may be incorporated into a special graphics programming language which is supplied separately. Many such languages offer the options of recording graphics instructions, recording screen patterns, and of reproducing the screen pattern on a printer of the dot-matrix type.

histogram, *n.* a form of data display showing sizes of quantities represented as lengths of bars. Also called *barchart*. Its merit is that its meaning is obvious and clear, but it becomes unusable if the ratio between the largest and the smallest quantities is too great. See Fig. 34.

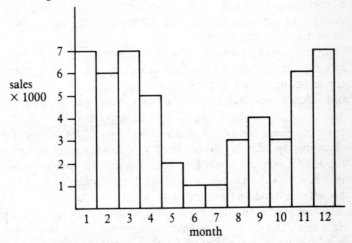

Fig. 34. **Histogram.** The lengths of the vertical columns represent the quantity size which is being plotted.

hit, *n.* a success in matching data. When a database is being searched for an item, a hit occurs when an item answering to the description is found.

holding loop, *n.* a LOOP which runs until broken by some action. Many machines run a holding loop in MACHINE CODE while being programmed, with the keyboard being checked repeatedly in a loop until a key is pressed. The machine returns to the holding loop each time a character has been put into memory. A holding loop can also be used in HIGH-LEVEL LANGUAGE to keep the machine inactive until the user presses a key. Such a loop is usually accompanied by the message Press any key to proceed.

Hollerith code, *n.* the standard code for PUNCHED CARD data storage. The code was invented by Hermann Hollerith, who devised the punched card system for analysing a late 19th century US census. The success of the system led to the formation of the Hollerith Corporation, which was later absorbed by IBM.

holographic store, *n.* storage in the form of a hologram. A hologram is a pattern created by LASER light on a photographic plate, with the distinguishing feature that the coding allows very high-density recording. Holograms are therefore a promising method of storage, though the COMPACT DISK offers more immediately usable systems.

home, *n.* a starting point on the screen. In many text and graphics systems, the 'home' position of the CURSOR is taken as being at the top left-hand corner of the screen.

hook address, *n.* an address for the first of two bytes which are in RAM and that can be changed. The principle is that these two bytes constitute the address of an OPERATING SYSTEM routine. By changing the address in these hook locations for another one in the RAM, you can insert (or 'hook') your own machine code routines into the operating system. Among other things, this allows you to add new commands to the BASIC language.

housekeeping, *n.* the actions that the computer must take to keep data intact and carry out program actions correctly. Housekeeping involves such items as correctly allocating memory space, ensuring that there is enough memory for a program to run, maintaining the screen display, keyboard, disk drive and so on. This forms a part of the operating system of the computer that must be used independently of the presence of any HIGH-LEVEL LANGUAGE. All housekeeping actions are TRANSPARENT to the user.

HRG, see HIGH-RESOLUTION GRAPHICS.

hub, *n.* the central part of a disk. A disk must be gripped at the centre, or hub, by the DISK DRIVE so that it can be spun at the correct speed. Most makes of floppy disks use hubs that are reinforced with mica to reduce the risk of tearing the thin plastic at this point. Disks without reinforced hubs should not be used for valuable programs or data. The miniature 3″ and 3½″ disks have hubs that are built up and need no further reinforcement.

I

IBM, *n. acronym for* International Business Machines, the largest and most powerful computer manufacturer in the world. IBM also manufacture a large range of office equipment, including the descendants of the celebrated GOLF BALL typewriter. The firm was a latecomer to microcomputers, since most of its computing business is in the manufacture of mainframes. The IBM Personal Computer (PC), though not technically very innovative, set standards which other manufacturers have copied.

IC, *abbrev. for* integrated circuit, a complete circuit in miniature which has been constructed on a small chip of SILICON. This is done conventionally by a combination of photographic printing, acid etching, and the deposition of semiconductor vapours. The result is an electronic circuit in miniature form in which all the connections between components have already been made in the manufacturing process. Since interconnections are generally the least reliable portions of electronic circuits, this approach has led to much improved reliability. Only the development of ICs has made the manufacture of microcomputers possible. See Fig. 35 on page 126.

icon, see IKON.

ICL, *abbrev. for* International Computers Ltd., a British firm that manufactures mainframe computers.

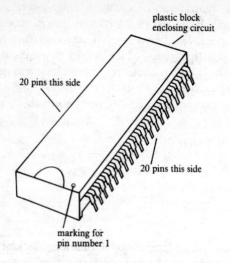

Fig. 35. **IC.** A typical small microprocessor IC. The actual working portion (the chip itself) is smaller than a fingernail, and the larger plastic casing (52mm × 14mm in this example) makes it easier to work with.

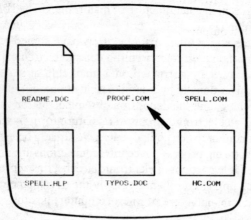

Fig. 36. **Ikon.** A typical ikon display. Each item which carries a title represents a program or file which can be called up by moving the arrowhead cursor, using a mouse, and then pressing a button.

ID, *abbrev. for* identification. Some disk systems insist on an identification code of a few letters being supplied when a disk is formatted (see FORMAT). The purpose of this is to prevent CORRUPTION of the disk when copying is carried out, because the system is arranged to prevent a disk being copied to another disk with the same ID mark.

identification, *n.* the coding for data. See also ID, IDENTIFIER.

identifier, *n.* a name or set of characters used to identify a number or a STRING or any other data type. Examples include FILENAMES and VARIABLE names, but many languages also permit names for CONSTANTS, RECORDS and other data types. See also DESCRIPTOR.

idle character, *n.* a 'do nothing' code denoting a byte that is sent down a line to inform the receiver that there is no data to be sent.

idle time, *n.* the time during which a machine is switched on but not in use.

IEEE–488, *n.* a standard for interface connections drawn up by the (American) Institute of Electrical and Electronic Engineers. Only data and HANDSHAKE signals are used, and the system is intended in particular for interfacing computers to measuring instruments. Most microcomputers can, however, be connected by means of interfaces to peripherals which provide IEE–488 inputs and outputs.

IF, *n.* the keyword that is used in BASIC and other languages as a CONDITIONAL. The test that is formed using IF will have a result that is either true or false, and the program must be designed to take different actions for these two possibilities. See also ELSE.

ikon, *n.* an image on the screen that is used to select an action. For example, the image might be of a dustbin. If you have finished working with a file, then moving the cursor to this ikon and pressing RETURN has the effect of deleting and closing the file. Ikons are often used in conjunction with a MOUSE and WINDOWS in machines that offer WIMP facilities (windows, ikons, mouse programs). The aim of these systems is not to replace the operating system of the machine, but to supplement it in ways that make the system more USER-FRIENDLY. See Fig. 36. See also GEM.

illegal character, *n.* a code that does not correspond to a valid character. The standard ASCII codes that are used for printer characters extend from 32 to 127. If the computer does not make use of codes above 127, then any code outwith the 32 to 127 range is illegal.

illegal operation, *n.* any action that the operating system of the computer will not permit it to perform. This might, for example, be a command which would corrupt the memory, misuse the printer, corrupt a disk etc. Programs which make use of machine code (or which use POKE statements) can generally carry out illegal operations.

image processing, *n.* the conversion of an image into DIGITAL data and its subsequent processing (see DIGITIZE). Once a TV type of image has been digitized into BINARY data, the computer can process this data in any way that the user wishes. This can be used to enhance the contrast of an image, to blend images, change colours, change shapes, and so on.

immediate addressing, *n.* a term in ASSEMBLY LANGUAGE to indicate that the data for an instruction is located in the byte of memory immediately following the instruction byte in the memory.

impact printer, *n.* any type of printer that strikes the paper. ELECTROSTATIC and THERMAL PRINTERS use special papers, and do not strike the paper. Similarly, the INK-JET and LASER PRINTERS rely on depositing material on the paper without direct contact. Impact printers, however, rely on the principle of needles or type shapes being pressed against inked ribbons which strike the paper. These printer types are comparatively noisy and slow, but they have the considerable advantage that they can be used with ordinary paper, and also with several sheets of interleaved carbons if copies are needed.

implementation, *n.* a scheme for making some idea work, particularly in HIGH-LEVEL LANGUAGES. These languages are defined in the form of rules (syntactical definition) and key-words, and programmers have to write COMPILERS or INTERPRETERS which will carry out the rules of the language. The resulting compiler or interpreter is an implementation of the language.

Though any implementation should obey the rules of the

language, it need not allow all of the possible language statements to operate, in which case it is said to be a SUBSET of the language.

improper argument, *n.* an error in FUNCTION use. When this phrase appears in an error message, you should look for a function whose ARGUMENT is an impossible one. For example, you cannot take the square root of a negative number, nor find an angle whose sine or cosine exceeds 1. An improper argument usually leads to a FATAL ERROR.

increment, *n.* an increase, usually by one. The conventional FOR type of loop implies that a counter variable will be incremented in each pass through the loop. Compare DECREMENT.

indent, *vb.* to insert a space in from the left-hand side. In word processing, the term is used to describe the action of leaving a larger than normal left-hand margin. A word may be indented, for example, to mark the start of a new paragraph.

index, *n.* a method of keeping track of an item. In text work, an index is a list of key words in alphabetical order, with page or reference numbers. In a HIGH-LEVEL LANGUAGE, the term is used as another word for COUNTER, meaning a variable subject to INCREMENTS or DECREMENTS on each pass through a loop. See also INDEXED ADDRESSING.

indexed addressing, *n.* a system used in ASSEMBLY LANGUAGE programming in which a BASE ADDRESS has been loaded into an INDEX REGISTER, and in which addressing is carried out by adding numbers to this address. A typical example of indexed command is LD A,(IX+3) which means that the accumulator is loaded from a memory address which is found by adding 3 to the number that has been stored in the IX register. Indexed addressing is particularly useful for implementing programs which contain tables of data, in particular, COMPILERS and INTERPRETERS.

index register, *n.* a REGISTER within the microprocessor. This type of register is generally one that can be used to store a BASE ADDRESS to which DISPLACEMENT numbers can be added. This is particularly useful in implementing the action of searching tables of data, since the index register can be used to store the address of the first item in the table.

(a) MNEMONIC INSTRUCTION LD A (7FA∅)

(i) Fetch 1st byte   ⟶   7FA∅ . .CF
    = CF   7FA1 . . 8∅
                                  7FA2 . . . .

(ii) Fetch next byte   7FA∅ . . CF
    = 8∅   ⟶   7FA1 . . 8∅
                                  7FA2 . . . .

(iii) Assemble into an address
      =8∅ CF (note high byte is second
         byte in store)

(iv) Fetch byte from this address
     = A1   ⟶   8∅CF . . A1
                                8∅D∅ . . B6

(v) Put A1 into accumulator

(b) LD HL, 7FA∅
    LD A (HL)

Fig. 37. **Indirect addressing.** The bytes are shown in hex
notation. (a) The address which is given in the instruction is
used to obtain the low byte of a new address, for which the
high byte is located at the next higher address. The new
address is then collected up and used. In practice, most
microprocessors use a different form of indirect addressing
in which the address is stored in registers first rather than
being used in a single instruction (b).

indexed sequential access, *n.* a disk filing method which is a
compromise between SERIAL and RANDOM access. This method
uses a second FILE as a form of index to the items in the main file.
When an item is required, the subsidiary file is searched, and the
result used to gain rapid access to the correct part of the main
file.

indicator light, *n.* a small light (usually LED) which is a method of indicating power on, disk drive active, or the state of a toggling key.

indirect addressing, *n.* a method of MACHINE CODE addressing. In ASSEMBLY LANGUAGE, this indicates a method of finding an address by referring to another pair of addresses. By reading a byte from each of these addresses, a new address is put together and can be used. A program which uses indirect addressing can be made self-modifying, because the bytes that are stored in the addresses can themselves be modified by the program action. The use of indirect addressing by a MICROPROCESSOR makes it much easier to implement HIGH-LEVEL LANGUAGE COMPILERS and INTERPRETERS. See Fig. 37 on page 130.

information, *n.* any data that is arranged and organized so that it has a meaning to a human reader.

information retrieval, *n.* any method of obtaining stored information. Information can be stored in a DATABASE, and retrieved by the request of the user. To retrieve information, the user has to provide the database program with some item from which the database management system can either calculate the location of the data, or carry out a systematic search. The item that has to be provided may simply be a reference number, or it can be a feature of the data, such as a surname. The system should be able to cope with items that are logically linked (all females of ages 21 to 35, blonde, secretarial experience) and often with FUZZY specifications.

information technology, *n.* a loose term that encompasses virtually all aspects of computing, data recording, TV, video, and communications.

information theory, *n.* a mathematical basis for treating information. This covers methods of coding data, and the most efficient ways of transmitting data.

initialize, *vb.* to prepare for use with a set of starting values. A computer runs through an initialization routine when it is switched on. In many cases this consists of clearing and perhaps testing the memory, and then reading a set of data from the ROM into RAM. Similarly, when a program starts running, some variables may have to be allocated with values, and this step is described as an initializing step. Large and elaborate programs may require many variables to be initialized by the user, and in this case, it is usual for the program to supply DEFAULT values which the user can then change if needed.

INK, *n.* an INSTRUCTION word that is used in some DIALECTS of BASIC to set the colour of characters. See also PAPER, FOREGROUND.

INKEY, *n.* a KEYBOARD scanning instruction used in several DIALECTS of BASIC to cause the computer to scan the keyboard and return with the ASCII code of any key that is pressed.

INKEY$, *n.* a keyboard scanning instruction used in most dialects of BASIC which tests the keyboard to find if a key is pressed, and returns with the character assigned as a STRING.

ink-jet printer, *n.* a form of NON-IMPACT PRINTER that 'draws' characters by squirting ink at the paper from a fine jet whose position and angle can be altered under MICROPROCESSOR control. The advantages include high operating speed, and the ability to form any character, including those of Chinese and Arabic. Some types can also operate with several jets, making colour printing possible. Disadvantages are that the jet can easily become clogged, and that it is impossible to make carbon copies.

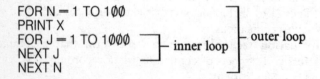

Fig. 38. **Inner loop.** In this BASIC example, the inner loop is used only as a time delay, preventing the printing action from being carried out too quickly. An inner loop like this is described as being 'nested' within the outer loop.

inner loop, *n.* a loop that is contained within another loop. When NESTING loops, the inner loop is the one which must run completely before the outer loop can make another run. In a piece of program which contains such nested loops, the inner loop should run as fast as possible, and any action in this loop that is not strictly necessary should be avoided. This is because all the actions in the inner loop will be repeated many times, making a disproportionately large contribution to the total time that the program takes. See Fig. 38.

input, *n.* an item of data that is entered into a computer. This may be from the keyboard, from a tape, or from a disk. The input can also be obtained directly from DIGITIZERS, GRAPHICS TABLETS, and other devices. An input may be of as little as a single byte, or it may consist of a long stream of bytes. Large input items are normally broken into sections of up to 255 bytes by the action of the programs that carry out input. When the input has been programmed in a HIGH-LEVEL LANGUAGE, the byte or bytes will be assigned to a VARIABLE NAME or IDENTIFIER. When the input is carried out using MACHINE CODE, the bytes will be placed in consecutive memory addresses, using a free part of the RAM.

INPUT, *n.* a BASIC keyboard input instruction forcing the machine to go into a HOLDING LOOP until the RETURN key is pressed. Any text or numbers that have been typed can then be assigned to a variable. PASCAL uses READ for a very similar purpose. The word must be followed by a variable name to which the input will be assigned. Most versions of BASIC allow INPUT to be followed by a 'CHANNEL' number, such as #3, which can be used to specify an input from another device, such as tape or disk, serial port and so on.

input bound, *n.* a computer action limited in speed because the speed of input of information is the main factor that determines the speed of the whole program. The usual cause of a program being input bound is excessive requirement for keyboard entry, but small computers which use cassette storage of data will suffer from being input bound in this way also. Compare OUTPUT BOUND.

input device, *n.* any device that can supply an input to the computer. This includes the keyboard, disk drive, tape unit, and any other PERIPHERALS that supply input signals.

input/output controller, *n.* a form of INTERFACE found on the larger computers, that controls the paths between the computer and its peripherals. This allows the peripherals to be used more efficiently, and speeds up the action of the main computer. Some types of input/output controller incorporate both memory and a separate microprocessor. They can therefore prevent the main processor from being INPUT or OUTPUT BOUND by carrying out input or output steps while the main processor is performing other tasks.

input statement, *n.* an INSTRUCTION that causes input. All HIGH-LEVEL LANGUAGES provide for the input of data, and the statement that is used for this purpose is the input statement.

insert, *vb.* to place between existing items. Editing often requires characters to be inserted, and many editing systems will insert by DEFAULT (see EDIT). This means that when the CURSOR is placed over a letter, any character that is typed will be inserted between this character and the previous one. Insertion is an essential feature of the editing system of a word processor. The alternative process is to OVERWRITE.

instruction, *n.* anything in a program that causes an action to be carried out. Strictly speaking, the term COMMAND denotes an entry which is made and immediately carried out, and instruction to something that is carried out only when the program is run, but the words are often interchanged. See also STATEMENT.

instruction set, *n.* the list of all the instruction words of ASSEMBLY LANGUAGE for a particular type of MICROPROCESSOR. Also called *repertoire*. A full instruction set will list for each word the ADDRESSING METHODS that can be used, the data that is required,

type	mnemonic	operand	object code	bytes	clock cycles	status

type	mnemonic	operand	object code	bytes	clock cycles	C	Z	S	P/O	AC	N	operation
R-R	AND	reg.	10000rrr	1	H	$\emptyset$	X	X	P	1	$\emptyset$	[A]∧[reg.]→A

Fig. 39. **Instruction set.** This is a typical entry in an abbreviated form for one microprocessor action. This example shows the type of instruction, mnemonic, operand, code, number of instruction bytes, number of clock cycles and the effect on status register flags. The right-hand column summarizes the action using the symbol for logical AND. The last 3 bits of the object code are allocated by consulting a table which shows the 3-bit code for each register.

and the time that is needed (in terms of CLOCK CYCLES) for carrying out the instruction. See Fig. 39.

instruction word, *n.* see RESERVED WORD.

integer, *n.* a whole number (no fractions), usually of a limited range. Most varieties of BASIC allow the range of integers to cover −32768 to +32767, and this range is also common in other programming languages, including Pascal, because it can be stored in only two bytes. The BBC machine, and a few others, permits a much wider range by specifying 4-byte integers for BASIC. Some other languages, including C , permit both short (2-byte) and long (4-byte) integers to be specified. The advantage of using integers is that arithmetic (but not division) with integers is always precise. See also REAL NUMBER, PRECISION OF NUMBER.

integrated circuit, see IC.

integrated database, *n.* **1.** a database that can supply data for several different requirements, but without any redundant information. **2.** a database program which is combined with other data handling programs.

integrated device, *n.* a device that is incorporated in another device. Some microcomputers are supplied with integrated disk drives, others with integrated displays, many with integrated keyboards. The main advantage is that no connecting cables are needed, but the user is deprived of the choice of how the equipment should be arranged.

integrity, *n.* reliability of data. Preservation of the integrity of disk files means that files have not been corrupted. Integrity of data has been maintained in an operation if none of the data has been corrupted in the course of the operation.

intelligent spacer, *n.* a word-processing symbol that can be placed in a line of text and which will ensure that words which belong together are not split at the right-hand of the screen. See also EMBEDDED BLANK.

intelligent terminal, *n.* an assembly of keyboard and screen which also includes some computing circuits. Also called *smart terminal*. An intelligent terminal can DOWNLOAD data from a main computer, and carry out some processing work, thus decreasing the load on the main system. Microcomputers can often be used as intelligent terminals for mainframe computers. Compare DUMP TERMINAL.

interactive processing, *n.* a processing system that allows 'dialogue' between computer and user. The system is used extensively in microcomputing in which the machine stops at intervals to allow the operator to enter data or instructions, and which will also pass messages to the operator about the data. All microcomputers are interactive, unlike many mainframe machines of the past. Mainframe machines used to be programmed by typing program instructions to a paper tape punch, and later feeding the tape into the computer. The program might compile, but if an error was found, compiling would stop with an error message, and a new tape had to be prepared. Contrast this with the programming of modern microprocessors, in which the program text is typed directly into the machine, and the text can be seen echoed on the screen. In addition, an interpreted language like BASIC is interactive, because it allows the user to test instructions by entering the instruction as a direct command and observing the result. See also BATCH PROCESSING.

interblock gap, see GAP.

interface, *n.* a circuit that allows otherwise incompatible items to be connected. This process is called *matching*. For example, a computer may work at a clock rate of 4 million pulses per second, and a printer with 20 characters per second. An interface is therefore needed to feed signals from the computer to the printer at the correct speed, and in the correct form, to allow the printer to operate.

Interfaces are needed to connect the computer to almost any other device, and in many cases, interfacing problems are the most intractable that a user can suffer. Many engineers believe that incompatibility is the natural state of all systems, and that correct interfacing is the exception rather than the rule. Interfacing would be considerably easier if manufacturers did not insist on making 'improvements' to established standard connecting methods, such as RS-232.

interleaving, *n.* anything in computing acting on slices of items alternately. For example, two programs can appear to be running simultaneously if the computer runs a small piece of each program alternately. Another form of interleaving is the use of a dual disk system, in which data is read from the disks alternately. See also TIMESHARING.

interlock, *n.* a form of security device. In computing, refers to a PASSWORD system which is part of a LOG-ON procedure and which is intended to prevent unauthorized use.

intermediate storage, see TEMPORARY STORAGE.

internal codes, *n.* number codes for characters, other than ASCII, used in the OPERATING SYSTEM but not transmitted externally.

internal language, *n.* a language that is used inside the machine and is not directly under the control of the operator. Many COMPILED LANGUAGES are compiled to instructions of an internal language, which is then interpreted. See P-CODE, COMPILE, INTERPRETER.

internal memory, *n.* the memory to which the processor is directly connected. Most of the ROM and RAM memory of a computer is of this type, but several machines allow also the use of EXTERNAL MEMORY which is connected through INTERFACES.

internally stored program, *n.* a program that is stored in a ROM within the machine. Other programs would be stored in disks or on tape, externally. The advantage of an internally stored program is that it can be run immediately, with no delay due to loading time. In addition, CORRUPTION of the program is impossible, because the bytes of a ROM cannot be altered. See also SIDEWAYS RAM/ROM.

interpreted language, *n.* a language that is implemented by an INTERPRETER.

interpreter, *n.* a program for running a language such as BASIC step by step. An interpreter reads an instruction from a program text, locates a set of MACHINE CODE bytes which will carry out the action, and then executes the instruction before reading the next instruction. This can be a comparatively slow process, because it means that each instruction word has to be analysed each time it is encountered, in order to find the memory location of its machine code. If the program contains a loop, for example, using a form such as:

```
FOR N = 1 to 50:PRINT A:NEXT
```

then the machine code for the action PRINT A will be looked up and activated 50 times. The looking up action is a time-consuming one, and this makes interpretation comparatively slow, although good design can mitigate this. See also COMPILER.

interrupt, *n.* a signal to the microprocessor which will cause it to suspend the piece of (machine code) program that it is carrying out and jump to another program. After the interrupt, the machine resumes its normal action. An interrupt system is often used to make the microprocessor respond to the keyboard, and if the interrupt system is disabled, the keyboard cannot be used (see DISABLE INTERRUPT). When an interrupt occurs, variable or register values may have to be saved for later use. This is done by using a reserved part of the memory which is called the STACK.

inverse video, *n.* a display that uses black text on white background when the normal display consists of white text on a black background. Also called *reverse video*. The name denotes any display that interchanges the background and text colours.

inverting, *n.* the interchanging of bits 0 and 1. Inverting the byte 11110000, for example, would give the byte 00001111. See also NEGATION, COMPLEMENT, TWOS COMPLEMENT.

inverted commas, *n.* the " sign used in BASIC to mark the beginning and the end of a text string. Also called *quotes*. Many other languages use a single apostrophe instead.

invocation, *n.* the calling up of a SUBROUTINE or PROCEDURE. The invocation of a subroutine is done by using GOSUB with a line number, the invocation of a procedure by using its name.

I/O port, *n.* an interfacing method in which the port allows signals to be passed from or into the computer, but only under program control. See INTERFACE.

item, *n.* a single unit of data. An item may be represented by one bit, one byte, or a large number of bytes, depending on the complexity of the item.

item size, *n.* the number of bytes needed to represent an item.

iteration, *n.* a method of solving problems by repeated application of a routine. Any iterative method is very well suited to computing, because it can be programmed in a LOOP. The routines which are used by the microprocessor to find logarithm, sine and similar values make use of iterative methods in which the actions are confined to addition and subtraction.

J

jacket, *n.* the cardboard or plastic cover for a disk. This has holes and slots cut into it so as to expose the HUB and also to allow the HEAD-OF-DISK DRIVE access to the disk. Floppy disks in the 8″ and 5¼″ sizes use stiff plastic or cardboard jackets, with glued or crimped seams. The smaller 3″ or 3½″ disks use rigid plastic envelopes, with spring-loaded sliding metal shutters to protect the disk surface from being accidentally touched. This makes for greater INTEGRITY of data.

jack plug, *n.* a form of audio connector of the COAXIAL CABLE type which is seldom used in microcomputing, except for a few machines which use a socket for stereo headphones.

jitter, *n.* a display fault on the screen. A displayed picture is said to jitter if it can be seen to be rapidly moving up and down by a short distance. This is very unpleasant to watch, and is usually caused by faulty SYNCHRONIZATION of the video field (vertical) signals. This can be due to the MONITOR itself or, more likely, to the VIDEO signals from the computer. Jitter is more common when TV receivers are used as monitors, because the circuits of TV receivers have been designed to make use of the more rigidly standardized TV broadcast signals. Some computers allow correcting bytes to be sent to the chip that controls video output in order to reduce jitter.

job, *n.* a complete piece of work, usually involving many processes on a large amount of data. A job may require one or more program runs, and may also require more than one program to be used.

job-oriented language, *n.* a computer language which is designed for programming a specific type of job. This implies a high-level language, and is often taken as meaning the COMMAND LANGUAGE of a complex program. There have, however, been several high-level languages that have been written in order to carry out specific tasks, often mathematical in nature.

joystick, *n.* a miniature version of the aircraft control stick, which can generate electrical signals. On computers which contain a joystick PORT, this allows position control of a cursor or a graphics character if a suitable program is running.

The type of joystick connection which is used by Atari has been standardized by several other manufacturers. Some joysticks offer no more than switch connections (up, down, left, right), but others can generate different voltages which can be used as position COORDINATES. The use of joysticks is by no means confined to games, and the principle of control without the use of the keyboard has been extended via the TRACKBALL to the MOUSE.

jump, *n.* a movement which is out of sequence. In ASSEMBLY LANGUAGE, a jump is a command which causes a program to move to an address which is not the next address in sequence. A jump instruction is an essential part of a machine code LOOP, and there are many CONDITIONAL jump instructions which allow a jump to proceed only if some simple condition is satisfied. This is the way in which alternative pieces of program can be arranged to run following a test. In high-level languages, a jump is a movement to an instruction which is not the normal following instruction. The word GOTO is used as a method of enforcing such a jump in practically all HIGH-LEVEL LANGUAGES.

justify, *vb.* to line up text by adjusting the spaces between the words. Text is normally left-justified, meaning that each line starts at the same position relative to the left-hand side of a page, with the exception of new paragraphs and other indented material (see INDENT). If only left-justification is used, the right-hand side of the text will appear irregular. When RIGHT-JUSTIFICATION is used, the last character in each line is placed at a specified position relative to the right-hand side of the paper. Right-justification is nearly always additional to left-justification rather than a replacement. Text which is right-justified will always fill the width of a page exactly. Right-justification can be carried out by any good WORD-PROCESSING program.

K

k, *abbrev. for* kilo. Outside computing, the lower-case k means one thousand, as in kilohertz.

K, *abbrev. for* computing Kilo. In computing, the upper-case K is used to mean the number 1024, which is two to the power ten. This is the unit that is implied in words such as kilobyte.

Kansas City standard, *n.* a standard of data recording. This was drawn up in the late 70s in the US to pave the way for exchange of data on audio cassettes. Several machines made use of the standard, but interchange of data was never fully achieved because of the different ways that the machines handled the data.

key, *n.* a touch-controlled button, or an unlocking device. The keys of the keyboard of a computer are buttons, each of which operates a miniature electrical switch. A key in programming is a code byte or group of bytes that assists identification. the key FIELD of a RECORD, for example, is the field (surname, perhaps) that is used to identify the record.

keyboard, *n.* the assembly of keys by which we communicate with the computer. Since the keyboard is the most-used part of the computer, a good keyboard is an essential part of any computer that will be used for business purposes. This generally implies keys with a reasonable range of movement, as on a typewriter. A few home computers and even so-called 'business machines' have made use of keys which operate tiny pressure pads. These keys feel very uncertain in action, and are totally unsuitable for extended use.

keyboard layout, *n.* the standardized position of keys. In English-speaking countries, the standard layout is described as QWERTY, from the characters on the top half-line of keys. In several continental countries, the AZERTY layout is followed. See also DVORAK, MALTRON.

keyboard lockout, *n.* disablement of the keyboard. The microprocessor action of servicing the keyboard must generally be switched out when a small computer services other inputs and outputs. The keyboard, with the possible exception of its BREAK key, cannot therefore be used while disk or tape loading is taking place, or while serial communication is being received or transmitted, or while a program that makes no use of the keyboard is being run. These restrictions do not apply to computers which use separate FRONT ENDS.

key matrix, *n.* a way of wiring key switches. Each key on the keyboard operates a small on/off switch. To avoid a mass of wiring, the key switches are connected in groups, so that they can be accessed by COORDINATES (rows, column numbers). This is known as a matrix connection, and it can sometimes cause odd effects, like finding that holding down three keys can simulate the action of another key. The computer OPERATING SYSTEM must contain routines that will interpret the matrix numbers and find the correct ASCII codes, using a LOOK-UP TABLE. See Fig. 40.

key number, *n.* the internal code for a key. This is the internal code number that is returned to the memory of the computer when a given key is pressed. The internal code number is not usually the same as the ASCII code number.

key overlays, see KEYSTRIP.

keypad, *n.* a small subset of keys, usually a set of keys for number entry. See also NUMBER PAD, HEX PAD.

key rollover, *n.* a system that allows fast typing. Simple types of keyboards respond to one key at a time, and may give nothing if two or more keys are pressed in rapid succession. Key rollover is

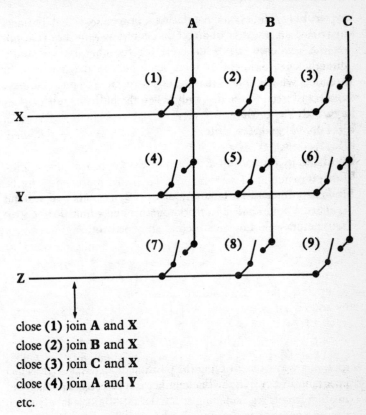

close **(1)** join **A** and **X**

close **(2)** join **B** and **X**

close **(3)** join **C** and **X**

close **(4)** join **A** and **Y**

etc.

Fig. 40. **Key matrix.** A simple key-matrix circuit. Each key operates an on/off switch that is connected between two lines. The closure of any one switch can be detected by the computer because each switch makes a connection between a different pair of lines.

a system that makes use of a BUFFER memory to hold the result of keystrokes that are made almost simultaneously. The buffer is emptied by the computer in the brief intervals when keys are not being pressed.

keystrip, *n.* a reminder of key action. This is a strip of paper which is placed next to PROGRAMMABLE KEYS so that the user can see what action these keys perform.

key stroke, *n.* the action of pressing a single key.

key to disk, *n.* a system of direct disk entry. When a key is struck on the keyboard, the ASCII code for the character is stored directly on a disk, rather then being held in the machine. In practice, what is done is that the codes are entered into a BUFFER, and transferred to the disk only when the buffer is full.

keyword, see RESERVED WORD.

kill file, *vb.* to delete a file.

kilo, see k, K.

kilobaud, *n.* a speed of one thousand BAUD.

kilobyte, see k.

kludge, *n.* **1.** an unsatisfactory mock-up. **2.** a connection of items which are not intended to work together and which do not do so satisfactorily. **3.** any trick used as an expedient.

L

label, *n.* a way of identifying the position of an INSTRUCTION in a program. In BASIC, the line number can be used as a label, but in other languages, including ASSEMBLY LANGUAGE, a label, which can be a number or a name, must be used. The label is separated from the instruction by some MARKER, often a colon. The label name may have to be declared as a label early in the program (see DECLARE). Once the label has been established, it can be used in a GOTO instruction in a HIGH-LEVEL LANGUAGE. See Fig. 41.

LAN, see LOCAL AREA NETWORK.

language, *n.* in computing, any way of passing instructions to the machine other than the direct input of number codes. Languages are classed as LOW-LEVEL or HIGH-LEVEL.

language translator, *n.* **1.** any program that permits conversion between languages. **2.** in computing languages, a program that rewrites the instructions of one language into the instructions of another. This can be done with reasonable success only if the languages are similar in concept, like BASIC and FORTRAN, or ALGOL and Pascal. **3.** a program that translates a NATURAL LANGUAGE into computer language.

Laser, *n. acronym for* Light Amplification by Stimulated Emission of Radiation, a source of coherent light. Normal light sources emit light waves which are not coherent, meaning that the light waves are emitted in bursts which do not behave like portions of a continuous wave. This lack of coherence prevents light from normal sources from exhibiting the physical features of a wave. A laser forces light waves to be emitted in step, of one single wavelength, so that it behaves in a way that accords with wave theory.

A further advantage is that the laser makes it possible to generate very small diameter beams of light which are almost perfectly parallel, with no measurable divergence.

```
(a)  LOOP: LD A,41H
           CALL ØA2H
           DEC BC
           LD A,B
           OR C
           JR NZ, LOOP
           RET
```

```
(b)  LABEL 1, 2, 3
     -----------------------
     1: WRITE (value);
     -----------------------
     IF SKIP = FALSE THEN GOTO 1;
```

Fig. 41. Labels. (a) In assembly language, a label word is declared by placing it in the correct position in a program. It is then taken to mean the address of the start of the instruction in that line. (b) In Pascal, the label is an integer number which has to be declared as being a label. It is then used in a very similar way. The use of GOTO in languages other than BASIC requires a label to be declared and put into position.

laser disc, see COMPACT DISC.

laser printer, *n.* a form of printer that depends on the use of laser light. The laser printer uses the principle of XEROGRAPHY, and is technically more like an office copier than a conventional printer. Laser printers are expensive, need the same type of copy paper as a copying machine, and do not necessarily provide the large range of type styles that can be obtained from a dot-matrix printer, nor the quality of a daisywheel. They are, however, very fast in operation and relatively silent. At the time of writing, few were available in the UK, and prices were high, but this can be expected to change considerably.

latency, *n.* computer waiting time. The latency of a program is the amount of time that is taken up in getting data from a disk or other store.

lateral reversal, *n.* the exchange of left for right in a picture, making it look like the image in a mirror.

LCD, *abbrev. for* liquid crystal display, a form of display using a material which can be changed from transparent to opaque or back by applying an electrical voltage across it. The display emits no light of its own, and depends for visibility on light from other sources. This makes it an ideal method of display for well-lit places, in which the conventional luminous type of display is less suitable. The very low power consumption of the LCD screen also makes it very useful for portable battery-operated computers. Colour displays have been exhibited, but are not yet commercially available. Early types of LCD display suffered from FLICKER, because the screen had to be refreshed (see REFRESH CRT), but later types used a 'latching' display in which the dots of the LCD pattern remained as set with no need for refreshing.

leader, *n.* **1.** tape which is clear or coloured plastic only, with no magnetic coating. The leader is used as a method of attaching the magnetic tape to the cassette spool, though leaderless tape can be obtained in cassette form. The significance of the leader is that it makes the first part of a cassette tape unusable. A cassette that has been rewound to one end must then be wound forward so that the leader has passed the recording head, and magnetic tape is now in contact with the head. **2.** the first FIELD of the record which carries information about that record.

learning curve, *n.* the rate of acquiring experience. Anyone learning a new programming LANGUAGE, a new word processor program, or any other new system will operate slowly at first, with reference to the manual. As experience is obtained, the manual has to be consulted less often, mistakes are fewer, and the speed of using the program or system improves. Finally, the ultimate speed of use is achieved. See Fig. 42.

If the effectiveness of use, as measured by speed of error-free output, is plotted against the time for which the program or system has been used, the curve shape always conforms to the same pattern, which is called the learning curve. This can be applied to predict how soon a new system can start to become effective in the hands of inexperienced operators.

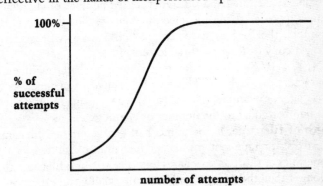

Fig. 42. **Learning curve.** This shows a rate of progress which starts slow, becomes rapid and then slows again as the system is almost completely understood.

least-significant bit, see BIT.
least-significant byte, see BYTE.
leaving files open, a phrase indicating that no CLOSE instruction has been used for a disk or tape FILE. This will leave data in the BUFFER, and no END-OF-FILE marker on the tape or disk. The file will be unusable, and data will be lost as far as the conventional reading system of the computer is concerned. Some data may be

readable from a disk by using a DISK DOCTOR, but data that was not recorded from the buffer cannot be recovered unless the buffer can be read before switching the machine off. Any good data-handling system should close all files when the program ends, and also when a fault stops the program prematurely.

LED, *n. acronym for* Light-Emitting Diode, a miniature low-voltage light source which has now replaced filament bulbs and neons for such purposes as INDICATOR LIGHTS. The LED is a SEMICONDUCTOR device, and the light is emitted with no significant amount of heat.

left-justification, *n.* the starting of each line of text at the left-hand margin. This is a DEFAULT arrangement used in all typewriters and in WORD PROCESSING programs. See also JUSTIFY.

LEFT\$, *n.* a BASIC instruction that copies part of a STRING starting at the left-hand side. A specified number of characters from a specified string is copied into a new string VARIABLE. For example, the BASIC statement A\$=LEFT\$(B\$,3) will make A\$ carry a copy of the first three letters of B\$.

LEN, *n.* a BASIC FUNCTION that returns with the number of characters in a STRING. This can be printed or assigned as an INTEGER. For example, N%=LEN(A\$) would assign to integer N% the number equal to the number of characters in A\$.

length of filename, *n.* the number of characters in a filename. Most disk or tape systems accept filenames of limited length, sometimes as short as six characters. The use of a filename that is longer than the acceptable limit will usually cause the system to stop with an error message, so that data is not recorded. A system which accepts longer filenames is much easier to work with, because it is then possible to use filenames which describe the data better. A filename such as NAMESOFFRIENDS is much more useful than NAMFRN, for example.

LET, *n.* a BASIC KEYWORD which is used for ASSIGNATION. For example, LET A\$="MESSAGE" would assign the characters of the word MESSAGE to the variable name or IDENTIFIER, A\$. The use of LET is optional in many DIALECTS of BASIC, so that the example could also be written as A\$="MESSAGE".

letter quality, *n.* a print quality that is suitable for office letter use. The output of a simple DOT MATRIX printer is acceptable for listings, but can make text like letters hard to read. For business letters, such output is completely unacceptable, and the print quality of a DAISYWHEEL printer is needed. Several dot-matrix printers, however, now offer near letter quality (NLQ) operation, though at much slower than normal speeds.

library, *n.* a disk-filing term. In some disk-operating systems, a letter can be designated as a library letter. Files which use this letter as their directory entry are normally program or subprogram files. These files will be given priority in any disk search for programs or routines. The DOLLAR SIGN is very often the DEFAULT library letter.

library function, *n.* a program FUNCTION that is supplied separately on disk and included into a program by using its name.

library routine, *n.* a program or subprogram stored in the LIBRARY group. This would normally be a well-tested routine which will be accessed by several main programs, or a well-tested program which will be chained (see CHAIN).

LIFO, *n. acronym for* Last In, First Out. A few types of memory operate on data in sequence, with the data being taken out in inverse order of storing. The STACK memory for the microprocessor is operated in this way, though this is a software form of LIFO. HARDWARE LIFO memory is seldom used in modern computers.

light pen, *n.* a device that detects light, usually from the screen, and can send signals to the computer. The light pen is normally a very simple device, and it sends a digital 1 signal to indicate the presence of light, and digital 0 to report the absence of light. The sensitivity of the device is usually adjusted so that background lighting has no effect on it. Since the pen is a simple light sensor, a program must be operated to make it useful. If a suitable program is used, a light pen can be used to create diagrams on the screen, or to make menu choices.

line, *n.* **1.** a long thin mark, or row of characters. **2.** in GRAPHICS, a mark made on the screen or on paper, joining a set of points. The line may be straight or curved, and its thickness depends on the RESOLUTION of the graphics display. **3.** one single trace of the cathode-ray beam across the MONITOR or TV screen. **4.** in a program LISTING, one complete set of statements. **5.** in BASIC, all the characters that follow a line number. Such a line may require more than one screen or printer line to display.

linear program, *n.* a program that proceeds from start to finish with no BRANCHES or LOOPS. A completely linear program is unusual, and most programs incorporate some repetition. It is possible, however, to have a main program which appears to be completely linear, because the loop portions are contained in PROCEDURES or SUBROUTINES.

linear programming, *n.* a specialized mathematical method. This is used to break down problems so that they can be solved by computer programs.

line editing, *n.* a system that requires the user to specify a line for alteration. See EDIT.

line feed, *n.* the selection of a new line. On the screen, this implies moving the CURSOR down to the next line. On a printer, feeding the paper up by one line spacing. In either case, a line feed (LF) code, normally ASCII code 10, is sent to the OPERATING SYSTEM. Most printers can be switched so that they line feed on the LF character, ASCII 10, only or also when the CARRIAGE RETURN code (13) is received.

line flyback, see FLYBACK.

line length, *n.* **1.** in word processing, the number of characters in each printed line. **2.** in programming, the number of characters permitted in each STATEMENT line.

line number, *n.* a reference number for a program line. BASIC, unlike most other languages, numbers its lines, and can use the numbers also as LABELS. This makes editing and the provision of error messages very easy, but can tempt programmers to make excessive and inappropriate use of the GOTO instruction.

line printer, *n.* a printer, used with large computers, that prints a line at a time. This form of printer is very fast (and noisy) in operation, and is very seldom seen on microcomputer systems, because a line printer costs more than most microcomputers.

line spacing, *n.* in word processing, the gap between printed lines, usually single or double.

link files, *n.* files that have some relationship to each other and which are used by the same program. On some compilers, to link files means that a number of OBJECT CODE files can be made into a single file.

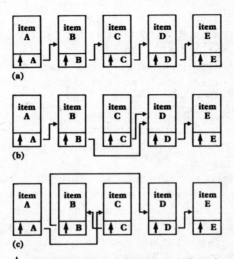

↑ = pointer; the arrows outside the boxes indicate the address of the item next in series.

Fig. 43. **Linked lists.** (a) A straightforward representation of a simple linked list. The pointer number in each record gives the position of the next record in the list by, for example, providing its memory address. (b) Deleting an item from a list can be done by altering the previous pointer. (c) Changing order in a list can also be done by changing pointers. Using pointers in this way avoids moving items about in the memory. In BASIC, the lines of programs are the data items, and the pointers consist of two bytes at the start of each line.

linked list, *n.* a form of list in which each item of data carries a reference number (or POINTER) that identifies the position of the next item in the list. BASIC program lines are usually stored in this form, but there is no direct provision in BASIC for using such lists as data. Other HIGH-LEVEL LANGUAGES provide a data type, the POINTER, which can be used in the construction of linked lists of data. Each RECORD in a file will contain a pointer number, which will allow the previous record to be found. With more elaborate programming, it is possible to create double-linked lists, in which each record carries a pointer to the previous record and also a pointer to the following record. See Fig. 43.

The use of pointers makes it very easy to locate a record, to eliminate a complete record from the list (by omitting its pointer), or to change the order of items.

LISP, *n.* a list-processing HIGH-LEVEL LANGUAGE which is mainly intended to make easy work of processing LISTS of items. A feature of LISP is the use of brackets (parentheses) as DELIMITERS, and the appearance of LISP programs has led to the remark that LISP means Lots of Irritating Silly Parentheses. LISP, which first appeared around 1959, has been used for text-processing systems, and also in AI work.

list, 1. *n.* a set of items in some order. This could refer to a set of characters in a word, words in a sentence, sentences in a book. It could also refer to items in a disk file. The use of lists as data types in computing has led to the evolution of languages for the specific purposes of LIST PROCESSING. See also LISP, LOGO, PROLOG. **2.** *vb.* to print in order. To list a program means to print out all of its INSTRUCTIONS in order of first to last. On microcomputers, a LIST command will normally cause the list to appear on the screen, and a slightly different command, such as LLIST or LIST#8 will be required to produce HARD COPY.

listing, *n.* a printed program produced by a LIST action.

list processing, *n.* actions on lists of data. The action of a word processor, for example, is almost entirely list processing. Many of the most important actions of computer programs are directed to the manipulation of lists, whether of numbers or of text. In general, PROCEDURAL LANGUAGES of the conventional type treat lists in terms of the individual items in the list, and require data types such as arrays to be specified to deal with lists. This makes for greater difficulty in programming actions on anything other than simple lists, hence the development of specialized list-processing languages such as LISP, LOGO and PROLOG.

liveware, *n.* human programmers and operators. Sometimes referred to as the weakest link in a computer system. The term started as a joke, but has been taken up seriously to refer to the most essential 'ware' of computing, which is often the most difficult to replace.

LN, *n.* a mathematical function. The term is used in a few languages to mean natural (or Napierian) logarithm, as distinct from the conventional base 10 logarithm. Just to make life more confusing, LOG is often used for the natural logarithm in other DIALECTS.

load, *vb.* to transfer a program from tape or disk into the memory of the computer. This will normally involve a command such as LOAD or GET, along with the filename for the program. The term DOWNLOAD is used when the loading takes place over telephone lines or other remote links.

load and run, *n.* a form of loading in which the program loads and then runs without any further command. Used for most COPY PROTECTION systems, because it can be combined with ways of preventing the program from being interrupted.

loader, *n.* a program that loads another program. The term usually denotes a very short program, often held in ROM, which is used to load the rest of a program, often an operating system. The CP/M system, for example, uses a loader to load the remaining sections of the program from disk. The term also denotes a program in BASIC which is used to load and place a MACHINE CODE program in the memory. This can take the form of BASIC instructions which specify a machine code load, or the direct placing of data bytes in memory, using POKE instructions.

local, *adj.* of or relating to anything in computing that has a temporary value in a procedure. A *local variable* in a PROCEDURE is a variable name or IDENTIFIER whose value is assigned within that procedure, and which has no value, or a different value, outside the procedure. For example, in a program, the variable name Count might be used in a main loop to count a number of items. In a procedure, the word Count could be declared as local, (a *local declaration*) and used for counting the number of letters in a word. This use of the word Count in the procedure would not interfere with the use of Count in the main program, nor corrupt its value. Compare GLOBAL.

local area network (LAN), *n.* a cable system that can be used to link suitable computers together. This allows, for example, one computer to be connected to disk drives and printers, and the other computers on the network to make use of these peripherals. A LAN is a very useful way of providing computing power among a group of users without needing to multiply the number of disk drives and printers in use. The drawback is that with a large number of users working together, the speed of computing for each user may become unacceptably slow. LANs have become very popular in educational computing, where resources are necessarily limited.

The use of a LAN is possible only if suitable HARDWARE, in terms of sockets on each computer, is available. For some computers, this may have to be added externally. Special SOFTWARE is also required, so that conflicting demands by different computers in the network can be resolved. A local network may be connected to external networks through the telephone lines.

local declaration, see LOCAL.

location, *n.* **1.** the position or ADDRESS of a byte in memory. **2.** the position of a byte of data in terms of TRACKS and SECTORS on a disk.

lockup, *n.* an inactive keyboard and/or screen, the state in which the computer ceases to respond to keys, and sometimes displays no further information on the screen. An unintentional lockup is usually caused by CORRUPTION of the OPERATING SYSTEM or of some RAM that is used by the operating system. Lockups are common when MACHINE CODE programs are being tested, particularly if the operating system is in RAM. Lockup is also deliberately built into the operating system. Most systems will lockup the keyboard and screen during a disk load or save operation, and also during any processing which does not require an INPUT. See also INTERRUPT.

locking file, *n.* the action of making a file inaccessible for writing. Many disk operating systems allow a file to be 'locked', meaning that no other file of the same name will be accepted. This deters accidental erasure of a file in a system that would otherwise allow a file to be replaced with any other file of the same name. Locking in this way is a software protection, applied by writing a code byte into the disk directory, and which can be released by deleting the locking byte. This form of local 'write prevention' should not be confused with the use of a WRITE-PROTECT label, which protects the whole disk surface and which cannot be released by software instructions.

log, *abbrev. for* logarithm, often meaning the base 10 logarithm. Several dialects of BASIC use LOG to mean the natural logarithm, see LN.

logic, *n.* a system for deducing a result from two or more items of data. In electronics and computing, the inputs to a logic device will consist of bit signals, 0 or 1, and the output will also be the bit 0 or 1. All logic actions, no matter how complicated, can be built up from a few fundamental actions, originally described by George Boole in 1836. These actions are the logical comparison instructions of AND, OR and XOR along with the inversion, NOT. See also GATE.

logic card, *n.* a CIRCUIT BOARD that provides digital logic actions on data bits. This normally applies to larger computers, as the microprocessor itself contains the logic circuits for microcomputers. The use of external logic cards can provide hardware logic for actions which can be much faster than computed logic, and is preferable for some devices. See also GATE.

logic circuit, *n.* an electronic circuit that carries out logic actions. These actions are carried out by GATES, and the circuit will be designed so as to use standard types of gates.

logical language, *n.* a category of programming language in which rules and relationships are manipulated rather than PROCEDURES. See also HIGH-LEVEL LANGUAGE.

LOGO, *n.* a language devised by Dr Seymour Papert as an alternative to the PROCEDURAL and more mathematically based FORTRAN and BASIC. The fundamental data type is the LIST, but the language has become very closely associated with TURTLE GRAPHICS, that are used to teach the principles of programming to the very young. This use of LOGO, along with lack of good record filing routines, has to some extent hindered its development and acceptance as a general programming language.

log on/off, *n.* the procedure for starting or ending use of a computer system. Several systems, particularly mainframes, demand that a user should go through an elaborate procedure of providing passwords, the date, names of files and so on before being granted access to the system. This is called 'logging-on'. Similarly, it is sometimes necessary to go through a routine of providing answers to questions in order to stop using a system, and this is called 'logging off'.

TABLE A	TABLE B
1	1 · 0274
2	3 · 6146
3	8 · 2012
4	15 · 4026
5	27 · 6134
6	68 · 7015
7	152 · 4617

Fig. 44. **Look-up tables.** As the name suggests, these consist of lists that are stored in memory and arranged in corresponding order. A look-up table is particularly useful when there is no simple relationship between one quantity and the other. Even if a relationship can be programmed, the use of a look-up table is often much faster than the use of a formula.

look-up table, *n.* a method of storing data for quick access. The data is kept in some ordered form in consecutive addresses in memory. The machine need only retain the address of the first item in the table, and a reference number can be used to generate the address for any other item. The use of a look-up table is often quicker than the use of a FORMULA for many computing purposes, but requires more memory. See Fig. 44.

loop, *n.* a part of a program which is run more than once in the course of the program. Each loop will contain a test of some sort which will allow the loop to be broken. The REPEAT .. UNTIL loop makes the test at the end of the loop, and the WHILE loop makes the test at the beginning. Some languages, notably C, allow for tests to be made in the middle of the loop, or for some items to be omitted. If no test is used, the loop is an ENDLESS LOOP. The provision of methods of forming a loop is an essential part of any programming language at any level.

loop check, *n.* a way of checking data that has been transmitted down a line. This consists of returning the data to the transmitter for checking. See also ECHO CHECK.

looping program, *n.* a program whose main action is a loop. Most programs are of this variety. See also LINEAR PROGRAM.

Lotus 1-2-3, *n. Trademark.* a well-known suite of business programs. These comprise a spreadsheet, a database, and graphics display programs. See also SYMPHONY.

loudspeaker, *n.* a device that converts electrical signals in the range of 20Hz to 20kHz into audible sound. A built-in loudspeaker is a useful warning device on a computer, and if the computer contains routines for generating sound signals, the loudspeaker is an essential part of the sound system. Some home computers which rely on a TV receiver for display can also make use of the loudspeaker of the TV receiver for sound.

low-level language, *n.* a language that is written for direct control of the microprocessor. Such a language can use symbols or command words in place of number codes, but can only be used if the action of the microprocessor is understood, and the configuration of the computer known. Each microprocessor type needs its own low-level language. See ASSEMBLY LANGUAGE, HIGH-LEVEL LANGUAGE.

lower-case, *adj.* of or relating to the 'small' as distinct from 'capital' letters. Compare UPPER-CASE.

lsb, see BIT.

LSI, *n. acronym for* Large-Scale Integration, a high density of packing of electronic circuits on a CHIP.

M

m, *abbrev. for* milli, one thousandth.

M, *abbrev. for* Mega, meaning one million.

machine, *n.* an alternative, informal term for **1.** Computer, **2.** MICROPROCESSOR, as in the phrase '16-bit machine'.

machine code, *n.* a number-code system for MICROPROCESSOR programming. The memory of a computer stores numbers in BINARY form, as a set of 1s and 0s. Each computer is programmed internally by number codes, which are instructions to the microprocessor or CPU, and are called machine code. The ROM of a computer contains a large number of SUBROUTINES which are written in the correct machine code for the processor. When you use an INTERPRETER for a language such as BASIC, the commands that you type are translated by the ROM into machine code instructions. If the high-level language is *compiled*, the whole of the program is translated into a machine code program by a COMPILER, and this machine code program is then recorded for later use.

It is also possible to program directly in machine code, thus bypassing BASIC, or any other HIGH-LEVEL LANGUAGE. Programming in machine code requires a detailed knowledge of the microprocessor and of how the computer has been designed. Such programming also requires considerably more planning than is needed for a BASIC program. One simple BASIC instruction, such as PRINT, might, for example, require hundreds of machine code instructions to execute. The instructions must also be put into the correct order, because the microprocessor works to very strict rules about the order in which number codes are fed to it.

Machine-code programming is made very much easier if an ASSEMBLER can be used. The advantages of writing and using machine code directly are that it executes much faster than interpreted BASIC, and that actions can be programmed which are not provided for in BASIC, such as reading 'protected' tapes and saving diagrams that have been made on the screen.

machine cycle, *n.* one cycle of the machine CLOCK. The processing speed of the microprocessor or CPU is governed primarily by the clock pulses. The time between two clock pulses is referred to as a machine cycle, because any of the actions of the microprocessor can be timed in terms of an integral number of machine cycles. An INSTRUCTION SET for a microprocessor will contain timings for all of the microprocessor actions in terms of the machine cycle. In this way, if the clock pulse timing is known, the time for any instruction or set of instructions can be calculated.

machine-oriented language, *n.* a programming language that is closely related to the way that the microprocessor works. ASSEMBLY LANGUAGE is the most machine-oriented of all low-level languages, but a few languages have been devised, mainly for specialized uses, that are only slightly higher in level than assembly language and therefore almost equally machine-oriented.

Even high-level languages can be described as machine-oriented if they have to be written in a way that depends on low-level activities like STACK use. FORTH is a language in this class.

machine-readable, *adj.* of or relating to anything that can be read directly by the computer. This applies mainly to storage forms like disks and cassettes. If an author is required to provide work in machine-readable form, this implies that a word processor should be used, with the output in ASCII code form on disks. These disks can be read directly into another computer, unlike printed text, and often set directly into print by computer.

Macintosh, *n. Trademark.* a trend-setting product by APPLE. The Macintosh (named after a variety of apple!) used the WIMP principles for the first time on a lower-priced machine, and has introduced other ideas that have been widely imitated. The main criticism of the machine itself is that its memory has to be expanded to cope with the demands of its excellent operating system.

macro, *n.* a compound statement of (usually) ASSEMBLY LANGUAGE commands that can be stored as a unit and inserted into several different places in a program. This should not be confused with a SUBROUTINE, a set of statements which are stored in one place and can be executed from several different places within a program. Macros are a convenience for the programmers which avoid having to retype a lot of instructions several times.

magnetic card, *n.* a storage system for small amounts of data. The magnetic card, as exemplified by credit cards and cash cards, uses a strip of magnetic material to store data. The card is written by automatic processes which can control the rate at which the magnetic strip is pulled past the head of a recorder. Reading can be equally well controlled, as used in automatic cash tills, but is sometimes done by pulling the card by hand past a reading head. The chance of errors is greatly increased when hand operation is used, because the speed of movement cannot be kept constant.

magnetic core, *n.* the memory system for a mainframe computer. The large MAINFRAME computers require memory storage which operates much faster than the SEMICONDUCTOR ROM or RAM of a microcomputer. One such system is CORE MEMORY, which has the added advantage of being a type of NON-VOLATILE MEMORY. See also MAIN STORE, RAM, ROM, FLOPPY DISK, WINCHESTER DISK, DESTRUCTIVE READOUT.

magnetic field, *n.* the magnetic effect in the space around a magnet. Anywhere around a magnet, magnetic materials will experience a force caused by the magnet, and the strength of the magnetic force in such a region is a measure of magnetic field. Strong magnetic fields are generated at TAPEHEADS and disk heads (see HEAD-OF-DISK DRIVE) so that magnetic materials can be magnetized. Equally strong fields elsewhere can remagnetize tapes or disks, causing CORRUPTION of data.

Alternating fields, in which the magnetism changes to an opposite direction many times per second, are particularly destructive. Disks and tapes must therefore be kept clear of magnets (such as the magnets of loudspeakers) and from any apparatus which generates alternating magnetic fields, including monitors, TV receivers and electric motors.

magnetic ink, *n.* a form of ink that contains magnetic powder. An ink which is made using fine particles of iron oxide will be magnetic. It is therefore possible for the ink to carry magnetic messages in addition to any visible text. The system has been widely used for the numbering of cheques, using digit shapes whose magnetic fields can be recognized by a set of reading heads.

mailbox, *n.* a computer system that allows messages to remain in memory until removed. A mailbox system is permanently connected to the telephone lines. By connecting your computer through a MODEM to the telephone lines, and using a set of passcodes, you can send or receive messages. The messages you send need not be received immediately by another subscriber, because they will remain stored until the other user gains access to the system. PASSWORDS should not be obvious (not your initials, or sequences like 123456), because HACKERS may be able to use a lot of telephone time which could be charged to your account.

mailing list, *n.* a form of DATABASE program which is used to keep a list of names and addresses in the style that will be used on envelopes. The use of a mailing list along with a word processor allows STANDARD DOCUMENTS to be printed.

mainframe, *n.* a term for the largest types of computers. These will usually take up a complete room or rooms, use MAGNETIC CORE storage, require air-conditioned surroundings, and be capable of dealing with very large amounts of data at very high speeds. Until the advent of INTEGRATED CIRCUITS, all computers were of this type, even though some were by modern standards of quite modest memory sizes, 8K or less. Programming of the traditional type of mainframe was noninteractive (see INTERACTIVE PROCESSING), in the sense that programs were written in the form of punched PAPER TAPE, or recorded magnetic tape, which were prepared on other machines. This made the mainframe very cumbersome to program, and also to use. The main reason for the rapid spread of computer technology in the 70s and 80s has been the development of machines which are smaller, interactive and USER-FRIENDLY. See also MINICOMPUTER, MICROCOMPUTER.

mains, *n.* the electrical supply for the computer and all its PERIPHERALS. Sudden changes of mains voltages (SURGES or SPIKES) can cause a REBOOT and loss of data.

main store, *n.* the storage system that is built into a computer, or accessed rapidly through cables. The main store is used to hold the current operating program, and any data that is being processed. Subsidiary stores such as TAPE or DISK stores, are used to hold programs which are not currently in use, and data which is not currently being processed. Small computers use SEMICON-DUCTOR memory for main store systems, large machines use MAGNETIC CORES. See also TAPE, DISK, FLOPPY DISK, WINCHESTER DISK, RAM, ROM.

male connector, *n.* the plug connector of a cable. Compare FEMALE CONNECTOR.

Maltron keyboard, *n.* a non-QWERTY keyboard. The Maltron keyboard is one of the two main systems (the other being DVORAK) which places the keys in a logical order, ensuring that both hands are equally occupied, and that typing speed and accuracy is greatly increased.

mantissa, *n.* the part of a number in STANDARD FORM that contains the significant figures. For example, in the number 1.23E6, the mantissa is 1.23. When a number is written in binary standard form, the mantissa is always fractional. See also EXPONENT.

manual, *n.* the instruction book for a computer. Ideally, this should be a form of reference book that allows the user to program more efficiently. Many manuals try to combine this function with attempts to teach programming languages, usually with the result that the manual is suitable for neither function.

manual entry, *n.* the entry of data from the keyboard. In many systems for which the computer is used, the data is obtained from measurements which are made by machines. These measure-ments can be digitized (see DIGITIZE) and entered directly into the computer through PORTS, eliminating the mistakes which a human operator can make.

map, *n.* a schematic diagram, usually of the computer's MEMORY. A MEMORY MAP for a computer shows the memory in ranges of ADDRESS number, with the use of each range noted. See also MEMORY MAPPING.

marker, *n.* **1.** a character that marks a place. **2.** in word processing, a shape such as a white block that marks the start and end of a piece of text. This allows the program to work with the marked portion, so as to save it, delete it, move it, or copy it.

mask, *n.* a number that is used to control the form of another number. For example, using the AND logic action with the binary number 01111111 on any byte will have the effect of resetting (to 0) the most significant bit of the byte which is being ANDed. This is called *masking the msb*.

masked ROM, *n.* a mass-produced programmed ROM. The ROM is a set of tiny contacts which may be open (logic 0) or closed (logic 1). The closed contacts are formed by depositing a conductor, usually a metal, through holes in a mask, hence the name for a ROM made in this way. The use of a masked ROM for an OPERATING SYSTEM, as distinct from an EPROM, implies that the 'final' version of the operating system has been evolved.

master disk, see SYSTEM DISK.

matching, *n.* the connecting of systems correctly together. See INTERFACE.

matrix printer, *n.* a printer that 'draws' a character from a set of dots. Often described as a DOT MATRIX printer. This is a type of printer that uses a vertical line of tiny NEEDLES to mark the paper. Each character is formed by shooting some of the needles against the inked ribbon, so that each needle prints a dot on the paper. The head is then moved slightly, and other needles fired, until the character shape is built up. Early printer designs used seven needles, and shifted the head in five steps to print a character. This design is known as a 7×5 printhead, and though capital letters are printed reasonably well, it distorts the shapes of any lower-case letters which have DESCENDERS. These are letters such as y, g, p which have descending tails. More modern designs use a larger number of needles, from 9 to 24, and make more steps across the paper for each character. This makes for better character shapes, at the expense of slower printing speed. Several types allow the choice of high-speed printing for listings (using capitals), and NLQ (near letter quality) slow printing for other office uses. The highest print quality, however, is obtained from LASER and DAISYWHEEL printers.

medium, *n.* **1.** anything that stores computer output, such as disks. **2.** anything on which output is printed, like paper.

megabyte, *n.* literally one million bytes, but in computing the term generally denotes 1048576 bytes. The reason is that a KILOBYTE is taken as meaning 1024, two to the power ten, so that a megabyte then means 1024 kilobytes, two to the power 20.

megaflop, *n.* **1.** a measure of processing power. The term *flop* means FLOATING POINT operation, an arithmetic action on floating-point numbers. One megaflop means that a million floating-point actions can be carried out per second. Since one floating-point operation can require a large number (perhaps hundreds) of MACHINE CYCLES, a speed measured in megaflops implies CLOCK rates of several hundred MHz. **2.** a colossal failure!

memory, *n.* a method of storing data in an organized way. Any physical effect which can be switched in one of two ways can be used to create a memory system. Microcomputers use SEMICON-DUCTOR memory, in which microscopically small components either pass electric current or do not, so signalling the storage of BINARY 1 or 0. Magnetic memory, in which direction of magnetism determines whether 0 or a 1 is stored, is also extensively used. BUBBLE MEMORY is a microscopic form of magnetic memory.

Memory can be VOLATILE or NON-VOLATILE; read-only (ROM) or read/write (RAM). The action of a computer depends on the use of both ROM and RAM types of memory, and an important factor is the speed with which memory can be read, because this determines how fast the computer can operate in practical programming terms.

memory edit, *n.* the process of looking at and changing computer memory contents. A memory edit is one possible method by which a compiled program can be checked, or errors corrected if the SOURCE CODE is not available.

memory map, *n.* a diagram that shows how memory is used. See Fig. 45. See also MAP, MEMORY MAPPING.

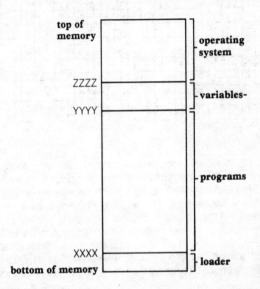

Fig. 45. **Memory map.** A memory map for an (imaginary) computer system. This shows which set of addresses in memory are reserved for particular purposes.

memory mapping, *n.* the correspondence between character position and memory ADDRESS. One example is the system in which each position on a screen corresponds to an address in memory. What is contained in that memory will then affect what is seen at that part of the screen. This system allows for both the shape and the colour of a point on the screen to be controlled by the content of memory.

The simplest memory mapping systems use the ASCII code for a character to provide the shape of the character on the screen. For

MEMORY MAPPING

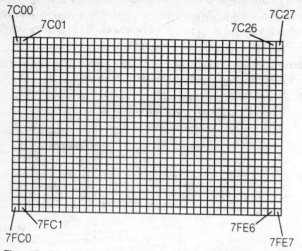

Fig. 46. **Memory mapping.** A simple memory-mapped screen layout. In this type of memory mapping (illustrated by the BBC Micro mode 7 screen) each address represents a character location on the screen. Placing a byte in an address will then cause a character shape to appear at the corresponding screen position. Many machines (including the BBC machine in other modes) use much more complicated screen mapping in which several dots in different positions are controlled by the bits in each byte in memory.

MENU
(Press number key to activate choice)

1. Enter new data

2. Read data file

3. Write new file

4. Leave program

Your choice —— ?

Fig. 47. **Menu.** A simple form of menu as it would appear on the screen. The choice is made by pressing a number key, and a mugtrap would be needed in the program to ensure that a number in the correct range was selected.

graphics work, much more elaborate memory mapping systems are in use, in which the shape of a character may be controlled by bits taken from several bytes located at widely differing addresses. Whatever system of memory mapping is used, both software, in the form of machine code programs, and hardware in the form of specialized cathode-ray tube signal generators, are needed to convert the stored numbers into signals which can cause a shape to appear on the screen. See Fig. 46.

menu, *n.* a set of choices that the user can take in a program. Menus are often set out with the different choices numbered. The user can then select by typing the chosen number. A useful variation is a pointer which can be moved by CURSOR keys or by the use of a MOUSE. When the chosen item is pointed to, then pressing the spacebar or other key will implement the choice. See also MOUSE, IKON, WIMP. See Fig. 47.

menu-driven, *adj.* (of a program) operating by making use of choices from a MENU. Such a program is usually easy for a programmer to follow, easy to alter or extend, and easy to use. It can, however, be time-consuming in use, particularly if one menu leads to another.

mesh network, *n.* a way of making connections. A network of connections is described as being a mesh if there are two or more connections between each pair of items in the network.

microfloppy, *n.* a name for miniature disks. If a minifloppy means a 5¼″ disk, then a microfloppy means the 3″ or 3½″ disks that are now well established.

microcomputer, *n.* a computer that has been designed to be as compact as possible. The CPU is a single-chip MICROPROCESSOR, the MEMORY consisting of a small number of SEMICONDUCTOR memory chips, and the whole electronics system is held in a casing which is little bigger than the keyboard. This type of machine has been available since the early part of the 1970s, and has been responsible for the sudden upsurge of interest in and the more widespread use of computers. Most microcomputers are designed to be programmed in BASIC or in MACHINE CODE, but other languages are available, particularly for machines with larger RAM memory and which can be fitted with DISK DRIVES. By far the most efficient machines to use are these which can be fitted with programs in ROM, since the machine is available for use almost as soon as it is switched on. The use of SIDEWAYS ROM is a great advantage in this respect. The alternative, of using a CLEAN MACHINE into which an OPERATING SYSTEM and LANGUAGE must be loaded from disk, offers more versatility but takes more time to load up, and always presents the risk of CORRUPTION of the operating system if anything goes wrong in a program.

microelectronics, *n.* a development of electronics which reduces the number of faults in a system by increased use of chips, thus eliminating large numbers of connections. Before the advent of microelectronics, electronics systems depended on assembling large numbers of components that had to be connected by means of copper wire or strip, and soldered joints. These connections were always the least reliable part of any system. Work by G.R. Dummer in 1954 led to experiments in which several transistors and other components were formed along with interconnections on one block of semiconductor. The technology developed rapidly in the 1960s, mainly because of the demand for ultra-reliable systems for space technology, and by the early 70s, it was possible to fabricate several thousand devices and all of their interconnections on one piece of silicon.

By the end of the 70s, several hundred thousand devices could be put on one chip. Though the reliability of these units was the main reason for the widespread adoption of microelectronics, the very small size of each chip led to the possibility of making computers which were very much smaller than any previously imagined. The technology also led to such items as calculators, digital watches, miniature TV receivers and video cassette recorders, electronic typewriters and a host of other consumer goods.

micron, *n.* a unit of length, equal to a millionth of a metre. Used mainly to describe the sizes of units and connections in ICs.

Micronet, *n. Trademark.* an organization which provides PRESTEL data to a fee-paying user group of computer enthusiasts.

microprocessor, *n.* the central processing unit of a microcomputer. We can imagine any computer as consisting of memory, input/output, and processor. In this division, the processor is the part which carries out actions such as ARITHMETIC and LOGIC that are the basis of all computing. MAINFRAME computers traditionally use a large number of fast-acting transistors to make up the processor section, and this approach was also used in the early MINICOMPUTERS. The microcomputer was made possible by the creation of processors in one-chip form, with all the temporary memory (REGISTERS) and arithmetic or comparison units (GATES) built in and interconnected. The type of design also permitted the actions of the microprocessor to be controlled by electrical signals, so that the whole chip was PROGRAMMABLE.

Early microprocessors could deal with only four binary digits at a time, but by the mid-70s, 8-bit chips were available, and by the end of the 70s the first 16-bit chips were in production. Several manufacturers are now turning out 32-bit chips, but the OPERATING SYSTEMS to make use of such chips effectively have not been developed so rapidly.

microprogram, *n.* a program used within a microprocessor. In order for a single number-code instruction to cause an action such as addition, the microprocessor has to execute several steps, such as reading, addition and storage. These individual steps are controlled by a built-in program, the microprogram, which has been devised by the manufacturer. This program cannot be changed, patched or avoided in any way.

Microprolog, *n. Trademark.* a 'cut-down' version (or SUBSET) of the PROLOG computing language. Microcomputers generally do not have enough memory to deal effectively with a complex list-processing language like PROLOG, and subsets such as Microprolog have been devised for the use of microcomputer programmers.

Microsoft, *n. Trademark.* a very influential SOFTWARE HOUSE. Founded by Bill Gates, Microsoft wrote the BASIC interpreters for most of the early microcomputers, such as the Commodore PET and Tandy TRS-80. Microsoft later developed the MS-DOS operating system which is the basis of most of the 16-bit machines currently in use.

Microsoft Word, *n. Trademark.* a word processor program designed for 16-bit computers. The program allows a variety of type styles to be displayed on screen, and can work on several documents at once.

milk disk, *n.* a disk that is used to gather data from a small machine with a view to processing the data in a larger machine later.

minicomputer, *n.* an intermediate stage between the mainframe and the microcomputer. It makes use of the electronics technology of the micro, but has memory capacity and speed which takes it closer to the mainframe in capability. A mini will consist of several cabinets of equipment, but these will not take up nearly so much space, nor require the elaborate cooling that is needed by a mainframe. The CPU of the mini will consist of sections of 4-bit microprocessors (BIT SLICES) which are assembled together to make up (usually) a 32-bit processing unit. Fast-acting SEMICONDUCTOR memory will be used as the main store, and WINCHESTER DISKS as the backing store. The keyboard and video monitor units will generally be remote from the main processor unit, often connected by serial links. There is often provision for MULTI-USER connections and NETWORK use.

minidisk, *n.* any disk in a size smaller than 'standard'. The term was at one time used to denote any disk smaller than 8″ diameter, and is now sometimes used to mean any disk smaller than 5¼″.

minifloppy, *n.* a name given to the 5¼″ size of FLOPPY DISK. Synonymous with diskette.

miniwinny, *n.* slang name for a miniature WINCHESTER DISK.

MIPS, *n. acronym for* millions of instructions per second, another measure of computing power. See also MEGAFLOP.

mirroring, *n.* the rotating of a graphics display by 180 degrees in a plane at right angles to the picture plane in order to produce the sort of image that you would see reflected in a pool of water.

mnemonics, *n.* abbreviated names for ASSEMBLY LANGUAGE instructions. Programming in MACHINE CODE involves using number codes as instructions and data. Because these numbers are difficult to remember, and easy to make mistakes with, symbolic language is used. The symbolic language consists of mnemonics, numbers and LABELS. A 'mnemonic' is a shortened version of a command word, such as LD A in place of LOAD Accumulator. In this way, the programmer can design the program using phrases such as LD A,KEYBD which are easier to understand and check than a stream of numbers. When a program has been written in this assembly (or assembler) language, it can be translated quickly into machine-code numbers by a program which is called an ASSEMBLER. An assembly language program, once written, can then be used to generate code for different memory addresses, and even for different machines which make use of the same type of MICROPROCESSOR. See Fig. 48.

Each different type of microprocessor, however, requires a different assembly language, and a different assembler program. A few microprocessors have built-in assemblers (the BBC Micro, for example), and users of CP/M machines have an assembler program (for the 8080 microprocessor) provided on the SYSTEM DISK.

68000	Z80	6502
ADDA	ADD	ADC
SUBX	SUB	SBC
CMPM	CP	CMP
DIVU	RR	ROR
LINK	XOR	LDA
MOVE	LD	STA
ROR	LDIR	TAX
SWAP	CPIR	RTS

Fig. 48. **Mnemonics.** A selection of mnemonics for different microprocessors. These are not for corresponding instructions except for the addition and subtraction examples.

MOD, *n.* a number FUNCTION which gives the remainder after INTEGER division. For example, 8 MOD 3 gives 2, the remainder after 8 has been divided by 3. If a number N is used in a loop count, then the expression N MOD J will continually cycle through the sequence 0, 1, 2, 3, ... J. This is often used in connection with ranges of numbers such as the colour code numbers which might have to be repeated in the course of a loop.

mode, *n.* one of a number of optional systems of operation. For example, a computer may offer several screen modes that allow different degrees of RESOLUTION and require different amounts of RAM. A very common choice for text is the choice of 40 or 80 characters per line.

modem, *abbrev. for* modulator/demodulator, a device which allows computers to communicate along telephone lines (see MODULATOR, DEMODULATION). Telephone lines are useful only for signals which change comparatively slowly, up to a few thousand changes per second. The normal signal change rates of computers are several millions of changes per second, so a program (the terminal program) must be used to change the computer signals into signals which can be sent over telephone lines. The modem does part of this, and also performs the conversion from telephone line signals to computer signals. Older modems used an ACOUSTIC COUPLER to convert the signals from the computer into sound at the microphone of the telephone, and the sounds from the telephone earpiece into computer signals. Modern modems allow direct connection of electrical signals, but in the UK must be type-approved by British Telecom.

modifier, *n.* a symbol or statement that modifies an action. Used mainly in connection with the PRINT STATEMENT of BASIC and the WRITE statement of some other languages. The plain BASIC PRINT statement, for example, indicates that a new line should be taken, and the output printed on to the VDU screen. By using print modifiers, this DEFAULT condition can be changed. The use of TAB can force the start of the printed text to a new position on the line. The use of a SEMICOLON following a piece of text will prevent a new line being taken for the next piece of text. The use of COMMAS will divide the text into preset columns. Some DIALECTS of BASIC also use the APOSTROPHE as a CARRIAGE RETURN signal, and adding a CHANNEL number, such as #8, to the PRINT statement can be used to force HARD COPY, or send the text to a DISK FILE.

MODULA-2, *n.* *Trademark.* a comparatively new computing language, developed from PASCAL.

modularization, *n.* the design of programs from established routines. A top-down design method lends itself well to this use of standard modules. If the programmer maintains a library of modules, a program can be written which will simply call up each module as it is needed. The language C is structured around this use of library routines.

modulation, *n.* a system that modifies some characteristic of a wave so as to carry messages. The oldest form of modulation is the starting and stopping of a radio wave, in the form of Morse code. Signals at sound wave frequency, as from a microphone, can be modulated on to a radio 'carrier' wave by using the signals to alter either the AMPLITUDE or the FREQUENCY of the radio wave, providing amplitude modulation (AM) or frequency modulation (FM) respectively. The opposite action, which recovers the original signal, is called demodulation. For small computers which use TV receivers in place of MONITORS, the VIDEO signal must be modulated on to a suitable TV carrier frequency. This will later be demodulated inside the TV receiver. This avoids the danger of making any direct connection to a domestic TV receiver other than through the aerial socket.

In computing, modulation generally refers to a system which codes a digital 0 as one audio tone, and digital 1 as another tone. This system allows the tone coded signals to be recorded on audio tapes or cassettes, and transmitted over telephone lines. These tones can, in turn, be modulated on to radio waves to be transmitted by radio.

modulator, *n.* **1.** any device that performs signal conversion. **2.** in computing the term usually denotes a device which allows signals to be transmitted by radio waves (an *RF modulator*) by way of MODULATION. The modulator of a MODEM converts digital signals into audio frequency tones.

monitor, *n.* a term for two methods of overseeing a computer action. **1.** a machine code program that allows you to trace what your computer is doing. A monitor should allow you to read what is stored in any part of the memory, and to change anything that is stored in RAM. It should also allow you to analyse the action of a machine code program, even to the extent of reading the contents of the REGISTERS within the MICROPROCESSOR. The best monitors allow a machine code program to be run step by step, analysing the contents of the microprocessor and the memory at each step. **2.** a display unit which can make direct use of the computer's VIDEO signals. Many home computers can send video signals to TV receivers only, using a miniature type of TV transmitter which is called a MODULATOR. This makes it impossible to use 80 characters per line of text, or HIGH-RESOLUTION graphics, because the domestic TV system is incapable of dealing with such fast-changing signals. A monitor is constructed so that the computer (or video-recorder) signals can be connected directly, rather than through an aerial input. This allows much better resolution, particularly of colour pictures, providing that the monitor is well-designed. Unfortunately, a lot of monitors which are advertised for small computers are little better than converted TV receivers, and do not compare with the professional type of monitor. See also COLOUR MONITOR, MONOCHROME MONITOR.

monochrome monitor, *n.* a MONITOR whose display is in one colour only. The traditional monochrome means white text on a dark screen, but colours such as green or amber are considered more restful to the eye. A monochrome monitor is more suitable than a colour monitor for HIGH-RESOLUTION graphics or for word processing with 80 characters per line.

most-significant, see BIT.

most-significant byte, see BYTE.

motherboard, *n.* a baseboard for a computer circuit. Many computers other than the cheapest 'home' types make use of a motherboard construction. This means that the main part of the computer is constructed with a number of silicon chip circuits soldered or plugged into a main connecting board. This 'motherboard' is also provided with connectors into which other boards can be plugged. In this way, the capabilities of the computer can be greatly extended, because the supplementary boards can contain extra memory, other OPERATING SYSTEMS,

INTERFACES to PERIPHERALS, communications circuits, or whatever else is developed.

If the connections to the motherboard allow every connection of the CPU to be available to other devices, then the computer can be expanded almost indefinitely. The most notable example of this technique is the APPLE-2, a design of the mid-70s which was so well thought out that it was still in use and extensively sold in the mid-80s.

mouse, *n.* a device for computer operation which partly dispenses with the use of the keyboard. The mouse is a miniature trolley which can be moved about on a desk surface. As the mouse is moved, a pointer on the VDU screen moves, and can be made to point at various symbols, the IKONS. Pressing a button on the mouse will then initiate the action related to that symbol. See also WIMP.

MP/M, *n.* a multi-user version of CP/M that contains the additional control features that are needed to allow networking (see NETWORK.)

msb, see BIT.

MS-DOS, *n. Trademark.* a disk-operating system (DOS) that is designed by the MICROSOFT corporation for use with 16-bit computers, notably the machines like the IBM PC.

MSX, *n. Trademark.* a Japanese scheme to standardize an OPERATING SYSTEM and LANGUAGE for 8-bit computers. The MSX standard uses a MICROSOFT OPERATING SYSTEM and BASIC, with a Z-80 MICROPROCESSOR, and agreed standards for SOUND and GRAPHICS. Though the machines are very capable, they came at a time when prospective customers wanted features such as built-in disk drives and 16-bit processors for the same price level. Later versions of MSX moved towards built-in disk drives, but the machines made surprisingly little impact on the British market.

mugtrap, see VALIDATION.

multi-access system, *n.* a system in which several users of one computer all have access to the same program and set of files. In some cases, only the files can be used by remote terminals.

Multiplan, *n. Trademark.* a SPREADSHEET program which is

175

particularly easy to use and to learn. Its features include the provision of helpful messages on the screen, the use of DEFAULTS in case of doubt, a good set of commands, and the use of names for quantities in FORMULAS.

multistatement line, *n.* a COMPOUND STATEMENT in BASIC. Each line is numbered, and the simplest BASIC INTERPRETERS allow one statement per numbered line. Because the line structure for a BASIC interpreter takes up at least four bytes of memory per line (the line OVERHEAD), considerable memory saving can be effected if several statements are placed on each line. This is normally done by placing a colon as a SEPARATOR between statements. There is no line overhead problem in a compiled (see COMPILE) language.

multi-user system, *n.* a computer system in which several users can run different programs with different data. This is done by a TIMESHARING system which is most effective when each TERMINAL has its own memory. While one machine is paused for printing or awaiting the operator, processed data can be fed to another terminal. If all users are operating intensively, however, the rate of processing can be very slow. Because of the speed factor, another scheme which has come into favour uses the master computer simply as a server of data to terminals each of which has its own MICROPROCESSOR and memory.

Murray code, *n.* a 5-bit code for TELEPRINTER machines. The Murray code, devised in the early 1900s, was an improvement on the older BAUDOT code, but permits only upper-case characters to be used.

N

NAND gate, see AND GATE.

NAK, *abbrev. for* negative acknowledgement, a code used by remote TERMINALS to indicate that data has not been correctly received, and should be retransmitted.

name, *n.* a title that represents data. Quantities that are being processed, whether numbers, letters or words, are often represented by names or IDENTIFIERS. Any action which is to be carried out on a number or other quantity can therefore be programmed in terms of the name. For example, if the VARIABLE name of X is used to represent a number, then a command such as PRINT X will mean that the number is to be printed. In this way, the program does not need to contain any details of what numbers or other characters are to be used, only what is to be done with them (the PROCEDURES of the program).

nanosecond, *n.* a unit of time equal to one thousandth of a millionth of a second, that is 1E-9 seconds. For very fast-acting computers, the time to carry out an instruction may be less than a millionth of a second (a microsecond) and is therefore expressed in nanoseconds.

natural language, *n.* the language that is spoken and written by humans, as distinct from computer programming languages. The closer a programming language comes to natural language, the higher the level of the programming language.

NCR paper, *n.* 'no carbon required' copying paper. 'NCR' is also an abbrev. for National Cash Register, the company which introduced the system.

needles *n.*, the printing elements of a DOT MATRIX printer.

negation, *n.* the inversion of a BINARY digit. Also called *complement*. Negating binary 1 gives binary 0, negating binary 0 gives binary 1. When this action is applied to a complete byte of 8 bits, negating the byte 00000000 (zero) will give the byte 11111111 which in DENARY represents –1. Many computers use –1 to represent TRUE and 0 to represent FALSE. See also TWOS COMPLEMENT.

negative, *n.* conventionally, a number that is less than zero. In DENARY, a negative number is represented by a special sign, the negative (or minus) sign, written as –. In binary code, there is no negative sign, and one bit of each number (the MSB) is used to convey sign. This is done by using a 1 to mean negative and a 0 to mean positive.

nesting, *n.* the enclosing of one action inside another, often used of LOOPS, SUBROUTINES, or PROCEDURES. For example, in BASIC,the lines:

```
100 FOR N%=1 TO 12
110 FOR K%=1 TO 31
120 READ D$(N%,K%):PRINT D$(N%,K%)
130 NEXT K%:PRINT
140 NEXT N%
```

form a loop system in which the loop that uses K% is nested inside the loop that uses N%. The use of nested loops can make a program run very slowly, and great care needs to be taken to put as few actions into the innermost loop as possible.

network, *n.* a system of interconnections between computers that allows them to share facilities, typically hard-disk drives and printers. A network also allows different users to communicate, and to pass data to and from each other. Networking can greatly increase the utility of a system by allowing different users to contribute data. The snag is that the use of a network can sometimes cause an unacceptable reduction in the speed of computing.

network diagram, *n.* a method of representing the connections of a NETWORK.

NEW, *n.* a command that is used in several languages to clear out a program from the memory in readiness for a new program. Very often, the old program remains stored, and only two POINTER bytes are actually changed. A LOAD from tape or disk usually performs a NEW automatically before the loading action starts.

NEXT, *n.* a statement in BASIC used as a TERMINATOR to mark the far end of a LOOP that starts with FOR. All of the actions up to the NEXT statement will be executed on each PASS THROUGH THE LOOP.

nibble, *n.* one half of a BYTE. The term is used to denote a set of four bits, normally either the most significant (see MSB) four or the least significant (see LSB) four taken from a byte. See also GULP.

NLQ, *abbrev. for* near letter quality, an attribute of a DOT-MATRIX printer that has been designed to produce characters of similar print quality to that of a DAISYWHEEL. See also MATRIX PRINTER.

NMOS, *abbrev. for* n-type metal-oxide semiconductor, a form of FET construction which is used for MICROPROCESSORS and memory chips. See also CMOS, PMOS.

node, *n.* a point where lines join, or a place where network signals are switched.

noise, *n.* unwanted electrical signals, such as those which radiate from fluorescent lights or electric motors. If a lot of electrical noise is present in mains supplies or is radiated, then computers may have to be shielded. The computer system itself radiates electrical noise which can interfere with radio reception, particularly on VHF bands.

nomenclature, *n.* any system of allocating names. In a program, for example, variable nomenclature would refer to a system of allocating variable NAMES so that the programmer could easily remember what each name applied to.

nondestructive, *adj.* causing no erasure. A *nondestructive cursor* (see CURSOR) is one that can be moved around the screen without erasing any characters over which it passes. A *nondestructive readout* denotes any system of reading memory which does not erase the memory. Nondestructive readout is a normal feature of SEMI-CONDUCTOR memory, but not of MAGNETIC CORE memory.

non-impact printer, *n.* one using a printing method in which paper is not struck. Non-impact printers are quiet, but cannot produce carbon copies. See ELECTROSTATIC PRINTER, THERMAL PRINTER, LASER PRINTER, INK-JET PRINTER.

non-printing codes, *n.* ASCII code numbers, usually in the range 1 to 31, that do not represent a character but an action like clearing the screen, taking a new line, switching the printer on and off, and so on.

non-volatile memory, *n.* any memory that retains its contents when electrical power is switched off. Also called *permanent memory*. The normal RAM of the computer loses all data within a millisecond of being switched off, and a different memory system must be used for any data that has to be retained. This is usually provided by ROM, but a few machines feature CMOS RAM, which can be connected to a small backup battery and which will then retain data after the main power supply has been switched off.

NOR, *abbrev. for* NOT OR, a logic action. In most computers, this action has to be programmed by using NOT and OR.

normalize, *vb.* to operate on numerical data in which each item has to be adjusted so as to make the data fit a specified pattern. A common example is the normalization of examination marks so that the average is 50% and the standard deviation (the average difference from the average mark) about 15%. Normalization of marks in this way compensates for the fact that some examinations may be difficult and others easy.

In programs which produce graphs or bar charts, quantities may be range-normalized. This means that the range of values is compressed or expanded to fit the graph scales so that the maximum value will correspond to the highest point on the graph or the longest bar, and the smallest value to the lowest graph point, or a single unit of bar.

NOT, *n.* a word that is used in most languages to mean NEGATION. The word can be used in LOGIC sense or in BINARY sense. In logic sense we can use program statements such as:

IF A$ NOT "Y"

to make a comparison. In binary sense, NOT means the inverse of the number, so that NOT(0) means –1.

NOT gate, *n.* a HARDWARE implementation of NOT logic. See also GATE, LOGIC.

notation, *n.* a formal method of expressing the SYNTAX of a computer language without the use of examples. The best-known notation is BACKUS-NAUR FORM.

notebook, *n.* a feature of office management programs that allows you to make notes which are then stored on a separate file. Also called *scratchpad* (US). The notes are usually arranged to appear in a screen WINDOW rather than on the main part of the screen.

notice board, *n.* a form of BULLETIN BOARD used in an electronic mail system that is intended to be read by all users.

NRZI, *abbrev. for* non-return to zero indicator. A system of recording digital data on to magnetic tape, using two possible directions of magnetization to indicate the bits 0 or 1.

null set, *n.* a SET of items that contains no members. In languages which allow a set as a DATA TYPE (PASCAL for example), different sets may contain different items, but some sets may contain no items, or two sets may have no items in common. For example, the set of computer users may contain those who possess printers and those who possess disk systems, but if we tried to find how many owners possessed a disk system and a printer but no computer, we might find that this was a null set.

number cruncher, *n.* a specialized chip or circuit that performs mathematical operations. This can be very much faster than using the normal programmed functions of a general-purpose microprocessor. Several microcomputers, notably the IBM PC, allow a number-cruncher chip (or COPROCESSOR) to be used, but only a few programs can actually make use of this chip. Most large MAINFRAME computers have separate number-cruncher sections which allow mathematical operations to be carried out at very high speeds.

numberpad, *n.* a separate set of keys or buttons for entering numbers. Usually placed on the right-hand side of the keyboard and therefore useless to left-handed operators. A few computers feature the use of 'floating' numberpads which can be placed to the right or to the left of the main keyboard.

numeric, *adj.* of or relating to numbers, as distinct from CHARACTER data.

numerical control, *n.* the control of machines by digital data.

O

object code, *n.* a program which is in the form of a set of number codes (or MACHINE CODE) that will affect the microprocessor directly. A program in object code will run faster than a program run by an INTERPRETER, and if the object code has been written in ASSEMBLY LANGUAGE, the program will run faster than one in object code that has been produced from a HIGH-LEVEL LANGUAGE by using a COMPILER . In addition, by working with the microprocessor directly, it is possible to program actions which are not provided for in a high-level language.

OCCAM, *n.* a modern HIGH-LEVEL LANGUAGE. OCCAM is intended to be used in AI applications, runs on mainframe computers, and requires enormous resources of memory and BACKING STORE.

OCR, see OPTICAL CHARACTER READER.

octal, *n.* a number system that is based on a scale of 8. This scale was formerly used in MAINFRAME programming, but is very seldom encountered on microprocessors, and is much less useful than HEXADECIMAL.

octave, *n.* a set of 8 notes (counting inclusively) which is the basis of Western music. The term is also used to describe any set of 8 objects.

odd parity, see PARITY.

OEM, *abbrev. for* original equipment manufacturer.

O.K., *n.* a screen PROMPT that is used by some OPERATING SYSTEMS in place of READY.

on/off line, *n.* terms that are used when part of a system is remote. 'On-line' means that connection is established, and the remote device can be used; 'off-line' means that there is no connection.

one-pass assembler, see ASSEMBLER.

OPEN, *n.* an instruction that is used, in several languages, to open a disk or tape FILE. The action of OPEN is usually to allocate a BUFFER and to INITIALIZE the part of the OPERATING SYSTEM that deals with filing.

open wire, *n.* a cable link that uses a wire or wires supported on insulators. A telephone line is a typical open wire, and is open in the sense of allowing easy tapping.

operand, *n.* in ASSEMBLY LANGUAGE the part of an instruction that specifies on what byte an action will be carried out. For example, the command ADD C means that the byte in REGISTER C will be added to the byte in the ACCUMULATOR, and the operand of this command is C.

operating system, *n.* the MACHINE CODE program, often in ROM, that controls all the main actions of the computer such as the use of the keyboard, screen, disk system and so on. The alternative to using ROM for the whole operating system is to keep a very small LOADER system in ROM and to load (BOOT) the rest of the operating system from a SYSTEM disk. Computers that are intended for business use normally make use of one of the 'universal' operating systems such as CP/M or MS-DOS.

operational amplifier (opamp), *n.* a unit of an ANALOGUE COMPUTER whose behaviour can be altered by connecting electronic components to two terminals. When a waveform which corresponds to a mathematical expression is applied as an input to such an amplifier, the output waveform represents the effect of a mathematical operation on the input. For example, if the opamp is arranged to carry out summation, the output waveform will be proportional to the sum of amplitudes of the waves at the inputs.

operational code (opcode), *n.* the part of an instruction in ASSEMBLY LANGUAGE that specifies the action. For example, in LD A,C, the word LD is the op-code that specifies the action of loading.

operational research, *n.* a method of analysing a SYSTEM. The method is usually applied to large organizations with a view to producing a computer SIMULATION of the organization. Working on the computer simulation can then suggest methods of improving the organization itself.

operator, *n.* an action on a number or character. Numerical operators of addition, subtraction, multiplication and division are represented by symbols such as +, −, * and /. Operations on characters and STRINGS of characters are not so standardized. In BASIC, such string operators include LEN and LEFT$.

Highest Precedence
unary −
unary +
NOT
function
brackets ( )
exponentiate
multiply *
divide /
DIV
MOD
addition +
subtraction −
equality =
not equal <>
less than <
greater than >
less or equal <=
greater or equal >=
AND
OR
XOR

Fig. 49. **Operator precedence.** This list indicates in which order a set of operations will be executed if no other form of priority exists. Normally we would program using brackets to enforce the order of priority that we need. Not all languages use exactly this order of precedence.

operator precedence, *n.* mathematical operations in computing, which are always carried out in a set order. This order is, in general, raising to a power (exponentiation), multiplication or division, addition or subtraction. For example, if you program: A+B*C^D, then C will be raised to the power D, the result multiplied by B, and then A added. The order of action is *not* the same as the order of writing the commands. Many computers transform the order of expressions internally into REVERSE POLISH NOTATION as part of their INTERNAL LANGUAGE. The order of precedence can be altered by the use of BRACKETS. Any expression that is contained within brackets will be carried out before actions that lie outside the brackets. See Fig. 49.

optical character reader (OCR), *n.* a device that by passing a 'reading head' over text will convert the characters of the text into ASCII coded signals that can be fed to the computer. An OCR which can handle a wide variety of text styles (typewriter text, printing in different sizes and in italics, etc.) can be very expensive, but simplified low-cost models which can read a few of the most common print styles are now appearing, and can be used with many small computers.

optical disk, *n.* a form of position TRANSDUCER. An 'optical disk' is a circular transparent disk that has a pattern of radial bars printed on it. The disk is attached to a shaft, and a set of lights and PHOTOSENSORS is arranged along one radius, so that the lights shine on the photosensors. Each photosensor is arranged to contribute one bit to a binary number, so that as the disk turns, different numbers are generated by the set of photosensors. This can be used to DIGITIZE the angular position of a shaft, and is widely used in machine control. The code that is used is more likely to be GRAY CODE than the conventional binary system.

optical fibre, *n.* a thin thread of glass. By using a coaxial system, with one type of glass enclosed by another, these fibres can be constructed so that a light beam will pass down the length of the fibre with very little loss of energy. This can be used for information transmission, because light is a waveform similar in nature to radio waves but with a much higher FREQUENCY. Optical fibres are generally used in conjunction with LASERS and are now employed in all types of DIGITIZERS.

optical transmission, *n.* a system of communication using LASERS and glass fibres. See OPTICAL FIBRE.

OR, *n.* a LOGIC action in which two bits are compared. The result is logic 1 unless both bits are at logic 0. When two bytes are ORed, corresponding bits are compared so as to provide each bit of the result. For example, 11110000 OR 11000011 gives the result

OR

11110011. The OR action can also be applied to actions in HIGH-LEVEL LANGUAGES. In such a case, the action is a test of alternatives, each of which must be either true or false. For example, if a statement reads:

IF A=5 OR J=10 THEN Fivout

the test is for variable A being equal to 5 or variable J equal to 10. If either or both of these conditions is true, then procedure Fivout is executed. If neither condition is true, then the next statement will be executed. See Fig. 50.

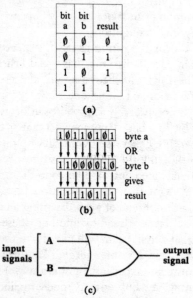

Fig. 50. **OR.** OR and OR-gate action. (a) A truth-table for the OR action, which shows all the possible results of ORing two bits. (b) When two complete bytes are ORed, the OR action is carried out on corresponding bits, that is bits in the same position in each byte. The result is put into the corresponding position in the result-byte. Each bit action is self-contained — there is no carry bit as there would be in an ADD or SUB action. (c) The symbol which represents an OR gate in an electronic circuit.

ordered list, *n.* a list of items in some order such as alphabetical or numerical order.

ORG, *n.* a keyword used in ASSEMBLY LANGUAGE to enter the starting ADDRESS at which object code is to be assembled. ORG is classed as a PSEUDO-OPERATION, meaning that it takes the same form as an assembly language statement, but is actually a command to the assembler itself.

origin, *n.* **1.** a reference point. **2.** in graphics, the point which is picked to be the zero of each axis. All positions in subsequent graphics instructions are measured from this point. **3.** in ASSEMBLY LANGUAGE, the first ADDRESS in memory at which code will be placed by the action of the ASSEMBLER. See also ORG.

out of range, *n.* an ERROR MESSAGE which means that a number has become unusable. This might refer to an INTEGER which has been incremented or decremented to an unacceptable value, or to a number used as a coordinate which has reached a value that corresponds to a position off the screen.

output, *n.* any signal that is passed out of a system. The term has to be used with care, because the signal that is the output of one system is often the input of another system. Typical computer outputs include the PRINTER, DISK SYSTEM, MONITOR, NETWORK, and MODEM outputs.

output bound, *n.* a computer system restricted in speed because of an output. The term mainly denotes a program which makes extensive use of a printer for output. Unless the printer is fitted with a large BUFFER, the computer will be forced to hang up during the time while the printer is operating. This makes the speed of computing as slow as the speed of printing. A useful method of dealing with the problem, apart from the use of a printer buffer, is to SPOOL the output. Compare INPUT BOUND.

overflow, *n.* the result of a number becoming OUT OF RANGE. The term usually denotes the result of a number becoming too large to store in the number of bytes allocated to it, and is of concern mainly to the ASSEMBLY LANGUAGE programmer who is working with mathematical functions. Some high-level languages deliver an overflow error message when an INTEGER variable is assigned

with a number that is too large. See Fig. 51. Compare
UNDERFLOW.

<table>
<tr><td>ADD</td><td>1 0 1 0 0 1 1 0</td><td>Denary: 166</td></tr>
<tr><td></td><td>1 1 0 1 0 0 0 1</td><td>Denary: 209</td></tr>
</table>

carried 1   0 1 1 1 0 1 1 1   result: Denary 119 and 1 carried

(a) unsigned single byte   carry but no error

<table>
<tr><td>ADD</td><td>0 1 0 1 1 0 1 0</td><td>Denary: 90</td></tr>
<tr><td></td><td>0 1 1 1 0 1 0 1</td><td>Denary: 117</td></tr>
</table>

1 1 0 0 1 1 1 1   result: Denary −49

(b) signed single byte   no carry, but overflow error

Fig. 51. **Overflow.** Overflow errors are caused by a number
needing more bits than can be fitted into or used in a register.
The examples show single byte overflows. In (a), an
unsigned addition has given a 9-bit answer of which only 8
bits can be stored in the register. The carry bit in the status
register will detect that this has happened. In example (b), an
addition of signed numbers has caused a carry into the msb,
which changes the sign of the result. This type of overflow
error can also be detected by the microprocessor, using an
overflow flag.

overhead, *n.* an unavoidable but undesirable extra, usually the
extra memory that has to be used to store 'organizing' codes. A
good example of memory overhead is provided by the numbering of lines in BASIC (see MULTISTATEMENT LINE).

overhead bit, *n.* a bit that is used for PARITY checking.

overlay, *n.* **1.** a pattern laid on top of something else. **2.** a pattern
that shows a different use of the keys (a *keyboard overlay*). For
example, a keyboard that can be used in word processing in
foreign languages will need key overlays to show characters that
are not present in English. See also KEYSTRIP. **3.** a pattern
superimposed on the normal screen display which, for example,

might show a scale (a *screen overlay*). **4.** a program which can be called up from a disk and run in order to provide variable values which the main program can use. See also CHAIN.

overstrike, *n.* a printer action. Overstriking means printing a character, shifting the paper or PRINTHEAD slightly, and then printing again. The effect is to emphasize the character, as if bold type had been used. Overstrike is a method of producing better character quality from DOT MATRIX printers, because by this method, the gaps between dots can be filled in. On a DAISYWHEEL printer, overstrike is used to produce bold or 'shadow' printing effects.

overwrite, *vb.* to replace a character by another on the screen or in memory. Overwriting on the screen means that one character that is typed will replace any other character in that space. This is the normal action of the screen, but when WORD PROCESSORS are used, this is changed to an INSERT action. Some computers allow non-erasing overwrite action, in which a typed character is added to the character that is already present. This can be used to form special characters, and to add ACCENT MARKS to characters on the screen. Overwriting memory means that when a byte is stored in a memory address, it replaces any byte that was formerly stored at that address.

P

package, *n.* a set of related programs. A commercial office package, for example, might consist of a spreadsheet, a word processor and a database program. These would not only be supplied as one set, they would nowadays normally be arranged so that each one could make use of data provided by another. Many packages also incorporate graphics display systems. See also SYMPHONY.

packed structure, *n.* a structure that makes the best possible use of memory. For example, ASCII codes take up only 7 bits of a byte. If memory is used as if it were not grouped in bytes, but could allow a grouping of 7 bits or less, then ASCII codes can be packed into less memory. Packing is efficient if the data can be retrieved in order of recording, but it can cause complications if random access to data is needed. Many high-level languages make use of a data type which is a packed array of characters.

packet, *n.* a set of bits. The term usually denotes a set of bits that is sent over a network or along a line. The data bits are accompanied by error check bits, and also by codes for start of packet and end of packet.

pad character, *n.* a word-processing character which prints as a space, and can be placed between words. The effect of using the pad character is to make the words appear to the program to be a single word, which cannot be split between lines. Many word processor programs allow the user the choice of pad characters, in case there is a special requirement to print the character that is used by DEFAULT as a pad. See also EMBEDDED BLANK.

padding to length, *n.* the adding of blanks to data. Many computer LANGUAGES accept STRINGS only if a definite length (such as 20 characters) has been declared. Any string that is input from the keyboard will be packed with blanks on the right-hand side to reach this preset length, or will have characters deleted from the right-hand side if the string is too long. Working with equal-length strings is wasteful of memory, but can make actions such as sorting into alphabetical order much faster.

paddle, *n.* a form of JOYSTICK, a controller which is held in the hand and used to control the position of an object, such as a CURSOR, on the screen. Used mainly in games at one time, but now superseded by the joystick. See also TRACKBALL, MOUSE.

page, *n.* **1.** a form of division into groups. *Screen paging* means that a full screen of information is presented to the user, and a new screenful will appear when a key is pressed. *Print paging* implies the division of text so that it will fit into separate sheets of paper. **2.** a set of bytes in memory, very often 256 bytes.

page-break, *n.* a command code to a word processor, usually an

EMBEDDED COMMAND which will cause the printer to take a new page. This means that any FOOTER will be printed on the current page, and the paper rolled out. When continuous paper, such as FANFOLD is used, the page-break action must ensure that the perforation between pages lies between the footer of one page and the HEADER of the next. When single sheets are used, the page-break action must stop the printer and the computer, and deliver a signal to the operator so that a new sheet can be fed in. If a single-sheet feeder is in use, this action can be made automatic, and printing will resume at once when the new sheet is fed in.

PAINT, *n.* a colour graphics statement that will fill in a closed area with a specified colour. Also called *FILL*. The statement must include the position COORDINATES of a point within the closed area, and a code number for the colour that is to be used in filling. Some types of paint instruction require the boundary of the closed area to be in the colour that will be used for painting, others require this colour to be specified in the paint statement.

paper, see BACKGROUND.

paper advance, *n.* part of the action of a printer. The two main methods of feeding the paper through the printer are SPROCKET FEED and FRICTION FEED. The sprocket feed method, also called pin feed, uses paper in continuous roll or FANFOLD form with a set of rectangular holes down each side. A pair of sprockets on the printer engages with these holes, and this allows the paper to be positioned very precisely by turning the sprockets. The friction system uses a roller which extends for at least the full width of the paper. The paper, which can be a continuous roll or cut sheets, is sandwiched between this main roller and a set of smaller rollers, and is moved when the roller turns. This feeding method is not so positive as the sprocket feed, and not so suitable for such actions as printing spreadsheets, in which alignment must be perfect.

Friction feed is particularly unsuitable when multipart paper (sheets of paper with carbons between) is used, because only one sheet is held reasonably well, and the others are likely to slip sideways. Most DOT MATRIX printers are fitted with sprocket

PAPER ADVANCE

Pin No.	Signal	Pin No.	Signal	
1	STROBE IN	9	D8	
2	D1	10	ACKNLG	
3	D2	11	BUSY	All
4	D3	12	PE	other
5	D4	13	SLCT	pins
6	D5	18	+5V	grounded
7	D6	31	PRIME	
8	D7	32	ERROR	

STROBE	Sent by computer to printer to indicate data to be read
D1-D8	Data bits of each byte
ACKNLG	Signal from printer at end of data, ready for next byte
BUSY	Signal from printer to indicate not ready for data
PE	Signal from printer — out of paper
SLCT	Signal from printer — printer working
PRIME	Signal to printer — initialize
ERROR	Signal from printer — error has occurred

Fig. 52. **Parallel-printer.** The parallel-printer interface Centronics standard connections. Not all printers will send or make use of all of the possible control signals, but signal paths are provided for. The standard connector is a Cannon type 36 pin.

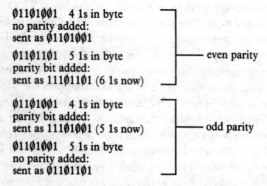

Fig. 53. **Parity.** Even and odd parity. The number of 1s in the byte is counted, and the msb allocated so as to make this total even or odd, according to which parity scheme is being used. On reception of the byte, the parity is checked again, and an error message will be given if the parity is incorrect. Several microprocessors contain parity flags in the status register.

feed as standard, and friction feed is an optional extra. The opposite is generally true of DAISYWHEEL printers.

paper tape, *n.* an old-established method of storing data, which replaced PUNCHED CARDS in many applications. The TELEPRINTER which was used as an INPUT/OUTPUT device by MAINFRAME computers incorporated a paper tape PUNCH and reader. The paper tape was of standardized width, with a set of sprocket holes running down its length, offset from the centre. An ASCII character was represented by punching holes in a direction at right angles to the line of sprocket holes.

Paper tape is a slow and very bulky method of storage, but it has two useful merits. One is that the system is standardized, so that any computer which is equipped with a paper-tape reader should be able to read a tape produced by any other computer. The other merit is 'archival quality'. Unlike magnetic media, paper tape signals cannot be corrupted, and short of physical destruction by fire, there is little that can make a paper tape completely useless. Even a torn tape can be mended and used to make a new copy, so that a paper-tape record has a permanence that is not attained by magnetic tape or disks.

parallel port, *n.* an INTERFACE for parallel signals. The parallel port, generally a single CHIP, is connected to the BUSES of the microprocessor, and can pass signals from the microprocessor to external peripherals, such as a printer or disk drives. The port also includes HANDSHAKING signals, so that the microprocessor action can be controlled by the speed of the peripheral. This means that the microprocessor can be held in a WAIT LOOP until a printer, for example, has dealt with a character code and is ready to process another. If the printer contains a BUFFER, the character codes can be fed very quickly through the port until the buffer is full. When the 'buffer full' signal is received at the port, the microprocessor is again forced into a waiting loop. The use of the port therefore requires both HARDWARE connections and SOFTWARE programming.

parallel printer, *n.* a printer that makes use of parallel signals. This implies that the connecting cable will use at least seven lines. The CENTRONICS standard of parallel connection requires the use of eleven active lines, though a number of additional 'ground' lines are often added to the connector. Because of the general use of the Centronics standard, a parallel printer can be connected to a computer that provides a parallel port with reasonable certainty that printing will be achieved. The main non-standard item is the form of connector and cable that is used, but a few manufacturers use one or more non-standard connections. See Fig. 52.

parallel processing, *n.* a method of increasing processing speed. The traditional design of computer uses SERIAL PROCESSING, which means that instructions are carried out one after another. Parallel processing is a system in which several instructions can be carried out simultaneously. This is much more difficult to program for, but is better suited to the more modern LOGICAL LANGUAGES. The FIFTH GENERATION computers are expected to be parallel types.

parallel signals, *n.* several signals sent along a set of wires at the same time. A parallel-printer connection, for example, uses seven wires, one for each bit in an ASCII character, as distinct from the SERIAL connection in which each bit is sent one at a time along one wire. Parallel connections are also needed when the computer is used to control external systems.

parameter, *n.* a quantity which takes a value for some time, after which the value can be changed. Sometimes jokingly defined as a 'variable constant'. When we pass a parameter to a PROCEDURE, for example, the same variable name might be used, but will be assigned with a different value each time the procedure is called. All VARIABLE names or IDENTIFIERS are parameters. Each can be assigned with a value, but that value remains assigned only until it is changed.

parent page, *n.* a page of information that contains an index which allows the user to select another page. Used particularly of TELETEXT systems.

parity, *n.* a method of checking a BYTE for one BIT being incorrect. The principle is to use only 7 of the bits in the byte to convey code, usually ASCII code. The 8th bit is the 'parity bit', and is set so as to make the number of logic 1 bits either even (even parity) or odd (odd parity) according to whatever scheme is desired. At a receiving device, the parity can be checked, and an error signalled if the number of logic 1s in a byte is odd instead of even, or even instead of odd. Even parity is more usual. See Fig. 53.

The use of a parity bit, as described here, is an example of a method of creating *self-checking code*, in the sense that a simple summation can check the correctness of each byte of code. More elaborate methods based on the same principles exist, and these are referred to as *self-redundant codes*, because these more elaborate systems make use of more bits than are strictly needed to convey each coded character, so making it possible for minor errors to be corrected automatically.

parsing, *n.* the filtering of a statement to separate out the instruction word from any argument. This is an important action in any INTERPRETER or COMPILER for a high-level language. It is in this parsing action that SYNTAX error will be discovered and reported. A few machines carry out this parsing action as a statement is being entered, so that time spent on DEBUGGING an entered program can be greatly reduced.

Pascal, *n.* a language invented by Niklaus Wirth, heavily influenced by ALGOL. The language has been designed to allow very easy compiling, and the programmer must therefore write a program in a very rigidly stylized form. This is a very valuable way of teaching structured programming (see STRUCTURE), and has led to Pascal being extensively used by academics. The language is very rich in DATA TYPES, but these data types are rigidly separated – there are no instructions corresponding to the use of VAL or STR$ in BASIC, for example. The handling of STRINGS is also less flexible than many BASIC dialects permit.

pass through the loop, *n.* the execution of the instructions of a LOOP.

passing values, *n.* arranging a program which is in sections so that the different sections can work with the same set of quantities. This is one of the most difficult problems in more advanced programming. Values of VARIABLES may have to be passed to a MACHINE CODE subroutine, to a PROCEDURE, or to other programs which are loaded by a CHAIN command. Some languages make excellent provision for this action, others make little or none. The most elementary method is to use a POKE form of statement to place values into memory, and arrange sections of the program to read these memory addresses. A simpler method is to make each program section record values on disk, to be read by other sections.

passive, *adj.* of or relating to: **1.** anything in computing not requiring power; **2.** an electronic component which has no amplifying action.

password, *n.* a set of characters that can be used as an access code to a computer system or database. The exploits of HACKERS have driven home the point that simple passwords, based on initial letters of names, or on simple number sequences, are completely inadequate as safeguards. See also EXCLUSIVE OR.

patching, *n.* the adding or inserting of new computing code. When a program is written in MACHINE CODE, or produced by a COMPILER it is difficult to make any changes in the program. Patching is a method which operates by replacing part of the machine code with an instruction that causes the program to jump to a different address. A piece of program, the patch, is placed starting at this address, and the patch ends with a jump instruction that returns control to the original piece of the main program. The patch will therefore run each time this particular section of the main program runs, and can be used to correct a BUG in the original program, or to add useful features. Some well-known programs, such as WORDSTAR, make built-in provision for patching so that the program can be 'customized' to the user's requirements. See also HOOK ADDRESS.

pattern generator, *n.* a circuit or program that can generate patterns, used normally for checking the performance of a monitor or TV receiver.

pattern recognition, *n.* a form of computer 'sight'. Pattern recognition systems use a matrix of PHOTOSENSORS. This can be connected to a computer, and by means of suitable SOFTWARE, can compare a pattern of light and dark on the sensors with predetermined patterns that are held as coded numbers in the program memory. This allows some patterns to be clearly recognized, and is the basis of OPTICAL CHARACTER READERS.

Pattern recognition is also a vital part of ROBOTICS, because it provides a robot with a limited form of sight. It also has considerable uses in medical diagnostic programs, automatic inspection of manufactured components, and in image enhancement. Pattern recognition is a vital part of AI studies. See Fig. 54.

msb	lsb	binary	denary
○○○○○○○○		00000000	0
○●●●●●●○		01111111	127
○○●○○○●○		00100010	47
○○○●○●○○		00010100	20
○○○○●○○○		00001000	08
○○○●○●○○		00010100	20
○○●○○○●○		00100010	47
○●●●●●●●		01111111	127

Fig. 54. **Pattern recognition.** In this example, a set of 8 × 8 photosensors has been placed over a shape. Where the shape reflects no light, the photosensor has been arranged to give a digital 1, so that the output of each row of sensors can be stored as a byte and the complete shape as a set of eight bytes. This set of numbers can then be compared, byte by byte, with a known set to find if the pattern matches.

pause, *n.* a short delay in a program. Also called *time*. The pause may be for a fixed time, or can be interruptable, meaning that pressing a key will end the pause. Some languages incorporate a PAUSE statement, or allow the use of a loop.

PCB, *abbrev. for* printed circuit board, the plastic board that carries the chips and the interconnections of a unit of a computer system. The smaller machines can be constructed on a single board, but larger machines normally use a set of boards with interconnections. See also EDGE CARD, MOTHERBOARD.

P-code, *n.* an intermediate code (or INTERNAL LANGUAGE) which is produced by PASCAL and many other COMPILERS. This code has then to be interpreted, but because of the compiling action, the P-code can be interpreted very rapidly. The benefit of using P-code is that it makes program exchange possible, since widely different machines can produce and work with the same P-code.

PEEK, *n.* a command in BASIC that returns the number that is stored in a selected byte in the memory. The argument of PEEK is the address of the byte in the memory . For example, PEEK(40250) will return the value of the byte that is stored in the address numbered 40250.

peripheral, *n.* a device that is not part of the keyboard-computer-screen system, but is connected to it separately and can exchange signals with it. Typical peripherals are a disk drive, a printer, and possibly a LIGHT PEN or OPTICAL CHARACTER READER. For each peripheral, hardware in the form of PORTS and suitable connectors will be needed. SOFTWARE will also be needed to allow the peripheral to operate. In some case, such as printers and disk drives, the computer's OPERATING SYSTEM will almost certainly contain the necessary software. For less standardized peripherals software on disk or in ROM form must be added.

permanent file, *n.* a file that is not wiped after completing a run. This does not necessarily imply that the file is recorded on disk. Compare SCRATCHFILE.

permanent memory, see NON-VOLATILE MEMORY.

personal computer (PC), *n.* a computer which is used by one person, as distinct from a shared MAINFRAME machine. The distinction is rather like that between the owner-driver of a car, and the user of a pooled chauffeur-driven car. The term PC implies a microcomputer, and at one time was synonymous with 'home computer'. The term PC later came to mean a machine which was primarily for business use, but with the additional facilities that had been pioneered by the home computer manufacturers.

At the time of writing, the term 'home computer' implies a machine which is used mainly for playing games, and 'personal computer' implies a machine for more serious uses which nevertheless can also be used for entertainment.

phoneme, *n.* a sound unit of language. Any spoken word or phrase can be broken up into a set of basic phonemes, and reconstructed by sounding the same phonemes in the correct order and with the correct timing. The analysis of sound into phonemes, and its

PIRACY

reconstruction are important in computer SPEECH SYNTHESIS, and also in DIRECT VOICE INPUT.

photocell, *n.* a device that is sensitive to light, and will generate a voltage or pass electric current when illuminated.

photosensor, *n.* any device which is sensitive to light. See PHOTOCELL.

pico, *n. prefix* denoting one millionth of a millionth, that is, 1E-12 (10^{-12}).

pinchwheel, *n.* the wheel, made of synthetic rubber, which on a CASSETTE recorder holds the tape firmly against the CAPSTAN spindle so that the tape can be moved at a constant speed. Any dirt on this wheel will cause speed error problems such as FLUTTER and WOW.

pinfeed, see SPROCKET FEED.

pipelining, *n.* a method of increasing processing speed. The principle is to reduce the difficulties that are caused by an INPUT BOUND system by having inputs arrive at a time when nothing else is happening. The word applies particularly to the microprocessor action. For many microprocessors, the input of a 2-byte address from memory is a time-wasting process, because nothing can be done until the second byte has been read. In a pipelined processor, TWO-PHASE CLOCK pulses are used, and data is read on one phase of the clock, with all processing being carried out on the other phase. In this way, there is always a byte being read, and 'in the pipeline'.

piracy, *n.* unlawful copying, particularly of software. Because magnetic recording methods are not totally reliable, computers are designed so as to make it easy to prepare backups of software. This, however, means that it is easy to make illegal copies of a program for sale. This has been possible because the law of copyright was formed at a time when magnetic recording was unknown and suitable changes in the law should ensure better copyright protection. Piracy has had the effect of forcing COPY PROTECTION on many software suppliers. This makes their products a poor bargain, because backup copies have to be paid for, and program PATCHING is usually impossible. It is very unsatisfactory to part with a lot of money for a program you

PITCH

can't back up, and which can't be patched to suit your requirements.

pitch, *n.* the effect on the ear of the frequency of a note of sound.

pitch envelope, *n.* a graph shape that shows how the pitch of a note changes with time. Computers which have advanced sound systems allow pitch envelopes to be defined by the programmer. See Fig. 55.

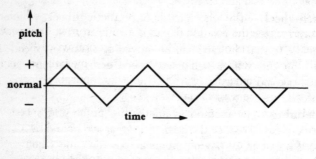

Fig. 55. **Pitch envelope.** This example shows a pitch which alternately rises and falls. An envelope like this provides tremolo on a musical note.

pixel, *n.* a unit of screen display. A pixel is the smallest size of spot on the screen which can be independently controlled by the computer. Many TEXT characters are built out of a 9×7 matrix of pixels, but in HIGH-RESOLUTION GRAPHICS, the machine may not be able to work with such small units. Most modern computers allow the colour of each pixel to be determined.

planning, *n.* the essential stage prior to programming. Professional programmers spend considerably more time in planning than in programming, because time spent in this way is usually less costly than time spent in testing and altering a program. Lack of planning is the main cause of amateurish and inadequate programs. Programming languages such as Pascal require a very high standard of planning before a program can be written, and this makes the language a favourite for academic purposes. BASIC, by contrast, can be written, usually very badly, with little or no planning. It can also be written very well and can produce excellent programs if the planning is carried out to the same standards as for other languages.

platen, *n.* the part of an IMPACT PRINTER which supports the paper at the point where the paper is struck.

player-missile graphics, *n. Trademark.* the Atari version of SPRITES.

PL/1, *n.* a HIGH-LEVEL LANGUAGE, used mainly on large computers for commercial and scientific work.

PL/M, *n.* a reduced version of PL/1.

plot, *vb.* to find the position of a graph point from its coordinates. Several DIALECTS of BASIC use an instruction word PLOT that will light a PIXEL at the position specified by two coordinate numbers. In some dialects, PLOT is a multipurpose instruction that can also be used in drawing lines.

plotter, *n.* a graphics PERIPHERAL that draws lines under computer control. See also PRINTER-PLOTTER, X-Y PLOTTER.

plugboard, *n.* a method of making temporary interconnections, also known as a patchboard. A set of lines to the plugboard ends with each line connected to a socket. By using sets of leads with a plug at each end, any socket on the board can be connected to any other. The system is used mainly for testing peripheral units.

plug-compatible, *n.* the ultimate in computer compatibility. If a peripheral can be plugged into the same socket of the computer as another peripheral, and will work, it is said to be plug-compatible with the other peripheral. Of all peripherals, parallel printers are most likely to be plug-compatible, though on a lot of small computers, joysticks use a standardized plug system.

PMOS, *abbrev. for* p-type metal-oxide semiconductor, a variety of FET construction used for LSI ICs. See also NMOS, CMOS.

pointer, *n.* a number that is stored in memory and which gives the memory ADDRESS of data. A pointer is a DATA TYPE in several languages, including PASCAL and C. Their use is particularly important for LIST handling. See also LINKED LIST.

POKE, *n.* a keyword in BASIC that allows the content of any part of RAM to be changed. The SYNTAX is POKE A,D, where A is an address number and D is a single byte data number, range 0 to 255. If this statement is used carelessly, the RAM may be

POLAR COORDINATES

corrupted, causing a REBOOT or a LOCKUP. See also PROTECTED LOCATION.

polar coordinates, *n.* a system for specifying position which uses the distance from an ORIGIN and the angle measured to a fixed direction. An alternative to CARTESIAN COORDINATES which sometimes is simpler to work with, but is normally more complex. Conversion formulas for Cartesian to polar and polar to Cartesian are available. See Fig. 56.

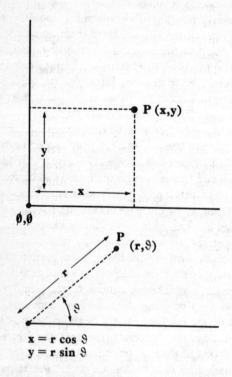

$$x = r \cos \vartheta$$
$$y = r \sin \vartheta$$

Fig. 56. **Polar coordinates.** Polar coordinates and Cartesian coordinates compared. The polar coordinate system uses the distance 'r' from a fixed point, and the angle theta from a fixed direction. The Cartesian coordinates X and Y which correspond to the polar coordinates can be found from the formula.

polling, *n.* the checking of a computer system at intervals. For example, the operating system of a computer may poll the keyboard at intervals while a program is running. This allows the machine to check if the BREAK or ESCAPE key is pressed. The alternative to polling is the use of INTERRUPTS.

POP, *n.* an ASSEMBLY LANGUAGE instruction to remove a byte or bytes from the STACK, and place it in a REGISTER or registers. Also called PULL. For example, the (Z-80) instruction POP AF means that two bytes are to be taken from the stack and placed in the A and F registers.

port, *n.* a circuit, usually in single CHIP form, that is used to connect the signals of the computer to other devices. A port is very often used to connect the keyboard and the screen, and for disk and cassette signals also. The port is usually a very complex chip, second only in complication to the microprocessor itself, and PROGRAMABLE to some extent. See also PARALLEL PORT.

portability, *n.* the ability of a language learned on one computer to be used on any other. The most portable programming languages are the most strictly defined, such as PASCAL.

postformatted, *adj.* of or relating to anything in computing arranged into order during printing. The term is usually applied to word processing commands that format the text at the printer, rather than on the screen.

postprocessor, *n.* **1.** anything that follows a processing run. **2.** a separate MICROPROCESSOR that handles data that has been already processed by another chip. **3.** a program that carries out a second processing of data following an earlier processing run. Compare PREPROCESSOR.

power supply unit (PSU) *n.* the source of DC power for the computer. Computers generally use low-voltage DC supplies, typically of 5V or 12V, and draw currents of up to a few amperes. The power-supply section is designed to provide steady and stable low-voltage supplies, using the mains 240V AC as a source. Small portable machines can use battery power, but if mechanical devices such as disk drives are incorporated, battery life is likely to be short.

power take-off, *n.* a socket on the computer that allows a limited supply of low-voltage power to be used for other units, such as the disk drive. Most systems use separate power supplies for each peripheral.

precision of number, *n.* the extent to which a number can be stored or expressed in exact form. Numbers can be stored as INTEGERS, as BINARY FRACTIONS, or in BCD form. Of these, the integer form is always exact, but of limited range. The BCD form is exact providing that a specified number of decimal places is not exceeded. The binary fraction form which is used on many computers to store floating-point numbers, however, almost always stores numbers in approximate form, called EXPONENT-MANTISSA form. The exceptions are numbers which are powers of 2. The reason is that the floating-point number is stored in the form of a BINARY FRACTION, multiplied by a power of 2. Unless a number happens to be an exact power of 2, its binary fraction form will not terminate, and no matter how many places of binary fraction are used, the stored form will never be exact. The approximations are disguised by ROUNDING when the numbers are displayed, but the numbers are not rounded while they are stored. This can lead to curious results when lines such as:

```
20 A=11:B=33:IF 3*A=B THEN PRINT TRUE ELSE PRINT FALSE
```

are run, because a line of this type can give a FALSE answer because of these approximations.

predeclaration, *n.* the definition of an identifier type before it is used in a program. Many languages, particularly PASCAL, require the use of an IDENTIFIER to follow stringent rules. One rule is that the DATA TYPE of any identifier must be predeclared by a statement such as:

```
Count:INTEGER
```

before any attempt is made to assign a value to the identifier.

preprocessor, *n.* any action carried out on data before processing. Compare POST PROCESSOR.

press any key, *n.* a message that can be printed on the screen when a HOLDING LOOP is being used. The holding loop continues until a key is pressed, and then the computer resumes normal action. Despite the message, pressing some keys may have no effect, and a BREAK or ESCAPE key may allow you to break out of the program completely. Loops of this type in BASIC make use of the GET, INKEY or INKEY$ statements.

pressure pad, *n.* a form of contact switch. A pressure pad will allow electrical contacts to close when pressure is applied to the unit. A form of miniature pressure pad can be used for a rather unsatisfactory type of keyboard. Pressure pads are also used in burglar alarm systems and as limit switches on mechanical devices such as printers.

Prestel, *n. Trademark.* a system operated by British Telecom for obtaining access to a very large database by way of the telephone system. Access can be very expensive unless the Prestel computer is within the local call area, and finding the correct page of the database can be a lengthy and frustrating experience because of the TREE structure. Prestel is just one of the databases which is open to the user of a MODEM. See also MICRONET.

preview, *n.* a word processor facility for a screen display of the text in the same form as it will appear on paper. A preview facility is not so important for word processors of the WYSIWYG type, but is essential for the type of program which, for example, uses 40 characters per line for text entry with maximum clarity.

primer, *n.* an elementary instruction manual. Many computers and peripherals come with a primer and also with a guide suitable for experienced programmers, but nothing of intermediate level. This gap is generally filled by books from independent publishers, who very often also publish more USER-FRIENDLY primers.

printer, *n.* a device that will print text on paper, producing HARD COPY. Very large MAINFRAME computers require fast printers in order to avoid being OUTPUT BOUND, and they will normally use some variety of LINE PRINTER. For smaller machines, the choice is between IMPACT or NON-IMPACT printers. Of the non-impact printers, only the INK-JET and LASER types will be considered for commercial work, though thermal printers are often used as built-in devices in computer-controlled equipment. Among impact printers, the DOT-MATRIX and the DAISYWHEEL variety are the main contenders. The daisywheel is used for the utmost print quality, but the standard of print that is possible on modern dot-matrix printers, combined with their versatility, makes them very useful. See also NLQ, PRINTER-PLOTTER.

printer-plotter, *n.* a form of combined printer and plotter. The mechanism consists of a penholder which can be moved under computer control in a horizontal plane, and a friction drive for paper which allows the paper to be moved in either vertical direction, also under computer control.

The machine is primarily a plotter, allowing diagrams to be drawn by simultaneous movement of both paper and pen. Many printer-plotters can use several pens, allowing coloured lines to be drawn, with the colour also under computer control. In addition, the ROM of the machine often allows ASCII codes to be accepted, causing a character to be 'printed'. The character is, in fact, drawn rather than printed, by movement of pen and paper. In the small sizes, such printer-plotters can be remarkably low-priced, and can provide very useful effects that are almost impossible by other means except at much greater cost.

print formatter, *n.* a program that is normally a part of a word processor. Also called *text formatter.* A print formatter arranges for printing to be carried out with the correct margin position, indentation, words per line, lines per page, HEADER, FOOTERS, etc. It is, in other words, concerned with how a continuous piece of text can be broken up into sections for printing. Some word-processing programs require the print-formatting decisions to be taken before the text is entered, others can leave this step until just before the printer is used. The most satisfactory system allows the print-formatting instructions to be kept like a piece of text on disk and added to the text at any stage.

printhead, *n.* the active portion of a PRINTER that produces the characters on paper.

print modifiers, *n.* instructions or PUNCTUATION MARKS that modify the way that printing is carried out. See MODIFIER.

print pause, *n.* an EMBEDDED COMMAND in a word-processed text that stops the printer, so that a daisywheel or ribbon can be changed.

printwheel, *n.* the printing part of a daisywheel printer. See DAISYWHEEL.

priority, *n.* the order of importance. In a NETWORK a method of assigning priority must be used to avoid clashes when two machines try to use the network together. The operating system of any machine must also determine priorities in the use of memory.

problem-oriented language, *n.* a language that is designed in order to solve a specific type of problem.

procedural language, *n.* a language that requires the programmer to define steps in the solution of a problem. Most of the well-known general programming languages are procedural in nature. An analyst will break the solution of a problem down into a number of steps which can be carried out in sequence. These steps can be programmed as PROCEDURES, and the solution of the problem is therefore carried out by applying these procedures in the correct order. See also LOGICAL LANGUAGE.

procedure, *n.* a set of actions forming part of a program that may be used more than once. A procedure is called into action by using its name, and VARIABLE values can be used by typing the appropriate variable names within brackets. For example, in a PASCAL program, the line:

PRINTOUT (Name,Address,Age)

would call up a procedure called PRINTOUT, which would work with the values of variables Name, Address, and Age. This procedure would have to be defined before being used, but the definition could use variables called A, B, C provided that these were of the same type as Name, Address and Age, and in the same order. See Fig. 57.

When a language permits the use of procedures, the solution of problems with that language is greatly simplified. This is because each procedure can be looked on, and worked on, as a small program in its own right, independent of the other parts of the program. This makes the MODULARIZATION of programs possible,

PROCEDURE

and also the maintenance of procedure LIBRARIES which can be called on if a method requires a procedure that has been written before. See Fig. 57.

BASIC
(BBC micro)

Definition:
```
11000 DEFPROCESSOR (A$)
11010 PRINT' "**"+A$+"**"'''': ("PLEASE TRY AGAIN ...")
11020 ENDPROC
```

Invocation:
```
100 IF N% ‹2 PROCESSOR ("NO COMMA!")
```

Pascal
(Oxford Pascal Compiler)

Definition:
```
PROCEDURE SPC (N:INTEGER);
VAR J; INTEGER;
BEGIN;
FOR J: = 1 TO MAX DO BEGIN
SPACE [J] : =  ;
END;
WRITE (SPACE:N);
END;
```

Invocation:
```
WRITE ('COLUMN 1'); SPC(15);
WRITE ('COLUMN 2')
```

C

Definition:
```
SQUARE (X)
INT X;

RETURN (X*X);
```

Invocation:
```
PRINT F(SQUARE(J);
```

Fig. 57. **Procedures.** In various computing languages, a procedure can be defined and called (invoked) by using the type of syntax that is illustrated here. Parameter values are passed to procedures by enclosing their variable names within brackets. Most languages insist that the data type of each parameter is defined, but this is not necessary in the dialects of BASIC that use procedures.

processor, *n.* the processing unit of a computer, see MICROPROCESSOR.

program, *n.* a set of instructions to a COMPUTER that will be carried out in order when a COMMAND such as RUN is given. See also INTERPRETER, COMPILER, HIGH-LEVEL LANGUAGE, LOW-LEVEL LANGUAGE.

program counter, *n.* in ASSEMBLY LANGUAGE, the REGISTER of the microprocessor that stores the ADDRESS of the byte which is currently being read or written. This register is responsible for addressing memory, and is the way in which the microprocessor can read and write data to and from the correct locations in the memory. A MACHINE CODE program is run simply by placing the address of its first byte into the program counter of the microprocessor.

program crash, *n.* see CRASH.

programmable, *adj.* of or relating to anything capable of being programmed. The microprocessor is a programmable device, hence its use in microcomputers. Some other chips, notably PORTS, SOUND CHIPS and VIDEO INTERFACE chips are also programmable to a lesser extent.

programmable key, *n.* a FUNCTION KEY whose action can be changed by a command or program instruction. Also called SOFT KEY.

programmer, *n.* one who programs a computer. For MAINFRAME computers, the operator will have coded and typed the program, the programmer will have written the program, and the systems analyst will have produced the ALGORITHM. These distinctions are less clear when microcomputers are used, and very often all the work of systems analysis, programming and operation will have been done by one person.

programming language, *n.* any method of writing a program for a computer. A programming language is a way of generating the number codes which can be interpreted by the OPERATING SYSTEM, or fed directly to the microprocessor so as to cause a program to run. In general, the use of a programming language implies typing instructions which are in order or which can be put into order. Languages are classed as LOW-LEVEL or HIGH-

PROLOG

LEVEL. See also MACHINE CODE, ASSEMBLER, ASSEMBLY LANGUAGE, BASIC, PASCAL, INTERPRETER, COMPILER, PROCEDURAL LANGUAGE, LOGICAL LANGUAGE.

PROLOG, *n.* a high-level programming LOGICAL language. The language is a derivative of LISP, and is the preferred language for FIFTH GENERATION machines.

PROM, *n. acronym for* Programmable Read-Only Memory, a chip that will retain data, but which can be written on and erased by suitable circuits. The erasable version should really be entitled EPROM, but 'PROM' is now used for either variety. A PROM is a very useful way of putting a program into permanent form without making it completely impossible to change. A computer which allows for insertion of PROM chips to replace or supplement a ROM is very much more adaptable than one which does not possess this facility.

prompt, *n.* a message on the screen for the benefit of the operator, usually a reminder that some action is needed. A prompt can also take the form of a BEEP. For business programs in which all of the output is to the printer, the screen will normally be used only for prompts and for input ECHO CHECK.

proportional spacing, *n.* a system used on a printer that allocates different sized spaces between letters, as distinct from the fixed space size that a typewriter uses. This produces better-looking copy, but the system is not easy to use with word processing programs, because so few WP programs cater well for the use of proportional spacing.

protected location, *n.* a piece of memory that cannot normally be used. For example, the OPERATING SYSTEM must make some use of RAM during the time when a program is running. This part of RAM must be protected against an OVERWRITE, because any CORRUPTION of the data stored in it would cause the program to CRASH. The part of memory that is used is protected by software methods, by placing the address of the start of the protected area in memory, and forcing the computer to check at each memory-storage step that none of the protected addresses is being used. This protection system operates normally for any HIGH-LEVEL LANGUAGE, but can be circumvented by the use of a LOW-LEVEL

LANGUAGE. This is why the use of a machine-code program so often causes a system crash.

protection, *n.* a system that is designed to make a tape or disk secure from copying. See COPY PROTECTION.

protocol, *n.* a set of computing rules. The term is usually applied to SERIAL transmission of data, which requires the receiver to be set up in exactly the same way as the transmitter. For example, a transmission might use the protocols of 7-bit code, no PARITY, one START BIT and two STOP BITS, 1800 BAUD. This set of protocols would have to be obeyed by the receiver also. The need for protocols in serial printer use makes serial printers much more difficult to use for a range of different computers than parallel printers.

pseudo-operation, *n.* an ASSEMBLER command. In ASSEMBLY LANGUAGE, instructions to the assembler program can be included along with the actual assembly language. These instructions are called pseudo-operations, because their form is the same as the form of the genuine assembly language instructions. The pseudo-operations are, however, peculiar to the assembler, not to the microprocessor. See also ORG.

pseudo-random, *adj.* (of numbers) appearing to be RANDOM, but actually patterned. The computer can generate numbers which appear to be random numbers. Because everything in a computer is programmed, however, these numbers do not satisfy strict statistical tests of randomness, and are described as being pseudo-random.

PSU, see POWER SUPPLY UNIT.

PULL, see POP.

punch, *n.* a device for putting holes in paper tape or in a card. See PAPER TAPE.

punched card, *n.* a way of storing computer data. A thick paper card is coded with data by using punched holes, with each hole in one of twelve possible positions. The cards are of standardized shape, size and thickness, and the holes can be punched in each of 80 columns, so allowing 80 bytes of data (80 characters) to be stored on each card. The advantage of this system is standardization – any computer which is fitted with a punched-card reader can read a card produced by any other card, providing that the data is in ASCII codes only. The system is clumsy and bulky, however, and is seldom used nowadays, because a very large number of cards are need to hold even a small amount of data.

punctuation marks, *n.* the marks such as COMMA, SEMICOLON, full stop and others which are used for punctuating NATURAL LANGUAGE. In computing languages these marks are used as SEPARATORS or MODIFIERS.

PUSH, *n.* in assembly language, the command which causes address or data numbers to be stored temporarily on the STACK. For example, the (Z-80) mnemonic PUSH AF means that the contents of the A and F registers are to be stored on the stack. See also POP.

pushdown list, *n.* a list in which the last item that was added is at the top of the list. This is a form of LIFO memory.

pushup list, *n.* a list in which the last item added is at the bottom of the list. This corresponds to the operation of a STACK.

Q

quad density, *n.* the highest density of disk recording, equal to four times normal density.

queue, *n.* a set of instructions awaiting execution, usually in computers which have a SOUND system. The execution of sound instructions is carried out by a separate chip which takes the sound instructions from memory and processes each in turn. Because a sound instruction might create a sound that lasted for a second or more, it would be undesirable to hold up the normal action of the computer while a sound was in progress. The sound chip can therefore deal with (typically) five instructions in a 'queue'. Of these, one will be in course of execution, and the other four are stored in the sound queue waiting to be executed.

Unless an extra sound instruction is issued, which would be unable to enter the queue, the normal processing action can continue, because the main processor simply places the data in the sound queue but does not carry out the subsequent processing on them. Special arrangements have to be made if you need to synchronize a sound with, perhaps, a screen action.

quicksort, *n.* an ALGORITHM for rapid data sorting. The quicksort is one of many methods of arranging number data into number order, or text data into alphabetical order. Like all of the rapid methods, the algorithm operates on a list, and compares items which are at different places, not adjacent, in the list. This type of sort is advantageous only when the number of items in the list is fairly large, i.e. several hundred or more. See also SHELL SORT, BUBBLE SORT.

quotes, see INVERTED COMMAS .

QWERTY keyboard, *n.* a keyboard laid out in conventional typewriter style, with the top line consisting of the QWER-TYUIOP keys. This layout was devised in the 1880s to ensure that typists could not type too fast for the machines. Various attempts to produce a better layout (DVORAK, MALTRON) have had little effect because the QWERTY layout is so widely used and entrenched. This is often quoted as a warning of the dangers of standardizing anything at an early stage in technical development.

R

RAM, *n. acronym for* Random Access Memory. In the early days of microcomputing, some memory systems operated in SERIAL form, with data being put in at one end and eventually emerging from the other. It was then impossible to gain access to a given piece of data without reading all of the rest of the stored data that had been recorded earlier, and the readout was generally DESTRUCTIVE.

Random access implies that any part of the memory can be read or written, and this is the only type of memory that is nowadays used for reading and writing. The readout is nondestructive, but the memory is usually VOLATILE, so that any data that must remain stored after switching off must be retained in a BACKING STORE, which is usually a disk system. One variety of RAM, CMOS, allows data to be retained providing a low-voltage battery is connected. The drain on the battery is very small, and data can be stored for several years in this way until rewritten. See also DYNAMIC and STATIC RAM.

random, *adj.* (of numbers) having no pattern, such as the numbers obtained from throwing unbiased dice. A set of truly random numbers will not favour any particular number or set of numbers, and no sequence will be repeated. If a large set of truly random numbers is generated, using a fixed range, like 1 to 10, then each number in the range should be picked an equal number of times. A truly random choice like this is very difficult to arrange. Compare PSEUDO-RANDOM.

random-access file, *n.* a method of storing files on disk so that any one RECORD can be read, written or changed without having to read or rewrite all of the others. This is done by allocating equal amounts of space to each record, and is possible only if the disk OPERATING SYSTEM allows some way of specifying at what part of the disk a set of items can be stored. This can always be done using MACHINE CODE, but is not always available in HIGH-LEVEL LANGUAGES. Random-access filing cannot be carried out in any real sense with cassette systems, nor with endless-loop (FLOPPY TAPE) systems. See also FIXED FIELD.

random access memory, see RAM.

range left, *vb.* to align text at the left-hand side of a page. See LEFT-JUSTIFICATION.

raster, *n.* the pattern of lines on a blank TV screen. The action which produces a picture on a cathode ray tube CRT is called *scanning*. The electron beam sweeps across the face of the tube, starting at the top left-hand corner. At the same time, the electron beam is being deflected downwards at a much lower rate, so that when the beam has swept or scanned from left to right, it will be slightly further down the tube face when it returns (in the FLYBACK) to the left-hand side. At the end of a complete FRAME, every part of the screen has been covered with this pattern of horizontal parallel lines. See Fig. 58.

The FRAME consists of two interlocking FIELDS where a TV receiver is concerned, with each field consisting of lines at double the normal spacing. This is done in order to economize in the rate at which video information must be fed to the receiver, and is not essential for a MONITOR, though most monitors adhere to TV picture standards. Normally, the line structure is invisible, because the electron beam is cut off or at a very low current during scanning. The picture is created by increasing the beam current, so making part of the screen surface bright, at various places in the scan. If no picture (VIDEO) information is used to brighten the beam, the screen remains dark. The pattern of lines is known as the 'raster', and it can be made visible by advancing the brightness control of the TV receiver or monitor. Making the raster visible is one way of checking for the presence of JITTER.

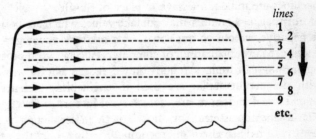

1st field (odd-numbered lines) takes 0.02 seconds.
2nd field (even-numbered lines) takes 0.02 seconds.
Hence 1 frame takes 0.04 seconds.

Fig. 58. **Raster.** The TV picture is produced by a spot of light which sweeps across and down the screen, tracing a set of parallel lines. One complete frame of the picture is produced in 0.04 second by two fields of interlaced lines.

raw data, *n.* data that has not been processed in any way. This generally refers to data as it has been entered at the keyboard, or obtained from DIGITIZERS or other input devices. Some programs are arranged so that raw data is recorded for later processing. This is particularly necessary if the amount of the data is likely to be more than the memory of the computer can hold. The recording of raw data is also useful in the event of a CRASH shutting down the system, because it avoids the necessity of entering all of the data again.

reader, *n.* a device that can convert data from paper tape or cards into electrical signals.

readout, *n.* the display of data on the screen. Also called *soft copy* as distinct from paper output, which is HARD COPY. To be legible, a readout should be paged (see PAGE), with the paging controlled by pressing a key.

read/write, *vb.* to allow data to be stored (written) or replayed (read).

read/write head, *n.* the magnetic head of a tape or disk recorder. See READ/WRITE, RAM.

READY, *n.* a screen message used in many OPERATING SYSTEMS to indicate that the machine is ready for programming. A few machines use the O.K. message in place of READY.

real number, *n.* a number that can take values which are positive or negative, whole or fractional, or a mixture of integer and fraction. Many applications of computers (such as word processing or GRAPHICS displays) require only INTEGERS, but for working with the numbers that are used in engineering, science or finance, real numbers are necessary. Most HIGH-LEVEL LANGUAGES include a 'real' or 'float' DATA TYPE, though a few SUBSETS of languages for microcomputers allow only the use of integers. A real number is stored in the form of a BINARY FRACTION, which can cause APPROXIMATION ERRORS. See also FLOATING POINT, PRECISION OF NUMBER.

real-time processing, *n.* computer processing 'as it happens'. Computing can be carried out on data that has been gathered in the past, like working with census data, or it may be required on data which is being typed at that moment, like hotel reservation requests. When the computer is working with data that is being typed or otherwise freshly input, and is expected to process that data and give a rapid reply, then the computer is said to be working in 'real time'. Compare BATCH PROCESSING.

reboot, *vb.* to start again as if just switched on (see BOOT). In a reboot, the computer starts afresh, which usually implies loss of data, and usually also loss of program unless the program is in ROM form. If the computer keeps its PROGRAMMING LANGUAGE on disk, a reboot will cause the language to be lost as well. Every effort must be taken in the design of a program to prevent accidental rebooting, particularly if this can take place when one key (a BREAK key) or a particular combination of keys is pressed. It is very unusual to encounter a reboot when a ROM-based operating system is used, and with an interpreted language like BASIC. A program which resists rebooting is known as 'robust' (see ROBUSTNESS).

receive, *vb.* to accept data from an external source, usually a remote source.

receive-only (RO) terminal, *n.* a TERMINAL that cannot transmit messages. In this sense, the domestic TV receiver is a receive-only terminal.

recognition logic, *n.* software for use with an OPTICAL CHARAC-TER READER.

record, 1. *n.* a unit of a FILE. A file consists of a collection of records which are themselves made up of FIELDS. For example, in a file of names and addresses, one record would consist of the name and address of one person. Several HIGH-LEVEL LANGUAGES treat a record as a DATA TYPE, so that a file consists of an ARRAY or a LINKED LIST of records. BASIC has no such data type, and records in BASIC have to be created by combining fields into a STRING, using a string array to form the file. See Fig. 59 on page 218. **2.** *vb.* to save data on tape or on disk. The word SAVE is more commonly used for computer data.

record gap, see BLOCK GAP.

recording density, *n.* the number of data bits recorded per linear inch of recording medium. See DOUBLE DENSITY, QUAD DENSITY, BPI.

RECOVERY SYSTEM

```
TYPE GOLFCLUB = RECORD                          ①
NAME: PACKED ARRAY [1 . . 2Ø] OF CHAR;
ADDRESS: PACKED ARRAY [1 . . 4Ø] OF CHAR;
BIRTHYEAR, JOINYEAR, ACAP: INTEGER;             ②
SUBSCRIP: REAL;
PAID: BOOLEAN;
END                                             ③
```

① definition

② items in record

③ end of record

Fig. 59. **Record.** This data type does not exist in BASIC and the example uses Pascal. The name of the record is defined, and this is followed by the definition of the items that will make up each record in a file.

recovery system, *n.* a method of CRASH investigation, a program, used mainly in mainframes, which keeps records of steps in a main program, so that in the event of a crash, the cause can be traced.

recursion, *n.* the action of a routine calling itself. Not all languages support recursion, because to be implemented correctly it requires the use of named PROCEDURES which can pass PARAMETERS to be implemented easily. Recursion is usually illustrated by mathematical routines that are seldom required, and the effects can always be programmed in other ways. For a few types of problem, however, recursion provides a solution which is neater and simpler than could be obtained in any other way.

redefine key, *vb.* to alter the action of a PROGRAMMABLE key so as to provide some desired action when it is pressed.

Redo from start, *n.* a useful message provided by some BASIC interpreters. In BASIC, an INPUT may call for a number to be entered. If a STRING quantity is entered, the 'Redo from start' message indicates that this entry is unacceptable, and a number should then be entered. It does *not* mean that the program has to be run again! Many interpreters, however, simply stop if an unacceptable entry is made, treating this as a FATAL ERROR. This can be avoided if all entry of data is to a string variable.

redundancy, *n.* the provision of excess capacity in a computer system. The use of 'redundancy' means that a system is organized so that at least two units are always available to carry out any task. In the event of failure or non-availability of one unit, the other can take over. Redundancy in a transmitted message applies to characters that can be omitted without losing the meaning of the message. Redundancy is an important topic in SPEECH SYNTHESIS, visual recognition, and AI.

redundant code, *n.* a method of error checking, see PARITY.

reformat, *vb.* to repeat the magnetic 'marking out' of a disk. This totally removes any data that was stored on the disk, and rechecks the material for DROPOUTS and other failures. Old disks should have their data backed up so that they can be reformatted at intervals. See also FORMAT.

refresh CRT, *vb.* to maintain a display of data on the screen. A cathode-ray tube (CRT) display exhibits a picture that is built up from a line pattern by brightening the beam at selected places. This picture is transient, because the glowing material (the phosphor) on the tube face glows only for a very short time after the electron beam has struck it. The process must be repeated at a rate of 25 times per second if the picture is to be shown continuously. This action is termed refreshing, and is part of the task of the VIDEO INTERFACE CHIP, or whatever circuits are used to carry out the task of controlling the video display. The earlier types of LCD screens also required refreshing, so that large displays suffered from FLICKER. Later types used LCD systems that required no refreshing.

refresh memory signal, *n.* a signal that is applied to DYNAMIC MEMORY chips to prevent loss of data. Several types of microprocessors can provide such refresh signals automatically to all of the memory that is connected to the chip.

register, 1. *n.* a form of RAM storage that is built into a MICROPROCESSOR. The registers of the microprocessor can be interconnected to allow data to be copied from one to another, and actions such as arithmetic and logic can be carried out in place of copying if needed. All of the actions of a computer depend on these few simple steps, which are PROGRAMMABLE. The internal connections between registers are made by electronic switches, controlled by the MICROPROGRAM. **2.** *vb.* to put the three colour images (red, green, blue) into alignment in, for example, colour printing or a colour TV tube.

relational database, *n.* a collection of data in which items are related in some way. The database program must take account of the relationships in the way that it operates by, for example, constructing LINKED LISTS or using HASHING codes that allow related items to be called up quickly in succession. You might, for example, call up data on a book title, and then be able to find other titles by the same author.

relational operator, *n.* a comparison symbol. i.e. the mathematical signs such as $=$, $>$, $<$, which are used to establish or test relationships between quantities.

relative addressing, *n.* a memory ADDRESSING METHOD that is used in ASSEMBLY LANGUAGE to denote a form of addressing in which a number is added to the contents of a REGISTER, usually the PC (program counter) register. Programs which make extensive use of this type of addressing are capable of RELOCATION, which means that they can be placed anywhere in the memory and will run without correction. Programs which use ABSOLUTE ADDRESSING are not so easily relocated, because each absolute address may have to be changed when the program runs in a new set of addresses.

relative coordinates, *n.* a set of coordinates that uses the current position of the CURSOR as an ORIGIN, rather than having a fixed origin at one place (such as the bottom left-hand corner). This can be very useful for GRAPHICS, and several DIALECTS of BASIC use graphics commands which exist both in absolute and in relative forms, such as DRAW and DRAWR.

release, *n.* a portion of a sound ENVELOPE. In the release section of the envelope, the sound AMPLITUDE dies away to zero.

relocation, *n.* the shifting of a program or other data from one set of memory ADDRESSES to another. Most computers allow a BASIC program to be loaded in at various different addresses, because the program consists of a LINKED LIST, but the term 'relocation' is usually applied to MACHINE CODE programs. Some machine-code programs cannot be easily relocated, because they contain address numbers which refer to the former position in memory. See also RELATIVE ADDRESSING, BLOCK TRANSFER.

relocator, *n.* a program used in relocation. This program loads the MACHINE CODE into memory starting at any of a range of selected ADDRESSES. It then corrects each address in the program which refers to another address within the program, so that the program can run. This applies mainly to ABSOLUTE ADDRESSING, and to CALL instructions. Once the program has run, the machine code can be used in its new range of addresses. The relocator program can be written in any suitable language.

REM, *n.* a STATEMENT in BASIC that is used to mark a reminder line. REMs are very useful as a guide to how a program is constructed, but their presence makes the INTERPRETER run more slowly. For this reason, many programmers who use interpreted BASIC will keep two versions of each program. The archive copy uses REM lines to maintain a set of notes on the actions of the program, but the working copy has been stripped of these lines, and also of any redundant spaces. In this way, the working copy runs fast, and the archive copy is used if any changes are needed to generate a new working copy

remote control, *n.* any device that allows something in computing to be operated at a distance, usually without connecting wires. Remote controls for TV receivers use either ultrasonic or infrared signals. A few computers use remote-control keyboards which are linked to the main processor by infrared signals. Similarly, a MOUSE can be linked to the main system in this way, because the ability to control a mouse free of connecting cables is much more important than being able to move a keyboard around while typing.

renumber, *vb.* to reallocate the line numbers in a program, usually a BASIC program. This is very useful if EDIT actions have left the program with inserted LINE NUMBERS or has resulted in line deletions.

REPEAT, *n.* the starting word for a form of LOOP which is used

REPERTOIRE

in most HIGH-LEVEL LANGUAGES, such as Pascal, and also in some varieties of BASIC. Unlike the FOR type of loop, the REPEAT loop does not depend on a number counter, and the loop runs until the result of a test of a number or character is true. The end of the loop is usually marked by the word UNTIL, and the test which will stop the loop is made following UNTIL. This implies that the loop will always run at least once, even if the condition for repeating is not true. For a loop that is tested at the start, see WHILE.

repertoire, *n.* **1.** the list of actions that can be carried out by a system. This list will be shown in a MENU for a program. **2.** see INSTRUCTION SET.

report program, *n.* a form of UTILITY that prints out information on a data file. This is usually quicker than any method that makes use of the main database handling program.

rerun, *n.* a repeat of a program run. A 'rerun' is usually carried out to check data, or to test for a fault in the program.

rerun point, *n.* a place in a program from which the run may be continued following a CRASH or FATAL ERROR. This is particularly easy when an interpreted BASIC program is used, because any line number can be used to locate a rerun point, as for example by using a command such as GOTO 1000. If a listing of the program is available, the user can decide which line to use as a rerun point. In general, a rerun should take place from a point which follows the point of the crash, otherwise the crash may be repeated. A rerun should not start in the middle of a SUBROUTINE or PROCEDURE.

Programs written in compiled languages (see COMPILE) can also use rerun points, but these are located by using ADDRESSES in the memory which need to be noted. In general, this is not information that will be available from a listing of the SOURCE CODE, and only a skilled programmer is likely to be able to find a suitable rerun point. Some compilers list the start addresses of each procedure in a program as an aid to looking for suitable rerun points.

rescue dump, *n.* a recording of data on to a disk when a CRASH occurs. If this can be programmed to take place automatically, then a crash of any type will not result in the loss of data. Large machines are often organized so that a rescue dump will be carried out if the main power supply fails or if the machine is switched off during operation.

reserved sector, *n.* a SECTOR of a disk which is used for HOUSEKEEPING purposes, such as the disk DIRECTORY. The disk-operating system (DOS) will maintain such sectors, often located on the first track, or first pair of tracks on the disk. Some operating systems, however, locate these sectors on central tracks on the grounds that this provides, on average, a shorter distance for the head to move from any other track. Programs which make direct use of the disk system (using MACHINE CODE) can designate their own reserved sectors.

reserved word, *n.* a word which is used in a PROGRAMMING LANGUAGE with a fixed meaning, and which cannot therefore be used as a variable name (IDENTIFIER) or FILENAME. Also called *instruction word, keyword.* The specification of any language must include a list of all of its reserved words, along with the SYNTAX for the use of each word. For a language such as BASIC, the list of reserved words is a good indication of the COMPUTING POWER that the language allows. For other languages, this is not necessarily true, and a better guide may be the standard LIBRARY procedures that are supplied with the language.

reset, *vb.* **1.** to restore anything in computing to its original state. **2.** In machine code, to change a bit from 1 to 0. **3.** to put the machine system into its normal or DEFAULT configuration. This can result in loss of data from a program, particularly if the machine is one in which the screen uses memory taken from the main block of RAM.

RESET, *n.* a graphics or filing statement. The term is used in BASIC to mean that a pixel is to be changed to background colour, thus made invisible. In Pascal and several other languages, it means that a file is to be prepared for reading by finding the address of the first item of the file.

resident, *adj.* of or relating to anything always present in computing memory as distinct from having to be loaded in from tape or disk. For example, a machine may be described as having a 'resident' BASIC. It is unusual to find any other language resident, and many machines require any language to be loaded from disk. See also LOADER, CLEAN MACHINE.

resident integer variables, *n.* variable type used in the BBC micro. These variables, A% to Z%, retain their values when another program is chained (see CHAIN) in, allowing a limited capability for passing PARAMETERS from one program to another.

resident software, *n.* software that is held permanently in memory. This may be in ROM, or in CMOS RAM, or any other NON-VOLATILE MEMORY which is permanently connected to the machine. Software which is usually resident includes the OPERATING SYSTEM and possibly a HIGH-LEVEL LANGUAGE.

resolution, *n.* a measure of the fineness of detail that can be seen on a screen. Often quoted in terms of the number of PIXELS that can be controlled. These are specified in two numbers, of which one represents the number across the screen and the other is the number down the screen. For example, 320 across by 200 down represents a fairly high resolution. This figure means that a total of 320×200=64,000 pixels can be controlled. If a two-colour system (foreground and background) is used, one bit will be needed to control each pixel, and with 8 bits per byte, this will require 8,000 bytes of memory. See Fig. 60.

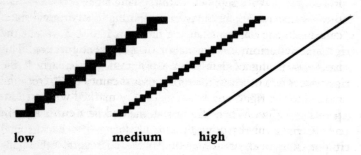

low   medium   high

Fig. 60. **Resolution.** A good test of resolution is to draw a diagonal line. Low-resolution displays or modes make a diagonal line look like a set of overlapping bricks, and only very high-resolution displays produce a line which does not look noticeably jagged.

response time, *n.* the time that is needed for a system to respond to some stimulus. Normally used of systems that include a mechanical action, because the response times for electronic systems are very rapid.

retrieval, *n.* the recovery, usually of data, from storage.

RET, *n.* an assembly language MNEMONIC for return from a machine-code ROUTINE.

RETURN, *n.* key or BASIC instruction. The key that is marked RETURN, or marked with a bent arrow, is used to terminate any DIRECT COMMAND, or to enter typed data. The RESERVED WORD RETURN is used in BASIC to terminate a SUBROUTINE.

rewind, *vb.* to wind a tape back to its start.

reverse polish notation (RPN), *n.* a system of arranging instructions and data in which the data is listed first. In a calculator which uses the RPN system, for example, the more familiar command sequence of 3×2= would be replaced by 3 2×. See also INTERNAL LANGUAGE, FORTH.

reverse video, see INVERSE VIDEO.

RF modulator, see MODULATOR.

RGB, *n.* a colour VIDEO signal system. Three colour video signals are used, corresponding to the three colours that are generated in the CRT. Computers and monitors that can operate with the RGB system will be capable of much higher RESOLUTION than those which use COMPOSITE VIDEO, in which the signals have been coded into one single signal.

right-justification, *n.* the arrangement of text so that the right-hand edge is aligned. See also JUSTIFY.

right-shift, *n.* a CURSOR-CONTROL KEY that causes the cursor to be moved to the right, and which is usually marked with a right-pointing arrow. When this key is omitted, the cursor can be moved right only by using the SPACEBAR.

ring, see CIRCULAR FILE, CAMBRIDGE RING.

ring-back system, *n.* a method of contacting a remote computer. This method is used by some BULLETIN BOARDS, and also for enforcing security. Taking the example of a bulletin board, you first ring the number and let it ring twice. You then hang up the telephone, prepare the MODEM and ring again. This time, you will get the tone that indicates that a computer is on line. This system is used in particular by a number of part-time BB operators so as to distinguish calls that need to access the BB from ordinary telephone calls on the same number. When used as a security method, it is the remote computer operator who rings back a number that has been supplied by the originator of the call. This discourages HACKERS, unless the hacker has managed to reroute calls through another number. See also PASSWORD.

RO, see RECEIVE-ONLY TERMINAL.

robot, *n.* any device that can be programmed, possesses some sensing functions, and which carries out mechanical actions.

robotics, *n.* the study of robot systems, incorporating many of the systems which are also of interest in AI.

robustness, *n.* a measure of the ability of a program or a system to resist a CRASH. A 'robust' program is one that you can use with confidence, knowing that if your little finger accidentally brushes against the BREAK or ESCAPE key, you won't lose either the program or your data. A robust program is particularly important for use with inexperienced operators, and for educational uses. The most robust programs require that the operating system, the programmming language, and possibly the program itself be in ROM form.

role indicator, *n.* a specialized code in data retrieval for the type of data that is to be recovered, allowing the data to be recovered selectively.

ROM, *n. acronym for* Read-Only Memory, a type of memory chip whose contents cannot be altered by writing data, nor by switching-off power. ROM is used for storing LOADERS and OPERATING SYSTEMS so that the system is available at the instant when the machine is switched on. The advantage of using ROM is that its contents are incorruptible; the disadvantage is that any errors cannot be changed except by plugging in a new ROM. See also MASKED ROM, PROM.

rotation, *n.* a microprocessor REGISTER action. In ASSEMBLY LANGUAGE the term denotes the shifting of data in a register, with the ends of the register connected so that no bits are lost, nor any new bits entered. Rotation is also often used in MACHINE CODE programs as a way of testing the bits in a byte, and also in programs that carry out multiplication or division. See Fig. 61.

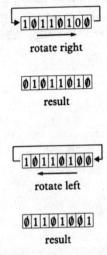

rotate right

result

rotate left

result

Fig. 61. **Rotation.** The rotation action in a register. The rotation consists of shifting all the bits by one place, but with the ends of the register connected so that bits can be transferred between the msb and the lsb. Most microprocessors include the carry bit of the status register as part of the accumulator when this type of action is executed. Various forms of rotation can be specified, of which the main types are left or right.

rounding, *n.* the adjusting of a number to a value that contains fewer places of decimals. This is done by adding or subtracting a very small fraction. For example, 4.9999999 can be rounded to 5.0 or 4.000000001 to 4.0. Rounding has to be carried out automatically when a REAL NUMBER has been stored, because such storage is always in an approximate form. Any test that has to be carried out on a real number should be preceded by rounding. See also PRECISION OF NUMBER.

routine, *n.* a part of a program that carries out some complete action. A complete program can be built up from a number of linked but separate routines, in which case the program is said to be modular (see MODULARIZATION). The word SUBROUTINE usually implies that the routine is carried out more than once. A PROCEDURE is a form of routine which is called into action by using its name, and therefore behaves as a program in its own right. Many HIGH-LEVEL LANGUAGES (C in particular) rely on collections of such routines on disk (the LIBRARY) to supplement the RESERVED WORDS of the language.

rows and columns, *n.* an arrangement of text displayed on the screen. The row number is the number of the line of text, starting from the top of the screen. The column number indicates the position of a character along from the left-hand side of the screen. Similar numbering is used for GRAPHICS, but the row number is then usually called the Y-COORDINATE, and the column number the X-COORDINATE. For graphics, some computers use Y-coordinates starting at the bottom of the screen (like a conventional graph), and others use a starting position at the top of the screen.

RS–232, *n.* the system that is used for SERIAL transmission of data. The connections and signals are standardized, but few manufacturers of the smaller computers pay much attention to the standards, with the result that few microcomputing RS-232 devices can be connected with any degree of confidence. The RS–232 signal consists of a start bit which is used to signal the start of a byte of data. This is followed by 7 or 8 bits of data, then by 1 or 2 stop bits. If only ASCII codes are used for data, with no PARITY checking, then 7 data bits can be used. The precise number of bits of data and of stop bits forms part of the PROTOCOL for the transmission. See Fig. 62. See also BAUD RATE.

rubber banding, SEE ELASTIC BANDING.

rule, *n.* a scale marked with character positions for WORD PROCESSING. Also called *ruler.* The scale shows the position of each character in a line, and is normally displayed at the top of the screen. Some WP programs allow a selection of rules, with each one used to display different information about the text as well as indicating positions.

run, 1. *n.* one complete execution of a program. **2.** *vb.* to command execution of a program.

RUN, *n.* a command in BASIC and other high–level languages that causes a program to be executed.

running head, *n.* a term in word processing to denote a line of title which is placed at the top of each page of a document. This might, for example, show such data as the page number, chapter number, document title, and possibly the author's name.

R/W video disc, *n.* a proposed form of COMPACT DISC that can be written by the computer as well as read by it. At the time of writing, all commercially available discs of this type were read-only. The attraction of the system lies in the enormous memory capacity of such a disc, measured in megabytes.

Pin Signal	Standard rates (Baud)
1 Ground	75
2 Data out	110
3 Data in	150
6 Data in ready	200
7 Ground	300
8 Data in detect	600
11 Reverse channel	1,200
20 Data ready out	1,800
17 ⎫ Ready/busy	2,400
24 ⎭	4,800
25 serial current loop	9,600
23 signals	19,200

Sequence of signals
Start bit
7 ASCII code bits
Parity bit (if any)
2 Stop bits

= 11 bits transmitted
per byte

Fig. 62. **RS-232.** The RS-232 standards. The 25-pin standard connector is normally specified, but few applications use more than 7 pins, hence the new proposed DiN plug standard. Each byte is transmitted one bit at a time, with a precise interval between bits. A start bit is sent to mark the start of a byte, and 2 (usually) stop bits to mark the end of a byte. The standard rates vary from a very slow 75 baud, used for old mechanical teleprinters, to the very fast 19,200 baud for terminals.

S

SAM, see SERIAL ACCESS MEMORY.

safety net, *n.* an emergency provision. This usually denotes a system that will save data in the event of a system CRASH. See also RESCUE DUMP, RECOVERY SYSTEM, RERUN POINT.

sampling rate, *n.* the rate of digitizing information (see DIGITIZE) by measuring the AMPLITUDE, or other characteristic of a signal, in times per second . Each measurement is converted into BINARY number form, and this comprises the digitized data.

SAVE, *n.* a COMMAND in BASIC that will cause a program to be recorded on disk or tape. Some languages use PUT instead of SAVE. Compiled languages (see COMPILE) require two forms of this command, one for the text file, or SOURCE CODE, and the other for the compiled MACHINE CODE, or OBJECT CODE.

scan, *vb.* to check each item of data to find if it belongs to a set that is to be accessed. See also RASTER.

scanner, *n.* a device that provides electrical signals from text or graphics characters on paper. Normally used to imply TV signals, though not necessarily at normal speed. The phrase 'flying-spot scanner' is used of a TV signal generator of this type.

scrambling, *n.* the encoding of data so that it is difficult for an unauthorized person to decode. The term originally denoted sound signals, in which frequency ranges were inverted so as to make the sounds unintelligible, and now usually denotes methods of coding and regrouping data bits into unintelligible bytes.

scratch, *vb.* to wipe out anything. The term is used in the disk systems of machines to mean deletion of a file.

scratchpad, see NOTEBOOK.

scratchfile, *n.* a temporary file on disk. This will often be deleted after use, or by the recording of the next scratchfile. In Pascal, TEXTFILES are often of this type. Compare PERMANENT FILE.

screen, *n.* the viewed surface of a cathode-ray tube (CRT) or LCD unit that displays text and graphics.

screen editing, *n.* an editing system that allows you to alter anything that you can see on the screen. See EDIT.

screen memory, *n.* memory that is used to store data for the screen display. On some computers, this is separate from the main RAM of the computer, on others it can take up varying quantities of the main RAM, leaving little room for programs. When the main RAM is used, a change of screen MODE can cause loss of data because of the reallocation of memory.

scroll, *vb.* to shift lines of text up the screen, so that a new line always appears at the foot. When the screen is clear, printing instructions will normally place text on the top line of the screen, taking a new line down as each line fills. When the screen is filled with text, the scroll action moves each line up the screen, so that the top line is lost, and the most recent line appears at the bottom.

Some computers allow this scroll action to be controlled easily by the programmer, and a few provide for inverse scrolling, so that lines of text scrolled out of sight can be recovered. Very rapid text printing, along with the scrolling action, can make text unreadable, so that paging is needed (see PAGE).

search, *vb.* to look through text for a given letter, word or phrase (see SEARCH AND REPLACE) or (in programming) to check a list of data items to find an item that corresponds to a description. See also SORT.

search and replace, *n.* an action, common in TEXT EDITORS and WORD PROCESSORS, that allows a letter, word or phrase to be found in a text and replaced with something else. This has to be used with care – it's easy to command that each 'smith' should be replaced by 'jones', but when you find words like 'blackjones' appearing you realise that the computer carries out these actions in a completely unthinking way. Most word processors allow the action to be *global* or *selective*. A global search and replace will find each occurrence of a word and replace it by the specified word. A selective search and replace will find each occurrence as

SECTOR

before, but prompt the user to make a Yes or No decision on replacement.

sector, *n.* a portion of a disk TRACK. A disk track is a circle on the disk surface, and the circle is magnetically divided into a number of sectors, often ten sectors per track. Sometimes called *segment*. Each sector will then store a set number of bytes, often 256. Programs or items of data that need less than a sector will nevertheless use the complete sector, because the disk system does not work in units of less than one sector. See Fig. 63.

sectoring hole, *n.* a method of locating a sector. The sectoring hole is a small-diameter hole that is punched in the disk and also in the jacket. This hole is located at a distance from the HUB which is clear of the innermost track on the disk. As the disk rotates, these holes will line up at some point. By passing a beam of light through the hole, detected by a PHOTOCELL, the drive can sense the position of this hole, and establish the position of the start of a sector. Disks which are hard-sectored require one hole in the disk for each sector. Disks which are soft-sectored use one hole in the disk, and the remaining sectors are established by recording codes onto the tracks. See SOFT SECTORING, HARD SECTORING.

segment, *n.* a portion of a circle. See also SECTOR.

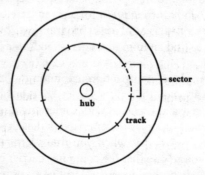

Fig. 63. **Sector.** A sector is part of a circular track on a disk. These tracks, like tracks on tape, are not physically visible; they are simply magnetized regions on the disk surface.

selective, see SEARCH AND REPLACE.

selective sort, *n.* a method of sorting large files on disk. The program picks out items in the order of the sort (numerical order, ASCII code order, etc.) and places the data into another file. This second file will be in the correct sorted order. The speed of sorting is slow, because the process is INPUT and OUTPUT BOUND by the speed of disk access. For very large amounts of data, however, which could not be held in an array in RAM, this is a preferred method.

self-checking code, see PARITY.

semicolon, *n.* a PUNCTUATION MARK that is used in many languages as a SEPARATOR. In BASIC, the semicolon is used as a PRINT MODIFIER, in Pascal it is used to mark the end of a STATEMENT.

semiconductor, *n.* a type of material whose electrical characteristics can be controlled by the addition of very small amounts of impurities. The intense study of semiconductors by the Bell Laboratories in the US in the 1920s and 1930s led to the invention of the TRANSISTOR in 1948. This in turn led to the development of ICs. Currently, the most favoured semiconductor material is the element SILICON.

semiconductor laser, *n.* a miniature and low power form of LASER. This makes use of the same principle as the LED. Semiconductor lasers are particularly suited as laser sources to be used with FIBRE OPTICS, and are found in COMPACT DISC readers.

separated graphics, *n.* graphics characters with spaces between them. Graphics characters drawn on a CHARACTER BLOCK which is smaller than the allowable size, such as using 7×7 instead of 8×8, will be printed with a space at one side and at the top or bottom. When a set of such characters is printed in adjacent screen positions, the spaces will separate the graphics characters just as they normally separate text characters. Compare CONTIGUOUS GRAPHICS.

separator, *n.* a character that is used to separate parts of a STATEMENT. This is done so that the OPERATING SYSTEM can distinguish the different parts. To take a simple example, the BASIC statement PRINT A means that the computer should print

SEQUENCE

the value of a variable which is called A. By contrast PRINT"A" means that the letter A is to be printed. In this second example, the quotemark (inverted commas) acts as a separator, indicating to the operating system the nature of what is to be printed. Typical separators include the SEMICOLON, COLON and COMMA.

sequence, *n.* an arrangment of items that ensures that the items are dealt with in order. A SORT is a method that is employed to put data into a sequence of ascending or descending value.

sequential, *adj.* of or relating to anything following a sequence, one by one.

sequential access, *n.* allowing access to a number of items one by one. See SERIAL FILE.

serial, *adj.* of or relating to anything using one bit at a time in data transmission. Most serial transmissions use the RS-232 system, and a PROTOCOL must be specified. For example, an 8-bit byte might be transmitted using 11 bits, with 1 bit to indicate the start, then 8 bits of the byte, and 2 bits to indicate the end. The protocol will also specify whether or not PARITY is used, and if so, whether even or odd. Serial transmission is possible only if both transmitter and receiver are using the same protocols.

serial access memory (SAM), *n.* any memory system that allows only serial access. In such a memory, to obtain the 5th item in the memory, you would first have to read items 0 to 4. At one time, memory of this type was all that could be obtained, but it has been replaced in computers by modern forms of random access memory (RAM). The action of the STACK simulates the action of serial access memory. See also LIFO.

serial file, *n.* a file on tape or on disk in which the items are recorded one after the other with one filename. When this file is read, the whole file must be replayed, because there is no method of obtaining any one item separate from the others. Disk systems usually permit some form of RANDOM ACCESS file to be used in addition to serial filing. Though serial files are simple to set up and use, altering such a file is time-consuming. To add, delete or change an item, the file must be read, amended, and saved again. The use of serial files makes a computer program INPUT BOUND and OUTPUT BOUND.

serial interface, *n.* an interface for transmitting and receiving serial signals. Such an interface would normally be of the RS-232 type, but a few manufacturers use other systems. The main merits of a serial interface are that it uses fewer connections. Serial interfaces have also been used for disk drives, but their use in this application has resulted in some disk drive designs which are slower in action than tape cassettes.

serial printer, *n.* a printer that uses a serial interface. The speed at which serial data can be received need not be as low as the speed of the printer. A printer which uses a serial interface will normally also feature a BUFFER, so that transmission can take place at high speed until the buffer is full. If the buffer is large enough, the rate of serial transmission can be fixed at a speed, such as 9600 BAUD, which will not cause the computer to become OUTPUT BOUND. Most of the low-priced popular printers which use CENTRONICS interfaces can be provided with a serial interface at extra cost. The interface must be set up by means of switches for the correct PROTOCOLS.

serial processing, *n.* the conventional processing action in which each action is carried out in a sequence. The alternative is PARALLEL PROCESSING. The phrase is sometimes also used to indicate actions on each of the items of a data file.

set, *n.* a group of related items. The pieces on a chess board constitute a set, as do the months of the year or the days of the week. Some PROGRAMMING LANGUAGES, such as PASCAL, allow you to specify a DATA TYPE of set and test for names being members of that set.

set-up option, *n..* a choice of MODE or of characteristics. The choice is made early on in the use of a computer or a program and will remain in use until specifically changed. For example, a short program could be used to establish set-up options for a word processor. These might include the choice of left-hand margin size, characters per printed line, lines per page, headers, footers and so on. See also DEFAULT.

sheet feed, *n.* the delivery of paper in single sheets to a printer. If a printer needs to use single sheets rather than roll or FANFOLD paper, the sheets have to be fed to the printer on demand. Most word processors allow the computer to deliver a prompt and then hang up until a new sheet has been inserted and a key pressed. For unattended operation, automatic sheet feeders can be bought for most printers, but they are expensive, particularly in comparison with the prices of most small printers.

Shell sort, *n.* a fast type of sorting routine in which a list is split into sections, and items in one section compared with items in the other. By repeating this action, using different sections, the complete list can be sorted with fewer comparisons and interchanges than a BUBBLE SORT. The Shell sort is particularly advantageous for large lists which can be held in memory. See also SORT, QUICKSORT, SELECTIVE SORT, BUBBLE SORT.

shift, *n.* a REGISTER action in ASSEMBLY LANGUAGE that moves all the bits in a register by one place in one direction, left or right. In any shift action, the bit which was at one end of the register will be lost, and a 0 bit will be placed in the other end of the register. See also ROTATION.

SHIFT, *n.* the key that is used to obtain upper-case letters from the keyboard when lower-case letters are obtained normally.

sideways RAM/ROM, *n.* a method of controlling extra memory. A trend in the design of microcomputers, pioneered by the BBC machine, has been to allow sections of memory to be switched by software instructions, so that a memory chip in one specified socket is used. This is normally used to permit a choice of programs in ROM to be run simply by typing the name of the desired program. If the ROM in one socket is replaced by RAM, it is then possible to store a program or data in this position temporarily. In this way, a program that might otherwise have to be held on disk, and accessed frequently, can be loaded into RAM and held there so that it can be accessed much more quickly. By switching between sockets, it is also possible to make use of several chips of RAM in this way. This can greatly speed up the action of a program which would otherwise be INPUT or OUTPUT BOUND.

signal, *n.* any method of communicating a meaning. Computers use electrical signals in a BINARY (on/off) code.

signal/noise ratio, *n.* a measure of signal quality. Electrical noise will always be present on any transmission system. The ratio of amplitudes of the desired signal to the noise must be above some minimum value for a system to operate successfully. If this is not attained for a digital system, data will be corrupted. See also PARITY, CORRUPTION.

$$01101001$$
— positive number, value 105 denary

$$11101001$$
— negative number, value −23 '

For 8-bit number:
  value range −128 to +127

Conversion of negative numbers to binary:
  (i)   Write value in binary
  (ii) Negate each bit
  (iii) Add 1 to lsb

Example: −23
  23 in binary is: 00010111
  negate:—   11101000
  add 1 to lsb: 11101001

— gives binary equivalent of −23

Conversion of signed binary to negative denary:
  $$10010111$$
  subtract 1: 10010110
  negate   01101001

— gives   −105 denary

For 2-byte numbers, the range in denary is −32768 TO +32767

Fig. 64. **Sign bit.** The sign bit which is used to indicate sign in binary numbers. This is the most-significant bit, and its use for this purpose can cause some curious effects when the computer reads and converts numbers that are stored in the memory. The examples show how numbers are converted to and from 8-bit signed binary. The processes are identical for 16-bit numbers.

sign bit, *n.* the BIT in a binary number that is used to indicate sign, positive or negative. By convention, the msb (most significant bit) is used for this purpose. If a binary number has a 1 as its msb, the number is negative. A 0 as the msb means that the number is positive. This can lead to an odd appearance if a set of integers is being printed out. Taking as an example 8-bit integers, the sequence 01111110, 01111111, 10000000, 10000001 will print as 126, 127,–128, –127. See Fig. 64.

signed, *adj.* (of a binary number) one in which the msb is used as a SIGN BIT. Compare UNSIGNED, SIGN BIT.

significance, *n.* the weighting of a digit, signified by its place in a number. For example in the number 123, the '1' means 100 and is the most significant figure. The '3' means 3 units, and is the least significant figure. BINARY numbers use a similar system of significance, but based on powers of two rather than on powers of ten. See BIT.

silicon, *n.* a common element which in its pure form is a SEMICONDUCTOR. Silicon is used for the manufacture of TRANSISTORS and ICs for computers, and also for PHOTOCELLS.

simplex, *n.* a data transmission system that allows signals to pass in one direction only. See also DUPLEX, HALF-DUPLEX.

simulation, *n.* the use of a system to create the appearance of another. For example, simple flying-simulation programs can give all the appearance of the cockpit display of an aircraft. More complex simulators can provide a full range of cockpit controls, and a projected scene through the windscreen, even some of the physical sensations of flying. The system that is simulated does not have to be a machine–control one, because items as different as the management of a large office, and the behaviour of water waves on a shore can be simulated. The essential feature is that the action must be capable of being represented by some mathematical function or 'model', and therefore by a program function. The programming is extremely complex but the technique can be very rewarding. Trying out changes on a simulation system does not incur any large costs, and allows experiment at low risk.

sine wave, *n.* the simplest pattern of wave motion, a wave whose shape is that of the graph of the sine of an angle plotted against the angle size. See also SQUARE WAVE.

single-key response, *n.* a way of MENU choice. In many HIGH-LEVEL LANGUAGES, an INPUT STATEMENT allows a reply to be typed, following which the RETURN or ENTER key has to be pressed. For actions such as making a menu choice from a limited number of items, this normal input action is clumsy, and should be replaced by a single-key response. This means that the choice can be made by pressing a single key, not using RETURN. In a BASIC program, this is usually achieved by using the GET or INKEY$ type of statement. Single-key response should not be used if some of the choices may have the effect of losing data, or of causing a fatal error by, for example, searching for a disk file which does not exist. In any case, when single-key response is used, VALIDATION of some kind is always needed.

single step, *vb.* to execute a program one instruction at a time. This is easily arranged with an INTERPRETER, but requires a good MONITOR program if the language is compiled, or in machine code. The ability to single step a program is very valuable as a method of DEBUGGING.

sink, *n.* a software way of 'losing' data. Most computers, when connected for printer output, will hang up if printing is not possible. This may be because the printer is not connected, or because there is no paper, or because the printer is not switched on. A *printer sink* allows the codes sent to the printer to be intercepted, so preventing the printer from hanging up.

skip, *vb.* to ignore and pass over. A faulty routine in a program, for example, can be skipped by using a GOTO statement. This allows the program to be used temporarily, providing that the action of the faulty routine was not essential to processing. A data-reading program can similarly be arranged to skip certain items, for example any invoices for a zero sum, which are not wanted.

slashed zero, *n.* a zero that has a thin bar diagonally drawn across it. This makes the zero much easier to distinguish from the letter 'O'. DOT MATRIX printers allow the option of using a zero in slashed or non-slashed form but it is not easy to obtain daisywheels with slashed zeros for some machines.

slave processor, *n.* a microprocessor that is under the control of the main microprocessor in a computer. See also COPROCESSOR, NUMBER CRUNCHER.

slice architecture, *n.* the design and construction of a mini-computer from 4-bit sections. See BIT-SLICE MACHINE.

slicing, *n.* copying part of a STRING into another string variable. For example, in Microsoft BASIC, A\$=RIGHT\$(X\$,2) will make A\$ consist of the last two letters of X\$. Other HIGH-LEVEL LANGUAGES do not use a string data type, and regard a string of characters as an ARRAY. This makes string slicing identical to array item selection.

smart, see INTELLIGENT TERMINAL.

SNOBOL, *n.* a HIGH-LEVEL LANGUAGE. A derivative of COBOL, SNOBOL is biased to the processing of STRINGS and the matching of patterns. It is not well suited to numerical applications, except for comparatively simple arithmetic.

soft copy, see READOUT.

soft, *adj.* (of a part of a computer system) able to be changed easily, like a program in memory. Compare HARD.

soft keys, see PROGRAMMABLE KEYS.

soft sectoring, *n.* a system in which a disk is magnetically marked out (see FORMATTING) by the computer in which it will be used, rather than by the manufacturers. In a soft-sectored disk, a small hole near the centre acts as an indexing mark, and the sectoring is numbered starting at the position in which a light beam passes through this hole. During formatting, a set of codes will be deposited on each TRACK of the disk, using the position of the sector hole as a starting point. Compare HARD SECTORING.

software, *n.* instructions to the computer in any form that can reasonably easily be altered. This includes PAPER TAPE, BAR CODES, printed listings, magnetic tapes and disks. If the instructions are on ROM or PROM, they are usually referred to as FIRMWARE. The software of a computer is by far the most valuable asset of the computer user, and for the smaller computers is very frequently of more value than the computer itself.

software engineering, *n.* the complete task of providing software. This includes analysis of the problem which the software is designed to solve, searching for methods that provide the minimum use of memory and the lowest running time at minimum expense to the user, programming and marketing. This is engineering in the sense that it involves the traditional engineering problems of reconciling conflicting objectives, and working with a view to acceptance by the ultimate user.

software house, *n.* **1.** a company that undertakes the writing of software. **2.** seller of software.

software piracy, see PIRACY.

software tools, *n.* program methods, such as specific PROCE-DURES, that are necessary to produce good software. Sometimes shortened to *tools*. These will include procedures for SORT, input, display, etc.

solid-state, *adj.* (of an electronic system) using non-moving 'solid' materials such as SEMICONDUCTOR devices in place of vacuum valves and mechanical components such as relays.

son, see FATHER.

sort, *vb.* to put anything into order, such as ascending number order or alphabetical order. The choice of a sort routine is one that must be made with considerable care. Several standard methods are well documented, and for general purposes, an array in memory is best sorted by a SHELL SORT. See also BUBBLE SORT, QUICKSORT, SELECTION SORT.

sort key, *n.* the item that indicates position in a sorted list. A RECORD may consist of a number of items, such as name, address and age of a number of people. These records can be sorted in several ways, such as by order of ascending age, alphabetical order of surname, and so on. The item that is chosen to be tested for sorting is the 'sort key'. For example, if age is selected as the sort key, then the list can be sorted in order of ascending age or in order of descending age.

sound, *n.* any wave-motion in air that is detected by the ear. Most MICROCOMPUTERS have commands that permit sounds to be generated, ranging from BEEPS to the operator to multi-channel music, with harmony. The electrical signals of sound are converted into sound waves by the LOUDSPEAKER.

sound chip, *n.* the IC that executes sound instructions. Modern microcomputers use specialized sound chips which are micro-processors in their own right. A distinguishing feature of the use

241

of these chips is the ability to SYNTHESIZE sound effects, and to accept data from the main microprocessor into a BUFFER called the sound QUEUE.

source code, *n.* the text of a program, usually in a HIGH-LEVEL LANGUAGE. A COMPILER will convert this source code to OBJECT CODE, which will be run by the microprocessor. The source code can be saved and loaded, and it can also be edited so as to generate a different object code. ASSEMBLY LANGUAGE is a LOW-LEVEL LANGUAGE which also uses source code that can be assembled to object code.

space-bar, *n.* the long bar-shaped key nearest to the keyboard user that generates the ASCII code of 32.

special character, *n.* a character that is not a normal part of text or a number. This includes the SEPARATOR characters, and characters such as the HASHMARK which are used for purposes other than printing as part of text.

speech recognition, *n.* a system that uses a microphone to pick up the sound of speech, and a set of circuits and software to convert this speech into text. This works well with languages like Japanese, in which the sounds of speech are standardized, but less well with flexible languages like English.

speech synthesis, *n.* a program that can be run in a computer that has sound capabilities and which will give speech-like sounds. The 'text' which controls the speech, however, does not look like English, and may not be particularly easy to learn. See also PHONEMES.

speed of loop, *n.* the time that is needed for a number of passes of the loop, often one thousand. Used as a method of BENCHMARKING.

spellcheck, *n.* a program used in conjunction with a word processor to compare each word in a text with words held in a dictionary on disk.

spikes, *n.* brief pulses of high voltage. These occur in the MAINS supply during thunderstorms or when work is being carried out on cables. A spike which affects the POWER SUPPLY of the computer can wipe out data by causing a REBOOT. Spike suppressors can be bought and fitted into the mains supply lead to reduce this problem. See Fig. 65 on page 244.

split screen, *n.* a display in which two or more parts of the screen are used for different purposes, and can be cleared and scrolled independently. See also SCROLL, WINDOWS.

spool, *vb.* to record on tape or disk for special purposes. The term usually means to record on tape or disk in ASCII codes only. Most microcomputers record BASIC programs in a coded form, with each KEYWORD abbreviated to one byte. In a spooled program, a word such as PRINT would be recorded as 5 ASCII codes rather than as 1 (non-ASCII) code or TOKEN. Some computers require a program to be spooled before it can be merged with another program. Another use of spooling is in preventing a program from becoming OUTPUT BOUND. When a program delivers a large amount of data to a printer, the computer may have to hang up waiting for the printer to finish before processing can resume.

In a spooled system, data is sent to a disk in ASCII codes, and fed to the printer in the gaps between processing actions. In this way, it is very often possible for the printer to operate continually during a program, and for the action of the computer also to appear continuous. Spooling in this sense is a form of TIMESHARING of the microprocessor.

spreadsheet, *n.* a type of display and forecasting system consisting of a display on the screen in which items appear in ROWS AND COLUMNS. Each individual position is called a CELL. The items may be text items, but for a large number of applications, they will be numbers. The number of cells can overflow the screen, because the use of CURSOR-CONTROL KEYS allows you to scroll the display in any direction. Some of the cells can be used to enter data, but other cells can be filled automatically by making use of relationships between items in other cells. For example, if a selling price for an item is entered in one cell, the VAT formula can be used to show the amount of tax in another cell, and the pre-VAT price in another. In this way, a complete analysis can be built up, even if a large number of cells is needed.

The advantage of using a spreadsheet of this type is that you can see at once what the effect of altering one item will be on the

SPREADSHEET

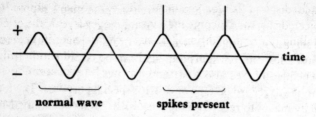

normal wave   spikes present

Fig. 65. **Spikes.** The sudden temporary changes of voltage can be very large and if they affect the voltages in the computer they can be very damaging. At best, the system will reboot, probably with loss of data. At worst, chips can be damaged so that the computer cannot be used until the damaged chips are located and replaced.

	1	2	3	4	5	6	7	8	9	10	11	etc.
1		Jan	Feb	Mar	Apr	May	Jun	Jul	Aug	Sep	Oct	
2												
3	Computers	2100	1300	900	800	600	200	600	800	1200	2400	
4	Peripherals	200	150	75	78	82	90	120	400	200	150	
5	Software	300	400	250	200	220	230	300	310	200	450	
6	Total Sales	2600	1850	1225	1078	902	520	1020	1510	1600	3000	
7	Direct Costs	960	1200	950	1000	1100	850	900	800	750	800	
8	Indirect	50	35	20	30	70	25	35	42	67	86	
9	Overheads	150	220	1200	450	210	120	60	75	1200	85	

etc.

Fig. 66. **Spreadsheet.** A typical spreadsheet in course of being filled with data. Rows and columns are assigned with names or data, and each intersection of a row and a column is called a cell. Some cells are filled with raw data, others by the use of formulas which are programmed when the spreadsheet is being set up. The width of the spreadsheet can be considerably greater than the width of the screen, and sideways scrolling is provided to allow you to view the otherwise hidden parts of the display.

whole display. If, for example, the spreadsheet shows the projected costs and income for a business over a year, the effects of falling demand, additional labour costs, changes in taxation, and so on can be seen very rapidly. If this type of action had to be carried out on paper, it would be very time-consuming and probably very inaccurate. Spreadsheet programs allow the spreadsheet display to be recorded so that it can be used again, and also to be printed on paper. See Fig. 66. See also VISICALC, SUPERCALC-3, MULTIPLAN, LOTUS 1-2-3.

sprite, *n.* a graphics pattern on the screen that can be moved under computer control without the need for the detailed graphics instructions of draw, wait, undraw, move etc. Sprite capabilities are essential if games programs are to be written in BASIC, or any other HIGH-LEVEL LANGUAGE, and can be useful for other purposes. Some computers, however, do not allow sprites to be controlled with BASIC commands. See also PLAYER-MISSILE GRAPHICS.

sprocket feed, *n.* a method of positioning paper in a printer. Also called *pinfeed*. See SPROCKET HOLES.

sprocket holes, *n.* the holes of square section which are punched in paper that is intended to be fed through a printer by sprockets or pins. The use of sprocketed paper allows much more precise control of paper position and is essential if the computer is working with preprinted forms.

square wave, *n.* a wave of square shape. The AMPLITUDE of a square wave switches abruptly between two limits, and the wave is one that is used very extensively in all DIGITAL circuits. All of the processing waveforms of a computer, for example, will be of this shape. Several SOUND systems of computers also generate a square waveform, which allows a wide range of sounds to be synthesized.

stack, *n.* the part of the RAM memory of the computer that is reserved for temporary storage of bytes by the microprocessor. Bytes are stored using a last-in first-out order, because this can be controlled simply, and is fast in operation. Control of the use of the stack is carried out by the STACK POINTER register. Any

STACK

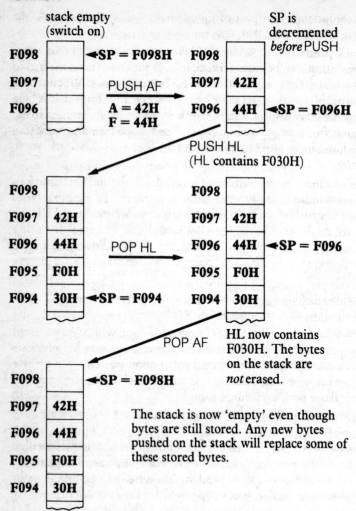

AF now contains 4244H

Fig. 67. **Stack.** Using the stack. This is a reserved part of the normal memory, and the address which is going to be used is stored in the stack-pointer register. The top-of-stack address (F098 in this example) is never used. All numbers are in hex.

corruption of this part of the memory will cause a CRASH. See Fig. 67. See also PUSH, POP.

stack pointer, *n.* in ASSEMBLY LANGUAGE, the REGISTER that stores the ADDRESS of the next free byte in the STACK. This is the means by which the stack is used for reading or writing. When a byte is to be placed on the stack, it is put into the address that is held by the stack pointer, and the stack pointer then decrements to the next free address. When a byte is read back from the stack, the pointer increments first, and then the byte is read. See also PUSH, POP.

stand-alone, *adj.* (of a part of a computer system) the ability to work independently. The term is applied, for example, to a MICROCOMPUTER which is on line to a mainframe but which can process data for itself. See also INTELLIGENT TERMINAL.

standard document, *n.* a word-processed document such as a letter which is held in outline form. A standard letter, for example, would be typed with abbreviations used in all places where different versions would require different text. The name and address, for example, might be represented by NME. and ADDR., so that the SEARCH AND REPLACE facility of the word processor could be used to insert the correct names and addresses for the different versions from a mailing list. With some planning, a large number of individual documents can be replaced by one standard document of this type, with the word processor inserting the changes that are needed for individual letters.

standard form, *n.* the method of writing a number as a single digit and decimal fraction multiplied by a power of ten. For example, 123.45 can be written as 1.2345E2, meaning 1.2345 times 10 to the power 2. Most computers will accept and print REAL NUMBERS in this form. The binary version of this form, also called MANTISSA exponent form, is used for storage and manipulation of real numbers in the computer. See also PRECISION OF NUMBER.

standard subroutine, *n.* a form of SUBROUTINE that can be used in a variety of different programs. The effective use of standard subroutines requires good DOCUMENTATION, particularly in respect of the variable values which have to be passed to and from the subroutine.

star network, *n.* a network of items that are all connected to a central point.

start bit, *n.* the opening part of a SERIAL data transmission of a byte. When the RS-232 system of serial transmission is used, each byte is preceded with a start bit, which is used to prepare the receiver for the first bit of the data byte. When the start bit is received, the receiver software will set a COUNTER so as to count in the correct number of data bits, usually 7 or 8. Compare STOP BIT.

state-of-the-art, *adj.* (of computer equipment) a rather pretentious modifier which means as up to date as possible. Cynics regard this description as a guarantee of unreliability.

statement, *n.* a single program instruction, complete with any ARGUMENT or data that it needs. In BASIC, one statement can be written on each line, or several statements in one line can be separated by colons to form a MULTISTATEMENT LINE. Other languages dispense with line numbers, and use a SEMICOLON to separate the statements. In such languages, it is usually possible to write a COMPOUND STATEMENT which consists of a group of statements that can be regarded as carrying out a task on a selected block of data. These parts of a compound statement are usually enclosed between words like BEGIN and END.

static RAM, *n.* a form of RAM that needs no REFRESH MEMORY signals. Static RAM was used in the early days of microcomputers, and is now returning to favour. Early versions required a considerable amount of electrical power to operate, but newer versions using CMOS are now available. Compare DYNAMIC RAM.

stationery, *n.* **1.** any paperwork used by the computer. **2.** preprinted forms which are sprocketed and joined to form CONTINUOUS STATIONERY.

status bit, see FLAG.

status line, *n.* a line of information at the top or the bottom of the screen that shows choices that have been made in terms of characters per line, lines per page, etc. The status line can also show the state of progress, such as current page number, current line number, word count etc. Several word processors allow a choice of status lines, according to what type of information you require.

status poll, *n.* signals sent out by a central processing system to find the status of PERIPHERALS, such as the printer, keyboard and screen. A status poll might, for example, reveal that the printer is off or out of paper, the screen needs scrolling, and a key is being pressed on the keyboard. See also POLLING, INTERRUPTS.

status word, *n.* a set of bytes that signals more than one status.

stepping motor, *n.* a motor which can move in precise and equal steps over a range. Each step is produced by a pulse of current to the motor, and the importance of the stepping motor lies in the fact that the pulses of current can be delivered from a suitable INTERFACE, under computer control. The stepping motor is used, for example, in disk drives to control the position of the disk READ/WRITE head, and in printers to control the movement of a DAISYWHEEL. It also has considerable applications in PLOTTERS and for ROBOTICS.

stop bit, *n.* the bit that follows the last bit of a byte in SERIAL data transmission, and is used as a signal to the receiver that all of the byte has been transmitted. Many PROTOCOLS make use of two stop bits. On reception of a stop bit, the microprocessor of the receiver will place the assembled byte into memory, and set up ready for another START BIT.

stop code, *n.* an EMBEDDED COMMAND code that is used to stop the printer. This might be used, for example, to take a piece of headed paper out, and put in plain paper. Most word processor programs can be programmed so that the stop action is automatic at the end of a page, thus enabling single sheets to be used with the printer.

stop list, *n.* a list of words that are not to be used. An automatic indexing program, for example, must be provided with a list of words such as 'and', 'but' and so on, which will not be indexed.

store, *n.* a memory location or REGISTER.

stream, see CHANNEL.

STR$, *n.* a BASIC instruction word that converts number codes. If a number is held as a set of ASCII codes in a string, the STR$

STRING

action will convert the number into the normal FLOATING POINT coding. See also VAL.

string, *n.* a DATA TYPE that consists of a set of characters. Most versions of BASIC allow a string to be represented by a variable name followed by the DOLLAR sign, with up to 255 characters in the string. Many other languages do not possess a string variable as such, using an ARRAY of ASCII codes (which requires DIMENSIONING) instead. Others treat a string as a LIST of characters. See Fig. 68.

(a) | S | T | R | I | N | G | 1 | S | T | R | I | N | G | 2 | S | T | R | I | N | G | 3 |

↑
start address for this
string of characters

Strings stored end-to-end in memory. Program stores start
address and number of characters for each string.
All codes ASCII.

(b) | S | T | R | I | N | G | 1 | 0̸ | S | T | R | I | N | G | 2 | 0̸ | S | T | R | I | N | G | 3 | 0̸ |

↑

Only start address needs to be stored. Each string ends with 0̸.
Other codes are ASCII codes 32-127 with no zeros contained.

(c) | S | T | R | I | N | G | 1 | | | | S | T | R | I | N | G | 2 | | | | S | T | R | I | N | G | 3 | | | |

↑

Only start address needs to be stored. Each string consists of
the same number of characters, padded with blanks.

Fig. 69. **String.** Strings of characters are stored as lists of ASCII codes in memory. (a) Most dialects of BASIC store a string in memory, with a variable pointer which consists of the starting address for each string along with the length of each string. (b) Strings in C are stored like arrays of numbers, but with a zero byte marking the end of each string. Only the starting address for a string needs to be known in this case. (c) Pascal strings are arrays of fixed length, so that only the defined length, along with a starting address for each string, needs to be referred to.

string area, *n.* a part of memory that is used for storing strings. This applies mainly to machines which use a BASIC INTERPRETER.

string function, *n.* an action that is carried out on a string, such as measuring length, or SLICING.

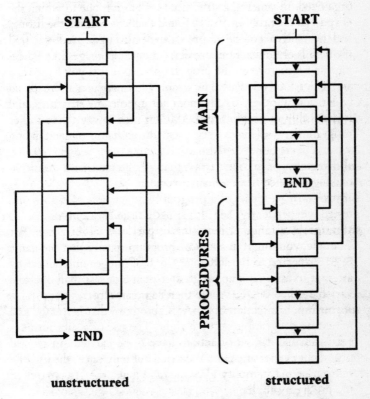

Fig. 69. **Structure.** A structured program consists of a recognizable main section with a clearly defined sequence of steps. If needed, these steps can invoke procedures to carry out actions, but each procedure will return to the step that called it. In an unstructured program, the steps are carried out in an irrational order and it can be very difficult to find out how variable values are passed and used, or even how the steps of the program are arranged.

string variable, *n.* a variable name used to represent a string.

stringy floppy, see FLOPPY TAPE.

stroke, *vb.* to press a single key on the computer keyboard. The term can also denote one side of a character shape.

structure, *n.* the way in which the writing of a program is organized. In general, a structured program is one in which the purpose of the program can be found easily by reading the listing, and the main part of the program can be used like an index to find the details of how actions are carried out. Languages like Pascal impose a structure on the programmer, so that if you have read and understood one Pascal program, you can in general read and understand another. BASIC does not impose any structure, and it is possible to program in BASIC in such a way that another programmer will have very great difficulty in understanding what is being done. See also MODULARIZATION. See Fig. 69.

subdirectory, *n.* a DIRECTORY that is obtained as a result of making a choice from a main directory.

subprogram, *n.* a part of a program which can be designed and tested independently. See also SUBROUTINE, PROCEDURE.

subrange, *n.* a range of items that is part of a larger range. For example, you might in a PASCAL program specify that the name SPOTS referred to the subrange 1 to 6 of integer numbers. Any attempt to assign a number greater than 6 or less than one to a variable called SPOTS would then cause an error.

subroutine, *n.* a section of a BASIC program that is treated as a miniature program in its own right. The use of a subroutine is very valuable if a set of actions have to be carried out several times, but even if an action is carried out only once, the use of a subroutine may simplify planning, and make the STRUCTURE of the program simpler.

All dialects of BASIC can use subroutines, but more advanced dialects, in common with other languages, prefer the use of PROCEDURES. In BASIC, the subroutine is called into action by using the GOSUB statement, followed by the line number for the subroutine. The end of the subroutine is marked by the RETURN statement. Any variable values that are used in the main program can be used and changed by the subroutine, and any variables that are assigned in the subroutine will also be present in the main program when the subroutine ends. In other words, all variables are GLOBAL and there is no automatic provision for creating LOCAL variables.

subscripted variable, *n.* an ARRAY variable that uses the same IDENTIFIER (name) along with numbers (SUBSCRIPTS) to indicate different values. For example, the array variable A$ might have members A$(0), A$(1), A$(2), A$(3), in which the numbers are the subscripts. Many programming languages permit arrays of all valid DATA TYPES to be used.

subset, *n.* a set of items that is itself part of a larger set (see SUBRANGE). In another sense, many LANGUAGES for microcomputers are described as being subsets of languages such as PASCAL, C, LISP and so on. This implies that several statements or facilities of the standard version are absent and cannot be implemented. This has traditionally been due to lack of memory, and is not so common nowadays. Users should beware of old implementations of these languages which are only subsets. One of the most common (and most irritating) omissions in many such subsets is the facility to use FLOATING POINT numbers. When this is omitted, it makes the use of the language for designing programs such as SPREADSHEETS rather pointless, because all the handling of real numbers will have to be carried out in MACHINE CODE.

substitution table, *n.* **1.** a list of substituted characters. **2.** in WORD PROCESSING, a table showing which keys or key combinations are needed to obtain accented letters, Greek letters, mathematical symbols, etc. **3.** in ASSEMBLY LANGUAGE, a set of lists that contains such items as TOKEN numbers, reserved words, and subroutine addresses.

suite of programs, *n.* a set of interacting programs. These are generally arranged so that they can be called into use as required, working on the same data. See also PACKAGE.

Supercalc-3, *n. Trademark.* a SPREADSHEET program. Supercalc was the first good spreadsheet for CP/M use, and is notable for offering an excellent range of facilities at a comparatively low price. See also VISICALC, MULTIPLAN, LOTUS 1-2-3.

supercomputer, see CRAY-1.

suppress, *vb.* to prevent the use of something in computing. Word processor programs may suppress the printing of some characters, because of undesirable effects on the printer. Other codes have to be suppressed before text is displayed on the screen, for the same reasons. See NON-PRINTING CODES.

surges, *n.* fluctuations of mains voltage that are slower than SPIKES. The power supplies of most computers can cope with mains surges without any risk of a REBOOT.

sustain, *n.* part of a sound ENVELOPE. The sustain section of the envelope is the region in which the sound amplitude is steady, preceding the RELEASE.

symbolic address, *n.* the use of a LABEL word in ASSEMBLY LANGUAGE to mean an address in memory. The label will at some stage have to be assigned (see ASSIGNATION), either by using the EQU PSEUDO-OPERATION instruction, or by the use of the word as a label at the correct part of the program. A well-designed assembly language program will make use of symbolic addresses as far as possible, because this makes the SOURCE CODE much easier to adapt to another set of addresses.

Symphony, *n. Trademark.* a suite of programs by Ashton-Tate, consisting of a SPREADSHEET, DATABASE and GRAPHICS package (like LOTUS 1-2-3) to which is added a WORD PROCESSOR, and communications routines. Symphony requires a minimum of 320K of RAM, preferably much more.

synchronization, *n.* the arranging of an action to take place at the same time as another. This is a common problem in fast-action graphics, because the TV display repeats at a rate of 25 times a second, and screen movement can appear to be jerky unless the movement is synchronized to the screen repetition rate. The synchronization is normally carried out by calling a machine code routine. Another synchronization problem concerns SERIAL transmission of data. Unless the receiver can assemble the bits that are transmitted into the correct bytes, the transmission will be hopelessly corrupted. The RS-232 PROTOCOLS ensure synchronizing by using standard BAUD RATES, number of START BITS, number of STOP BITS, number of data bits and so on. Providing that both transmitter and receiver are set up to the same protocols synchronization is automatic. See also USRT.

syntax, *n.* the 'grammar' of a program STATEMENT. A program statement must take a fixed form, called the syntax, and any departure from this form will cause an error message. Important points of syntax include the correct spelling of KEYWORDS, use of BRACKETS, PUNCTUATION MARKS and spaces. Several computer manuals show the syntax only in an abbreviated form, such as BACKUS-NAUR form.

synthesizer, *n.* the sound system of a computer which allows the sounds of musical instruments to be simulated. A synthesizer will also allow sound effects, and a SPEECH SYNTHESIS facility is also obtainable for most types of microcomputers. Another option is the use of the MIDI interface, a way of linking synthesizers together, which is available on a few modern computers. The provision of the MIDI interface allows a computer to be linked to a full-scale music synthesizer system.

system, *n.* the computer and all of its attachments, its actions, inputs and outputs, considered as a whole.

system disk, *n.* the disk which contains the OPERATING SYSTEM for the computer when this is not contained in a ROM. Also called *master disk*. The disk usually contains a large number of UTILITY programs in addition to the operating system. The name is often also used for a disk that contains a disk-operating system (DOS) only. The system disk should be used only to make a pair of backups, because the original itself is too precious to risk in everyday use.

systems analysis, *n.* the task of learning how a complicated system works so that a program can be written to control it. In microcomputing, the systems analysis is often carried out by the programmer, but for users of larger computers the jobs are separated.

system variables, *n.* the quantities that are stored into RAM by the OPERATING SYSTEM so as to run a program. In the event of a CRASH, the program can be continued only if the values of the system variables are uncorrupted.

T

TAB, *n.* a RESERVED WORD in BASIC used as a print MODIFIER to position the CURSOR to the required column during a printing operation. TAB has to be followed by a column number in brackets, and then by the item which is to be printed. For all machines, TAB(0) is the left-hand column position, but a few machines use TAB(1) also to refer to this position.

tab memory, *n.* memory that is devoted to storing TABULATION settings. The term is used in word processors to indicate that each press of the TAB key will take the cursor to a new screen position, preset by the tab memory settings.

tab stops, *n.* the preset and fixed tab positions of the cursor on the screen, usually of 8 columns each.

table, *n.* a list of data which is stored in memory. See also LOOK-UP TABLE.

tabulation, *n.* the action of moving the cursor to a preset place, the TAB setting.

tape, *n.* a method of storing data as magnetic signals, using a long narrow strip of plastic tape coated with magnetic material. The tape may be open-reel, carried on a large plastic or metal reel, or in a cassette, with two reels that are enclosed in a case. When a cassette is used, the cassette also contains the PRESSURE PAD which presses the tape against the TAPEHEAD.

Several sizes of cassette can be used, from the standard audio cassette size to the miniature data cassette size. In addition, tape can also be used in the 'endless' tape cartridge. The main disadvantage of using tape is that it is a SERIAL system, and to gain access to any required part of the tape may require fast winding in either direction. See also FLOPPY TAPE.

tape counter, *n.* a form of revolution counter that is connected to one shaft of a cassette or tape recorder. The readings of the tape counter can be used as a rough indication of position on the tape.

tape deck, *n.* the mechanical mechanism of a tape recorder. Also called *tape transcriptor*.

tape guide, *n.* a smooth bar, roller, or plastic cylinder which acts to guide TAPE past a TAPEHEAD. The tape guide normally uses shoulders to prevent the tape from moving sideways. Any side movement of the tape will cause incorrect placing of tracks, leading to crosstalk. A tape cassette contains some plastic tape guides, but the tapehead also has its own guides.

tapehead, *n.* a magnetic read/write head that works on the same principles as a HEAD-OF-DISK DRIVE. The main difference is that a tapehead does not move across the width of the tape but is fixed while the tape moves past it. Audio tape recorders do not fully magnetize the tape, so that an erase head is also needed to remove previously recorded signals before a new recording is made. This erasure is very seldom thorough enough for use with computer signals, and a BULK ERASER should be applied to cassettes which are to be reused.

teleprinter, *n.* the old-fashioned electromechanical type of keyboard and printer which uses the principles first laid down by Baudot, and improved by Murray in 1903. In computing, these machines formed the only link between operator and machine until DEC introduced the interactive video TERMINAL. Teleprinters for computing use were normally fitted with PAPER TAPE readers and punches.

teleprinter roll, *n.* paper for computer listings. The paper is plain, 214 mm wide, and wound on to a roll 88 mm in diameter. This paper can be used by any printer which is fitted with FRICTION FEED.

telesoftware, *n.* software that is transmitted by means of the spare capacity in the TV signal. One method makes use of the TELETEXT principle, in which the unused lines of the signal carry digital information. Another method uses a small flashing dot at the corner of the normal picture to carry digital signals which can be picked up with simpler and less costly equipment than is needed for decoding the teletext signals.

teletext, *n.* a system of transmitting information, using spare capacity of the TV signal. In the time when the receiver is executing the frame flyback, no picture information can be sent. This time can, however, be used to transmit data, which can be stored and assembled as needed. Teletext is designed to make use of this spare capacity in a standardized data-transmitting system, which can also allow the use of colour graphics. The BBC system is termed Ceefax; the ITV version is Oracle. The systems are technically identical, and they also use the same methods for transmitting computer programs. See TELESOFTWARE.

teletype, *n.* a remote-operated typewriter. The main difference between this and a TELEPRINTER is that the teletype uses larger diameter rolls of paper.

teletype roll, *n.* a TELEPRINTER roll with a diameter of 127 mm.

temporary storage, *n.* storage in computer memory that is used only momentarily. Also called *intermediate storage, working storage.* During calculations, for example, intermediate results may have to be stored, and this is done in temporary storage. See also SCRATCHPAD.

terminal, *n.* a remote display and keyboard that is connected to a computer by a data link, often a SERIAL link. See also INTELLIGENT TERMINAL, DUMB TERMINAL.

terminal block, *n.* a set of connections that can be broken. In computing, this is normally either a set of connectors for cables which allow the connections to be changed or a set of addresses in the RAM memory which can be changed so as to allow new routines to be inserted. See also HOOK ADDRESS.

terminal junky, *n.* a slang term for a computer enthusiast. See also HACKER.

terminator, *n.* a byte or other piece of data that indicates that a process is to be ended. For example, entering a 0 in a number-summing program could cause the program to halt. The zero byte or the carriage return code of ASCII 13 are often used as terminators in MACHINE CODE text-handling programs, including operating systems.

test, 1. *n.* a program statement that will cause a BRANCH in different directions according to the value of a variable. A test must be included as part of a loop if it is not to be an ENDLESS LOOP. See also IF. **2.** *vb.* to run a program with dummy data to find if the action is correct.

text, *n.* any non-graphics display of alphabetical or numeric characters on the screen, including punctuation and other marks.

text editor, *n.* a program that will allow the entry of text appearing on the screen into memory. The text can then be amended, deleted and enlarged as necessary (see ECHO CHECK). Several programming languages require the use of a text editor to enter the program instructions, so creating a SOURCE CODE or textfile. A text editor combined with a PRINT FORMATTER constitutes a word-processing program.

textfile, *n.* a file that consists of only ASCII codes, usually on tape or disk. One of the standard data types of PASCAL, and used by many other languages.

text formatter, see PRINT FORMATTER.

text processor, see WORD PROCESSOR.

text screen, *n.* a display mode for text only, that needs much less memory than a graphics display. Many small computers allow the use of a text screen, with little or no provision for graphics display, and a graphics screen, with no provision for displaying text.

thermal paper, *n.* printing paper that discolours on heating. Thermal paper is used by some types of printers because it allows silent printing.

thermal printer, *n.* a printer that uses THERMAL PAPER. This is a form of DOT MATRIX printer in which the NEEDLES of the printer are hot. Where each needle touches the paper, it will leave a mark caused by the chemical reaction in the paper. The advantage of thermal printing is that the needles do not have to strike the paper hard, so a thermal printer can be very quiet. Another advantage is that no inked ribbon is needed, so the print is easily kept clean. The disadvantages include high paper costs, one copy only, and little choice of print colours.

thesaurus, *n.* a system that searches for synonyms. A thesaurus program is usually packaged along with a word processor and a spelling checker. The thesaurus action allows the text to be scanned, and words with similar meanings to be used to replace marked words in the text.

thimble printer, *n.* a variety of DAISYWHEEL printer. The difference is that the type is carried on stalks which are arranged in a thimble shape, hence the name. The best known printer of this type is the NEC Spinwriter.

thin film, *n.* a constructional technique for semiconductors, particularly for LCD displays.

thin window, *n.* a form of LCD display used by a few computers to display information on a small subsidiary screen on the keyboard.

thread, *n.* a program that consists of a set of independent units, or BEADS connected together.

threaded language, *n.* a language in which the programmer can devise reserved words, and then write a program as a string of these reserved words. FORTH is one of the best-known examples of a threaded language.

time, see PAUSE.

timeout, *n.* a cancellation action that will take place if the user waits. Many tape systems include a timeout action, which will stop the tape with an error message if a file is not located on the tape within a given time. If this method is not used, the computer will keep searching the tape until the whole of the tape has been wound.

timesharing, *n.* the use of a computer by several users, apparently all at the same time. This is done using TIME-SLICING techniques.

time-slicing, *n.* a method of allocating the use of a MICROPROCESSOR to several actions. This involves switching the microprocessor from one program to another at short intervals, particularly when the microprocessor would otherwise be idling in a WAIT LOOP. Time-slicing is easy when all the actions make use of keyboards, because the time that is needed for a microprocessor to service a keyboard is very small compared to the time that a human operator takes to press a key. Time-slicing is less easy when all the uses involve running looping programs, and the method becomes cumbersome if all the users require frequent disk access.

title of disk, *n.* a word used as a FILENAME for a complete disk. Some disk systems allow each disk to carry a title which is stored on the disk and which appears in the disk DIRECTORY. This is very useful for quick identification.

toggle, *n.* a switch action. A key is said to be used as a 'toggle' if pressing the key switches an action on, and pressing again switches the action off. For example, in CP/M, the CTRL P key action toggles the printer on and off. The advantage of using toggle action is that fewer key combinations have to be remembered. The disadvantage is that it is not always possible to know whether an action is, at any given time, on or off.

token, *n.* a single byte that is used to represent a RESERVED WORD. Tokens are very commonly used along with an INTERPRETER to save memory and to speed up processing. When a LIST is required, each token must be 'expanded' into the reserved word that it represents. This is done by making use of a LOOK-UP TABLE. Similarly, when the program is run, each token is used to find the address of a machine-code SUBROUTINE which will carry out the action for that token. If the tokens are saved on tape or on disk as part of the program, the program is said to be saved in encoded form, as distinct from the spooled form, see ENCODER, SPOOL.

toolbox, *n.* a type of program that adds useful programming facilities to a computer. See also UTILITY.

tools, see software tools.

top-down, *adj.* (of a program design) dealing with outlines first and details last. Top-down programming is very popular for designing in some types of HIGH-LEVEL LANGUAGE, though some others tend to encourage 'middle-out' methods, in which a main action is designed, and then the actions which come before and after. *Bottom-up programming,* which starts with details first, is usually confined to machine-language programming in which a higher-level language is being constructed. See also MODULARIZATION, STRUCTURE.

top of stack, *n.* the highest ADDRESS of the part of memory that is used in machine-code programming for the STACK. This address is not normally used for data, because the normal action of stack use is to decrement the address before placing data into stack memory. See also PUSH, POP.

touch pad, *n.* an INPUT device that uses switch contacts placed under a plastic pad which may be inscribed with symbols. The device is sometimes used as a keyboard substitute and is also used as a way of controlling a program, with specialized inscriptions on each of the pads. The system also has applications in graphics as a method of transferring diagrams to the screen. See also GRAPHICS TABLET.

touch screen, *n.* a system of making computer inputs without using the keyboard. When a finger interrupts a pair of infrared beams which cross the screen, the position of the finger can be 'digitized' (see DIGITIZE) into X and Y coordinate numbers, and used by the operating system. The method is particularly useful for menu choice, and is an alternative to the more popular and much less expensive MOUSE.

trace, *n.* a method of checking the action of a program in BASIC which uses an INTERPRETER. The command TRON or TRACE ON is used, and when a program runs, each LINE NUMBER is placed on the screen as the line is executed. In the event of a fault, the lines that have been executed are known, and any BRANCHES are obvious. The action is cancelled by using the command TROFF or TRACE OFF.

track, *n.* a circle on the surface of a disk that stores data. This is not a physically identifiable circle in the way that the track of a conventional gramophone record can be identified. The track of a disk is determined by the construction of the disk drive and not by any marking on the disk itself. A track is usually subdivided into SECTORS. Conventionally, FLOPPY DISKS in the 5¼" size use either 40 or 80 tracks, and the diameter ranges from (approximately) 60 mm to 129 mm. The diameter of track is the same irrespective of the number of tracks used, so that the tracks of an 80-track disk are at half the spacing of the 40-track disk.

trackball, *n.* an inverted MOUSE, a ball surface, mounted in a box, which can be rotated by the fingers or the palm of the hand in any direction so as to control the movement of the screen CURSOR. Also called *trackerball*.

tractor feed, *n.* a method of feeding perforated or sprocketed paper into a printer. This allows the paper to be precisely positioned, and is essential if continuous forms are to be used. See also SPROCKET HOLES, FRICTION FEED.

traffic, *n.* computer signals passing by means of a data link.

trailer, *n.* **1.** the piece of non-magnetic tape at the end of a length of recording tape (see also LEADER). **2.** a final RECORD, that may consist only of TERMINATOR bytes, or that may carry information on the rest of the file.

transaction, *n.* any updating work on a FILE. This can include entry of a new RECORD, amending a record, deleting a record, etc. Any transaction on a SERIAL file, apart from adding a record at the end of the file, normally requires the whole of the file to be read and rewritten.

transducer, *n.* a device that converts one type of signal into another, for example, magnetic to electrical, light to electrical and so on. A disk or tape READ/WRITE HEAD is a transducer, as is a LOUDSPEAKER, microphone or a cathode-ray tube (CRT). A transducer is often an essential part of a DIGITIZER.

transfer rate, *n.* the rate at which data can be moved to and from disk, or the rate at which data can be moved along a SERIAL link to other computers. The rate is often expressed in BAUD, but a measurement in bytes per second is more useful. This is because the relationship between the baud rate and the number of bytes per second is not fixed, it depends on the PROTOCOLS for the link.

transistor, *n.* the simplest SEMICONDUCTOR amplifying device. A transistor can be of bipolar or FET construction; the FETs form the basis of most of the ICs used in small computers, but for larger computers in which high speed is an overriding factor, bipolar principles are used.

transmit, *vb.* to send out data.

transparent, *n.* anything in computing not obvious to the user, i.e. any complicated action which is dealt with entirely by the OPERATING SYSTEM, and needs no effort on the part of the user. For example, the user may specify a filename and a disk drive number, but the action of checking DIRECTORY, selecting a

TRACK and SECTOR and recording a file is done 'transparently' by the disk operating system.

transputer, *n.* a single-chip computer consisting of the MICROPROCESSOR, ROM and RAM memory and PORTS, all constructed onto one single chip.

tree, *n.* a DATA STRUCTURE in which each piece of data can lead to (at least) two more. Trees are used extensively in DATABASES, particularly in large databases such as PRESTEL. You might, for example look up 'travel', and be given the choice of 'air', 'road', 'sea' or 'rail'. When you select 'air', you are given a list of airlines. When you select an airline, you are given a list of airports. When you select an airport, you are given a list of destinations, and when you select a destination you are given a list of flight times. It can be fascinating to browse through, but infuriating if you just want to find if there is a 1.00 flight to Geneva on a Tuesday. For such an application, the type of database which accepts the key words 'flight', 'Geneva', and 'Tuesday' to find an entry which contains each word is better. See also BINARY TREE.

TRUE, *n.* one of the two BOOLEAN conditions of TRUE or FALSE, corresponding to the two possible BINARY digits. Several HIGH-LEVEL LANGUAGES allow you to define a variable as Boolean, meaning that it can take only these two values.

truncation, *n.* the transforming of a REAL NUMBER into an INTEGER by omitting the fractions. In some languages, the key word TRUNC is used. An alternative keyword that is often used is INT, meaning integer part.

truth table, *n.* a table of inputs and outputs for a LOGIC circuit. The truth table shows what the output or outputs will be for every possible combination or sequence of inputs to the circuit. Of interest mainly to logic circuit designers, but often a useful way of defining what you want of a series of tests within a program.

Turing test, see AI.

turnkey, *n.* a computer system requiring initially little or no user participation. A turnkey system of installation means that the supplier of a (large) computer system will see to its installation, wiring of peripherals, including any changes to buildings, provision of software, and training or provision of operators. The name comes from the phrase that the owner only has to 'turn the key'. Turnkey is also applied to hardware or software which requires no understanding of the computer on the part of the user.

turtle graphics, *n.* a graphics system in which a cursor (the 'turtle') appears on the screen, and can be guided to any point on the screen, leaving or erasing a trail as commanded. Some systems provide also for a mechanical trolley, also called a turtle, carrying a pen to be guided over a flat sheet of paper. Turtle graphics are widely used in teaching the principles of guidance and programming, often in association with the LOGO language. Turtle graphics provide the learner with simple methods of illustrating the concepts of PROCEDURES and RECURSION.

TV, *abbrev. for* television, or television receiver. 'Television' ('far vision') is the production by means of electrical signals of a series of transient visible images on a distant screen. Some computers make use of a domestic TV receiver as a MONITOR, but this permits only 40 characters per line of text, and rather low RESOLUTION graphics, with colour displays that are greatly inferior to those which can be obtained from a MONITOR. In order to make use of a TV receiver, the video signals from the computer must be modulated on to a UHF carrier signal, see MODULATION. This causes complications if the computer has to be exported, because three different colour standards exist, and many minor differences in specifications and in frequency ranges.

two-phase clock, *n.* a technical term in MICROPROCESSOR design and use to denote a CLOCK system using the main clock pulses to generate a set of alternate pulses, lying between the main clock pulses. Most of the actions of the microprocessor are carried out at the time of the main clock pulses, but some actions are carried out in time with the secondary pulses. This permits actions such as PIPELINING to be executed.

twos complement, *n.* a method of forming the binary equivalent of a negative number. The number value is written in binary, and each digit in the number is inverted (0 becomes 1, 1 becomes 0).

TYPE

When 1 is added to this, the result is the twos complement of the original number. For example, the denary number 67 is, in 8-bit binary, 01000011. To find the binary equivalent of –67, we invert to get 10111100, and then add 1 to get 10111101, which is the twos complement of 01000011. Integer numbers for most languages are stored as two bytes, using the convention that any number whose most significant bit is a 1 will be a negative number. This is why the range of integers is normally given as –32768 to +32767. Some small machines which use an INTERPRETER will print LINE NUMBERS normally on a listing, but will show line numbers greater than 32767 as negative numbers in some applications. See also NEGATION.

type, *n.* a form of variable or data. See DATA TYPE.

typo, *abbrev. for* typographical error, for example, misspelling, or any other error made at the keyboard.

U

UART, *n. acronym for* Universal Asynchronous Receiver Transmitter. This is a type of PORT chip, that allows communication to and from the computer using SERIAL links. 'Asynchronous' means that the serial signals do not have to be transmitted continuously, only when data is being sent. Many serial port chips are manufactured so that they can be used either in synchronous or asynchronous form. Compare USART, USRT.

UCSD, *abbrev. for* University College of San Diego. This college of the University of California has specialized in computing languages, and several versions of high-level languages bear the UCSD prefix. The best known of these is probably UCSD PASCAL, which differs in several respects from the standard that was originally laid down by Wirth.

UHF, *abbrev. for* ultrahigh frequency, the range of radio frequencies that is used for transmitting TV signals in Britain and in many other countries. If a computer is to be able to make use of a TV receiver for display, it must be able to transmit signals on one of the UHF frequencies, in the range of approximately 300MHz to 1000MHz. Direct connection of computer signals to an unmodified TV receiver is *extremely* dangerous, because most TV receivers are powered directly from the mains supply, with no isolating transformer. See also RASTER, MONITOR, MODULATOR.

ULA, *n. acronym for* Uncommitted Logic Array, a chip in which the signal paths are left unconnected and on the surface after the main manufacturing processes. This feature allows a customer to specify what he wants, so that a chip can be made at low cost but yet custom-designed to fit a specialized purpose. This is done by making surface connections between various points. The extensive use of ULAs was the design method by which computer prices were forced down so spectacularly in the early 80s.

underflow, *n.* a number result which is too small to represent. REAL NUMBERS are represented in the form of a binary fraction and a power-of-two multiplier. If a number is smaller than can be represented by the most negative power of two that can be used, this constitutes an 'underflow', and the number will appear as zero. Compare OVERFLOW.

underline, *vb.* to draw a line under text on paper or on the screen. An action which is useful in word processing programs, particularly if the underline can be shown on the screen. Underlining is usually achieved using EMBEDDED COMMANDS to the printer, but each make of printer generally requires a different code sequence. The normal action is to use one code for the start of underlining, and another for the end. In some systems, underlining automatically stops at the end of a line, in others it always continues until cancelled.

unjustified text, *n.* text of uneven line length. See JUSTIFY.

unprotected software, *n.* software which can be copied by making use of the normal BACKUP features of the machine. Unprotected software allows the user to take the normal precaution of working with backups, retaining the original software for emergencies. The use of software for business purposes that cannot be backed up is very risky.

unprotected field, *n.* the part of a RECORD that can be changed. See FIELD, RANDOM-ACCESS FILE.

unsigned, *adj.* (of a binary number) one in which the msb is used as a value bit rather than as a SIGN BIT. For 2-byte numbers, this implies a number range from 0 to 64436 rather than from –32768 to +32767. Compare SIGNED.

UNTIL, *n.* the word that marks the end of a LOOP which starts with REPEAT.

update, *vb.* to amend a file with recent data. Files often have to be updated daily, weekly or monthly according to how rapidly the data becomes out of date. Easy updating requires the use of RANDOM-ACCESS FILES, rather than SERIAL FILES.

upper-case, *adj.* of or relating to the capital letters as distinct from 'small' letters. Some systems allow only upper-case letters to be used for program instruction words, others treat upper and LOWER-CASE letters alike, or convert all lower-case letters to upper-case.

upward compatibility, *n.* the ability of a simple computing system to work along with more advanced equipment. A computer is upward-compatible if a program written for it can also be used on a more advanced machine. The reverse is not necessarily true. Compare DOWNWARD COMPATIBILITY.

USART, *n. acronym for* Universal Synchronous/Asynchronous Receiver Transmitter. This is a type of PORT chip which can send or receive signals along serial links with either synchronous or asynchronous PROTOCOLS. Compare UART, USRT.

user area, *n.* an area for storage of data which is available for the computer user. The term applies to storage space either in RAM or on disk on which the user can store data. In RAM, the OPERATING SYSTEM will take up some memory space even if the main operating system is in ROM. Space will also be required for screen use, and what is left is user space. Similarly on a disk, two TRACKS may be needed for DIRECTORY data, and the rest of the disk surface is available for the user. See Fig. 70.

user-friendly, *adj.* (of a part of a computer system) being easy to work with. A system can be said to be truly user-friendly if the first-time user can make use of it without continual reference to a MANUAL. Unfortunately, most manuals are even less user-friendly than programs, and OPERATING SYSTEMS often seem to be designed to be user-unfriendly. Because of this problem, some software producers have devised INTERFACE programs which manipulate the operating system, but present a user-friendly aspect to the user. Typical of these programs are GEM, Windows, and Topview.

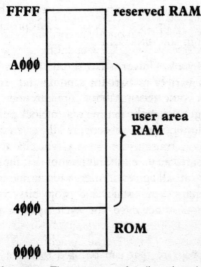

Fig. 70. **User area.** The user area of an (imaginary) computer. This is the range of addresses which can be used by the programmer, as distinct from ROM and reserved RAM addresses. The whole of the user area may not always be available.

user group, *n.* a set of users of one make of MICROCOMPUTER who band together to help each other, sometimes in the hope of persuading the manufacturer to support the machine better. An active user group is a very important factor in deciding which personal computer to buy, because it is often easier to find out details about the inner workings of the computer from the user group than from the manufacturer. The user group is often a good source of free software, and of useful guidance as to the usefulness or otherwise of commercial software. In the event of the computer going out of production, the user group often acquires spares so that the life of the machine can be extended. Many manufacturers, realising how useful such a group can be, have set up their own user groups.

user port, *n.* a PORT at which the main data and other signals of the computer are available for any other equipment that you wish to connect. Both inputs and outputs are available, but a program may be needed to operate the port, and this program may have to be written in MACHINE CODE.

USRT, *n. acronym for* Universal Synchronous Receiver Transmitter. This is a variety of port for sending and receiving SERIAL signals, with SYNCHRONIZATION. 'Synchronous' implies that signals are sent continually in time with a clock pulse. This is also true of asynchronous transmissions, and the essential difference is that synchronous transmissions send a 'sync character' byte even when there is no data to send. This ensures that the signal remains synchronized at all times. In an asynchronous system, the transmitter must send start and stop bits to ensure that synchronization is achieved for each byte. Compare UART, USART.

utility, *n.* a program that can be used to make programming easier. For the larger type of machine, these utilities will relate to such actions as formatting disks, copying programs, and setting up links to other computers. A set of these utilities will generally be included with the operating system on the SYSTEM DISK. For the smaller computers, some utilities provide functions which are missing in the computer, such as AUTO line numbering, others allow the action of the machine to be analysed, others allow you to design games, particularly 'adventure' type games. Other very common utilities include graphics design programs, and sound editors. Most utilities assume a greater knowledge of the machine than would be possessed by a casual user.

V

VAL, *n.* a BASIC instruction that finds the number value of a STRING, if there is one. Strings are stored as ASCII codes, whereas numbers are stored either as 2-byte INTEGERS, or in FLOATING POINT (REAL NUMBER) form, and VAL converts from ASCII form to real form. The syntax is X=VAL(A$), where X is a number variable and A$ is a string variable. The value of X will be zero unless A$ starts with a digit. The presence of VAL allows all inputs of data to be assigned to a string variable, allowing more useful manipulations for display and data testing purposes. Many programming languages do not permit this sort of conversion, because it infringes rules on DATA TYPES. See also STR$.

validation, *n.* a checking action in a program which is aimed at finding out if data is genuine. Also called *mugtrapping*. Validation should be carried out on any data that is entered from the keyboard, even when this is simply a Y or N response. The simpler types of validation are used to ensure that answers are within an acceptable range.

Validation becomes less easy when the user is not entering items from a fixed range. You might, for example, want to ensure that no-one entered a date of 31st. February, or claimed to be born in 1830. Some types of validation like this are comparatively simple, others almost impossible (there might, after all, be a claimant for Social Security whose name *was* Mickey Mouse). When exact validation is impossible, the typed answer should be placed on the screen with a message such as Is this correct?, asking the user to press Y or N.

variable, *n.* a quantity which is represented in the computer by a name (IDENTIFIER), and whose value can be changed by such actions as ASSIGNATION. Many versions of BASIC allow only

271

two-letter 'names' to be used for variables, but more advanced DIALECTS (and other HIGH-LEVEL LANGUAGES) allow 8-character (or longer) names to be used. The importance of variables is that the data which is being processed will at various stages be assigned to variable names. It helps considerably if these names can be 'meaningful' in the sense that the name will remind the programmer or user of what quantity is represented.

variable list table (VLT), *n.* the region of RAM memory in which a computer stores the values of VARIABLES and the variable names. For a BASIC INTERPRETER, this space is usually just above the last byte of the program text. See also STRING AREA, GARBAGE COLLECTION.

VARPTR, *n.* a reserved word in MICROSOFT BASIC. The use of VARPTR shows where a VARIABLE is stored in the memory, and is very useful for the programmer who wants to combine BASIC with machine-code SUBROUTINES. This is the only example of the use of a POINTER in BASIC.

VDU, *abbrev. for* visual display unit, the MONITOR, SCREEN, or TV display unit.

vector graphics, 1. *n.* a graphics diagram system. A vector graphics system allows lines to be drawn and then manipulated by using the keyboard, LIGHTPEN, or MOUSE. The alternative scheme uses individual PIXELS. **2.** *n. Trademark.* a make of computer.

Venn diagram, *n.* a method of visualizing relationships between SETS. A Venn diagram shows each set of items as a circle. Intersection of circles implies intersection of sets, meaning that several items belong to more than one set.

verify, *vb.* to check a recording. When ordinary CASSETTE recorders are used for data and program storage, it is desirable to be able to check that a file has been correctly recorded before the file is erased. Data which is written on disk is usually verified automatically, and a 'disk fault' message is delivered if a fault is found. This allows another disk to be used. Automatic verification is also a feature of FLOPPY TAPE systems.

vertical blanking interval, *n.* the suppression of VIDEO SIGNAL in the time of field or frame flyback. See RASTER.

video, *adj.* (of an electrical signal) carrying picture information. The video signals from a computer are the signals which a MONITOR will use to form a picture, whether of TEXT or of GRAPHICS. See also COMPOSITE VIDEO, RGB, MODULATOR, VIDEO SIGNAL.

video bandwidth, *n.* the range of frequencies that is needed for VIDEO signals. The video bandwidth is measured in MHz, and implies that any frequency from zero up to this limit will be present in a signal. For high resolution graphics and 80-column text, a video bandwidth of 18MHz is desirable. This contrasts with the 5MHz which is normally available on a domestic TV receiver. Most good-quality monitors can achieve a bandwidth of 18MHz, some more than 24MHz. A few displays that are titled 'monitors', mainly for small computers, are in reality converted TV receivers, and have bandwidths of little more than 7MHz.

video disc, *n.* a disc that is written on by means of a LASER with a bit pattern that represents a VIDEO signal. The information is stored in digital form, and can be read using a low-power laser. A huge amount of information can be written on one disc and the system is now being used in computing as a form of ROM. This allows huge databases to be used much more conveniently than, for example, by using telephone lines,a nd also has applications in interactive computer displays and in very advanced games. A combination of magnetic recording and laser writing is also being used experimentally in a read/write system. See also COMPACT DISC.

video interface chip, *n.* a specialized processor chip that produces a VIDEO SIGNAL from the text and graphics codes from the computer. This carries out many actions which would otherwise require the use of several boards of components, and also much of the time of the main processor.

video memory, *n.* a section of memory that is reserved for the use of the screen-display bytes. See also SCREEN MEMORY.

video signal, *n.* a signal that can be used by a MONITOR or TV unit to produce a picture on the screen. This signal is not a purely digital signal, hence the need for INTERFACE chips to generate the signals. Many colour monitors require three sets of video signals, one for blue, one for green and one for red. This system is known as RGB, and provides the best quality colour displays. The alternative is COMPOSITE VIDEO, in which the three colour signals are coded into one signal. If a domestic TV receiver is to be used, the composite signal must in turn be modulated on to a UHF carrier (see MODULATOR). The highest possible display RESOLUTION is achieved by RGB signals, the least with a modulated signal.

virgin, *adj.* (of tape) having never been recorded on. When audio cassettes are used, virgin tape is required for any valuable program or data, and the next best option is bulk-erased tape (see BULK ERASE). Reliable recording is seldom achieved on tape when one file is recorded over another, even when digital recording methods are used. This problem does not exist with disks because of the methods of recording that are used.

virtual address, *n.* an ADDRESS in an ASSEMBLY LANGUAGE listing that will be changed when the program is assembled into MACHINE CODE.

virtual memory, *n.* the use of a DISK as if it were part of the main RAM memory of the computer. Since the capacity of a disk can be much larger than the memory of a small microcomputer, this can allow very large programs to operate in small machines, just as if the machine had a very much larger memory than is physically present.

Visicalc, *n. Trademark.* the pioneer SPREADSHEET program. This was written for the APPLE-2 microcomputer in 1979, after the idea had been rejected as impracticable by the software houses for mainframes. One mainframe manufacturer went as far as to predict that the program was a hoax. The subsequent reaction was to find as many ways as possible round the copyright, and to invent new names. Though a vast number of copies of Visicalc are still in use, the program is showing its age now, despite the introduction of a later version, Advanced Visicalc.

VLT, see VARIABLE LIST TABLE.

voice grade channel, *n.* a signal-transmitting system that can use only a very limited BANDWIDTH, about 100Hz to 2000Hz. This is the range which is used by telephone systems for speech. In order to make use of voice grade channels, which include telephone lines and cassette recorders, the computer signals must be encoded as tones, using one frequency to represent digital 0 and another frequency to represent digital 1. The rate at which data can be sent using this coding is very slow.

voice input, *n.* a system that uses a microphone and an INTERFACE unit so that a limited number of commands to the computer can be carried out by speaking to the microphone. See also DIRECT VOICE INPUT.

voice recognition, see DIRECT VOICE INPUT.

voice synthesis, see SPEECH SYNTHESIS.

volatile memory, *n.* a memory system that loses data when power is switched off. RAM memory is volatile, ROM is not. Some varieties of RAM, notably CMOS RAM, can make use of a backup battery which maintains data storage when the main power supply is removed. This allows programs or data to be retained for as long as the battery can provide power, which may be up to five years. The memory is still volatile, however, in the sense that disconnecting the backup battery will clear the memory at once. See also ROM, PROM, EPROM.

volatility, *n.* the measure of how 'volatile' a data storage system is.

volume, *n.* loudness, or sound amplitude.

W

wafer, *n.* the thin SILICON disc on which CHIPS are formed. Constructional actions on the wafer are described as being *wafer-scale*. Chips that are formed on the wafer, and then interconnected, are described as being *wafer-scale integrated*.

wait loop, *n.* a LOOP that runs until broken by the user. At various stages in a program, computing may have to be halted until the user carries out some action, such as putting a disk in a drive, changing paper on a printer, or switching on a MODEM. During this time, the computer has to be kept waiting by programming a loop. No action needs to be carried out in the loop, though a message to the operator is often flashed by means of STATEMENTS in the loop. The loop must contain a statement which will detect the pressing of a key to indicate that the required action has been carried out (see PRESS ANY KEY). A waiting loop is sometimes combined with a timing loop, so that a DEFAULT action will be carried out after some time has elapsed. See also TIMEOUT, INKEY$.

warm start, *vb.* to restart the computer, but without loss of data. The use of a BASIC INTERPRETER allows a warm start to be carried out after any normal interruption of the program, or in the event of a FATAL ERROR. Compare COLD START.

Warnier-Orr, *n.* a method of program design that makes use of TOP-DOWN methods, and uses curly brackets to indicate how the details of each step are arranged. The Warnier-Orr diagram, despite its name, is less visual than a flowchart, and relies more on written descriptions. In many ways, this method of planning is very much more appropriate to modern high-level languages than the use of flowcharts. Named after Warnier, who invented the technique, and Orr, who made it popular. See Fig. 71.

warning, *n.* a visual or audible message to the operator to indicate potential danger, such as overwriting of data or destruction of a disk file. Audible warnings are often more useful than visual ones, though FLASHING messages can also be useful.

wash PROM, *vb.* to erase data from a programmable ROM. For the usual type of PROM, this is done by removing the label from the window over the chip, and exposing the PROM to ultraviolet light for about 30 minutes, depending on the intensity of the light. This should be done in an enclosed unit, because the ultraviolet wavelengths that are used are very harmful to the eye.

waveform digitization, *n.* the representation of an electrical waveform by a set of numbers. For control and measurement purposes, virtually every quantity that can be measured can be expressed as an electrical signal. The numbers represent the value of the amplitude of the wave at regular intervals. The interval size has to be chosen so that the waveform can be reasonably well reproduced. A rule of thumb is that the SAMPLING RATE at which measurements are made should be at least four times the highest FREQUENCY present in the waveform. Waveform digitization is required mainly for REAL TIME analysis of waveforms, and requires very fast computing speeds.

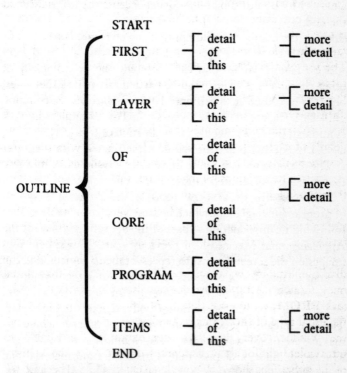

Fig. 71. **Warnier-Orr.** The form of the Warnier-Orr program-planning method. The amount of detail increases as you read from left to right. The sequence of each step and substep is read from top to bottom. This type of diagram is very well suited to the planning of structured top-down programs.

weighting, *n.* the assigning of more importance to some computing items than to others. Used in data processing to indicate that some terms used in a search may be more 'significant' than others.

WHILE loop, *n.* a LOOP in which a TEST is made at the start. In BASIC, the end of the loop may be marked with the word WEND (an abbreviation of WHILE END). Other languages mark the loop with the words BEGIN and END. Because the loop is tested at the start, it is possible for a WHILE loop not to run at all. By contrast, a REPEAT loop must run at least once, because the test is made at the end.

width, *n.* the number of columns that can be printed on screen or on paper.

wild card, *n.* a symbol that can represent one or any group of other characters. The term is used particularly of disk filenames, but it is also used in specifying database searches. A common wild card character is the asterisk, *. For example, the disk command, DELETE L* would cause deletion of files LONG, LAME, LIMB, L123 or any other file whose name started with the letter L. The ? character is often used as a single wild card, meaning that it can be substituted for any single character.

WIMP, *n. acronym for* WINDOW, IKON, MOUSE Program. A system of program management which became very fashionable in 1985 following its introduction as part of the operating system of the Apple Lisa and Macintosh in previous years. The system uses images on the screen (ikons) to represent menu choices, and can present different sets of choices by means of screen windows. The mouse is used to move a pointer cursor to the desired item, and pressing a button, or the mouse body, to execute the choice. The system can be produced on a variety of other machines by making use of software such as GEM, Windows or Topview.

Winchester disk, *n.* a DISK that is made of rigid material and normally permanently encased in its drive. Also called *hard disk*. This allows the disk to work in a dust-free space, spinning at high speed, with a head placed very close to the disk surface. A disk of this type can offer very large amounts of storage, typically 10 MEGABYTES, and very fast access. The problem of backup is dealt with by backing on to other Winchesters, FLOPPY DISKS, or to long open-reel tapes or on to video cassettes, but data loss from a Winchester is, fortunately, rare.

window, *n.* a section of the screen that can be defined by its coordinates, and used as an independent screen. This allows a set of instructions, for example, to be displayed independently of displays on the rest of the screen, because the window is unaffected by the clear-screen command or by scrolling on the main screen. Some form of window control has been a feature of most modern small computers and is normally handled by commands to the operating system. Most window systems allow multiple windows, which can be in different colours, and featuring actions such as sideways and backwards scrolling. Different windows can also be moved about on the screen. Windows are used extensively along with IKONS and the MOUSE in the WIMP system.

wipe file, *vb.* to erase the file. This may mean erase from memory, or from disk. In most cases the file is not actually erased, only its memory POINTERS or its disk DIRECTORY entry. The file will be destroyed when it is overwritten, or in the case of a file in memory, when the computer is switched off.

Wirth, Niklaus, the inventor of PASCAL, who has greatly influenced the progress of programming. Wirth's later language, Modula-2 is now available for microcomputers.

word, 1. *n.* two bytes. **2.** – *n. Trademark.* a MICROSOFT word processor program. See also DOUBLE WORD, BYTE.

word break, *n.* the splitting of a word at the end of a line. Most word processors do not do this, preferring to take the whole word into the next line. See also WRAP AROUND.

word count, *n.* a word processor action that counts words in a document. In fact, most word counts operate by counting the number of times that the space-bar has been pressed, but a few make a count of the actual words. This feature is often omitted in word processors, even very expensive types, but it is very important for many authors and journalists. A displayed running word count is one of the excellent features of the WORDWISE-PLUS WP program for the BBC machine (see WORDWISE).

word processor, *n.* a combination of TEXT EDITOR and PRINT FORMATTER that is used for typing letters, documents or books. Also called *text processor*. Because the system is computer-based, it is much easier to edit so that text can be made perfect before being printed. Word processors fall into two distinct classes, the WYSIWYG (pronounced wizziwig) and the 'postformatted'. For either kind, you would type your text and see it on the screen, but what you see depends on the type of program. WYSIWYG is an acronym for 'what you see is what you get', and the term implies that what you see on the screen represents the text almost exactly as it will appear on paper. This requires the use of an 80-column display on the screen. Such a display may not be easy to read, particularly if colour is used. On the other hand, it's very much easier to see how your text will look. You have to specify how you want the text formatted before you start typing. The alternative system can use 40-column displays, because what you see on screen bears absolutely no resemblance to how it will look on paper. The text is typed, and a set of formatting instructions will be used *after* the text has been typed in order to format the printed version. In some programs, you can also use a 'preview' facility to see what the text will look like on paper.

Any type of word processor will allow you to enter text, record it, replay recorded text, merge text, and format text for printing. For many authors and journalists, a WORD COUNT is essential, yet surprisingly few programs provide one. See also BLOCK OPERATIONS, BOILERPLATE, CENTRING, FORMAT, HEADER, FOOTER, STANDARD LETTER, INDENT, JUSTIFY, LINE SPACING, LINE LENGTH, MARKERS, PAGE-BREAK, PRINT PAUSE, PROPORTIONAL SPACING, RULE, SEARCH AND REPLACE, SPELLCHECK, TABULATION, UNDERLINE, WORD COUNT, WORDSTAR, WORDWISE, WORD WRAP.

WORDSTAR, *n. Trademark.* an early and very successful word processing program of the WYSIWYG variety. WORDSTAR became a standard for business use despite the need to learn very complicated key sequences for control. Modern computers that use SOFT keys allow word-processing programs to be used with

KEY STRIPS and other features which make their actions more USER-FRIENDLY.

WORDWISE, *n. Trademark.* a WORD PROCESSOR of the POSTFOR-MATTED type in ROM chip form for the BBC machine. This was the first word processor for the BBC machine, and many users consider it superior to programs costing four or five times the price. Because the program is in SIDEWAYS ROM, it takes up no RAM memory space and is very robust. The latest version, WORDWISE-PLUS offers programmability as well as a full range of normal word-processing actions. It is one of the few word processors to offer a running word count at the top of the screen, and is handicapped only by the relatively limited memory capabilities of the BBC machine in its older 'B' forms.

word wrap, *n.* a word processor action to move a word from the end of one line to the start of the next so that it is not split between lines. See also WORD BREAK.

word disk, *n.* a disk used for temporary storage of data during the running of a program. Some languages demand the use of a work disk for keeping files, even if the files are never permanently recorded. See also TEMPORARY STORAGE.

work station, *n.* **1.** a microcomputer system with communications facilities. **2.** a complete system which can offer all of the business applications of a microcomputer in one package. **3.** a computer stand, with all the computer peripherals kept in one place.

working storage, see TEMPORARY STORAGE.

wow, *n.* slow fluctuations of frequency on a signal replayed from tape. Compare FLUTTER.

wrap around, *n.* **1.** a system of displaying text in which words are never split, see WORD WRAP. **2.** in screen GRAPHICS, the term signifies that the CURSOR is never off screen. If the cursor is moved too far to the left of the screen, it appears at the right-hand side and so on.

write, *vb.* **1.** to store on disk or tape. **2.** in screen graphics, to cause graphics shapes to appear on screen.

write-protect, *vb.* to protect data on an individual file or complete disk. Some disk systems allow individual files to be write-protected (or locked), and any attempt to record another file of the same name will cause an error message, with no write action. For complete disk protection, a label or shutter is used to prevent the disk being used for anything other than reading.

WYSIWYG, see WORD PROCESSOR.

XYZ

X-coordinate, *n*. a number representing the distance measured in a horizontal direction along the screen.

X-direction, *n*. the horizontal direction of the screen.

X-distance, *n*. the distance measured in a horizontal direction. On screen, the X distance is measured horizontally starting at the left-hand side of the screen. The units of distance are screen PIXELS or column widths, depending on the screen MODE. See also Y-DISTANCE.

xerography, *n*. a copying system that depends on an 'image' formed from electrostatic charges. Powdered ink will be attracted to the charged parts of a surface, and can then be pressed on to paper. The method is the basis of most forms of office copiers, and also for the LASER PRINTER for computer systems.

X-Y plotter, *n*. an automatic graph plotter which is fed with X and Y position signals, and will plot the point at the corresponding position on a piece of paper. Particularly useful in scientific and engineering applications. See also FLAT-BED PLOTTER, CHART RECORDER.

XOR, see EXCLUSIVE OR.

Y-coordinate, *n*. a number representing the distance measured on the screen in a vertical direction.

Y-direction, *n*. a vertical direction, or any direction at right angles to the X-DIRECTION.

Y-distance, *n.* a distance measured in the Y-DIRECTION. On a screen the term often denotes a distance measured from the top of the screen downwards. The unit of distance will be the vertical size of the screen PIXEL, or the width of a text row, depending on the screen MODE that is used.

zap, *vb.* to remove something in computing. For example, 'zap memory' means to clear the memory of data.

zero, *n.* the digit 0. This should not be confused with the ASCII code for zero, which is 48. Files which use ASCII codes can therefore use the zero character as a TERMINATOR without any risk of confusion with the ASCII coded zero.

zero compression, *n.* the removal of unnecessary leading or trailing zeros from a number. A number which was entered into the computer as 001.120 would, for example, appear as 1.12 after zero compression.

zeroize, *vb.* to set memory or number variables to zero, thus ensuring that the memory will contain zero bytes, and number variables will all be assigned with the number zero.

zero, *n.* a region of the screen that can be divided into columns or print-zones.

APPENDIX

Teletype control characters

```
0  NUL  = null character
1  SOH  = start of header
2  STX  = start of text character
3  ETX  = end of text character
4  EOT  = end of transmission
5  ENQ  = query character
6  ACK  = acknowledge data or ready for data
7  BEL  = sound bell
8  BS   = back space
9  HT   = horizontal tab
```

APPENDIX

10 LF   = line feed
11 VF   = vertical feed
12 FF   = form feed
13 CR   = carriage return
14 SO   = shift out (alternate character set)
15 SI   = shift in (standard characters)
16 DLE   = data link escape
17 DC1   = display console 1
18 DC2   = display console 2
19 DC3   = display console 3
20 DC4   = display console 4
21 NAK   = negative acknowledgement
22 SYN   = synchronizing character
23 ETB   = end of transmission block
24 CAN   = cancel character
25 EM   = end of medium (tape finished)
26 SUB   = substitute character (can't print code)
27 ESC   = escape
28 FS   = file separator
29 GS   = group separator
30 RS   = record separator
31 WS   = wait separator

32 = [space]	56 = 8	80 = P	104 = h
33 = !	57 = 9	81 = Q	105 = i
34 = "	58 = :	82 = R	106 = j
35 = #	59 = ;	83 = S	107 = k
36 = $	60 = <	84 = T	108 = l
37 = %	61 = =	85 = U	109 = m
38 = &	62 = >	86 = V	110 = n
39 = '	63 = ?	87 = W	111 = o
40 = (	64 = @	88 = X	112 = p
41 =)	65 = A	89 = Y	113 = q
42 = *	66 = B	90 = Z	114 = r
43 = +	67 = C	91 = [	115 = s
44 = ,	68 = D	92 = \	116 = t
45 = -	69 = E	93 =]	117 = u
46 = .	70 = F	94 = ^	118 = v
47 = /	71 = G	95 = _	119 = w
48 = 0	72 = H	96 = '	120 = x
49 = 1	73 = I	97 = a	121 = y
50 = 2	74 = J	98 = b	122 = z
51 = 3	75 = K	99 = c	123 = {
52 = 4	76 = L	100 = d	124 =	
53 = 5	77 = M	101 = e	125 = }
54 = 6	78 = N	102 = f	126 = ~
55 = 7	79 = O	103 = g	127 = ■